WHY is BLOOD RED?

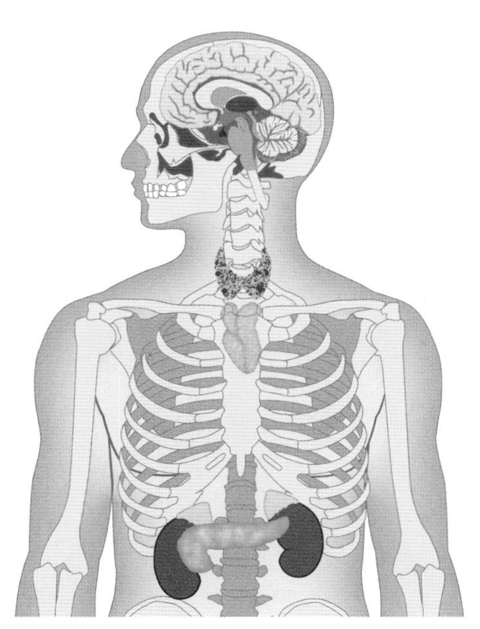

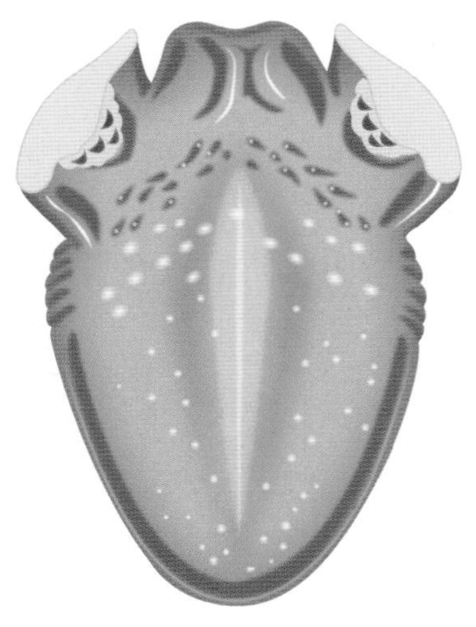

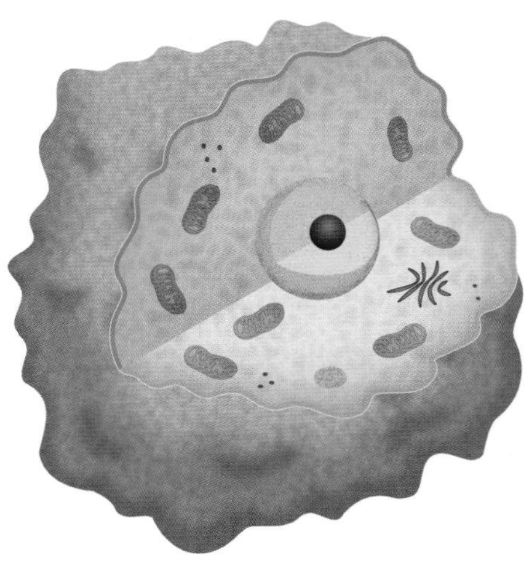

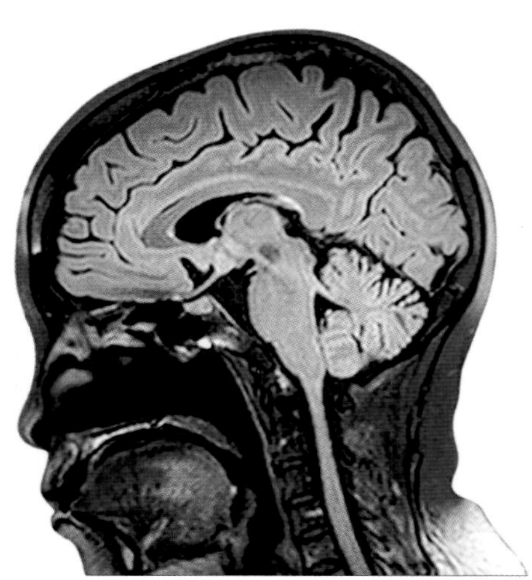

WHY is BLOOD RED?

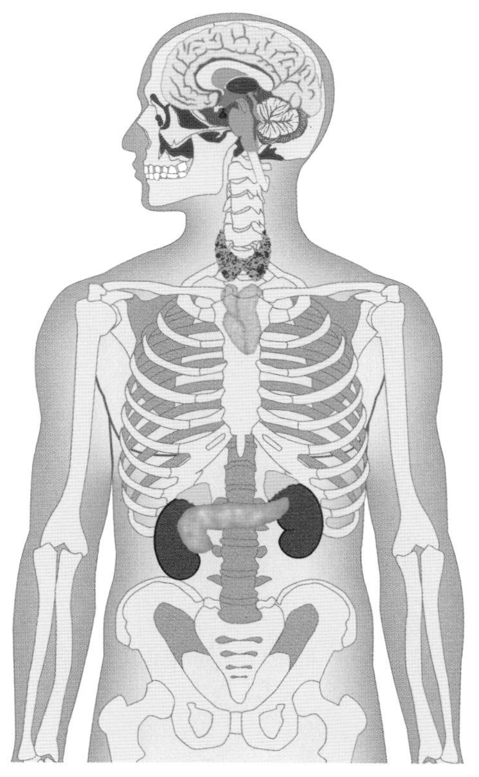

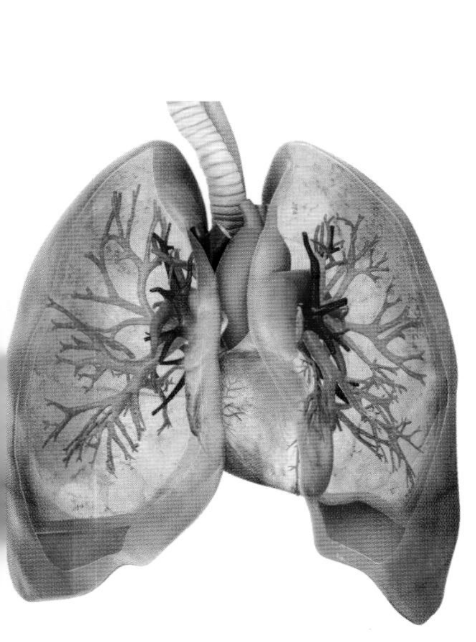

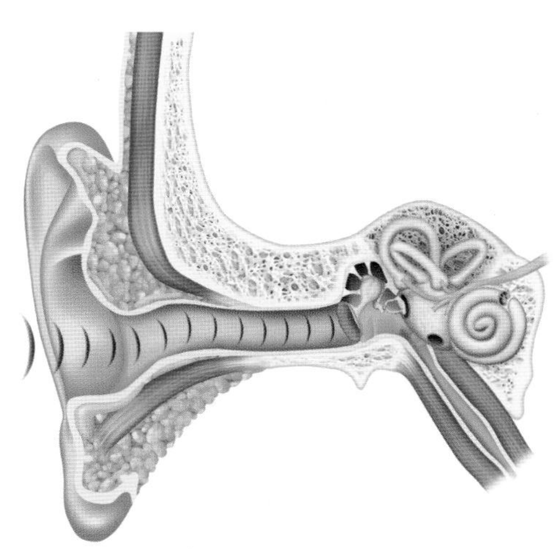

Emily Dodd

Author Emily Dodd
Consultant Dr Bipasha Choudhury
Illustrators Dan Crisp, Arran Lewis

DK LONDON
Editor Katie Lawrence
Senior art editor Ann Cannings
Additional editing Manisha Majithia, Olivia Stanford
Managing editor Jonathan Melmoth
Managing art editor Diane Peyton Jones
Senior production editor Robert Dunn
Production controller Barbara Ossowska
Jacket designer Ann Cannings
Jacket coordinator Issy Walsh
Publishing manager Francesca Young
Creative director Helen Senior
Publishing director Sarah Larter

DK DELHI
Project editor Radhika Haswani
Senior art editor Nidhi Mehra
Project art editor Bharti Karakoti
Managing editor Monica Saigal
Managing art editor Romi Chakraborty
Jacket designer Rashika Kachroo
Jacket editor Radhika Haswani
DTP designers Sachin Gupta, Vijay Kandwal
CTS manager Balwant Singh
Production manager Pankaj Sharma
Project picture researcher Sakshi Saluja
Delhi creative heads Glenda Fernandes, Malavika Talukder

First published in Great Britain in 2021
by Dorling Kindersley Limited
One Embassy Gardens, 8 Viaduct Gardens,
London, SW11 7BW

10 9 8 7 6 5 4 3 2 1
001–321271–Mar/2021

A CIP catalogue record for this book is available from the British Library.
ISBN: 978-0-2414-6141-9

Printed and bound in China

For the curious
www.dk.com

This book was made with Forest Stewardship Council™ certified paper - one small step in DK's commitment to a sustainable future. For more information go to www.dk.com/our-green-pledge

Contents

Body basics

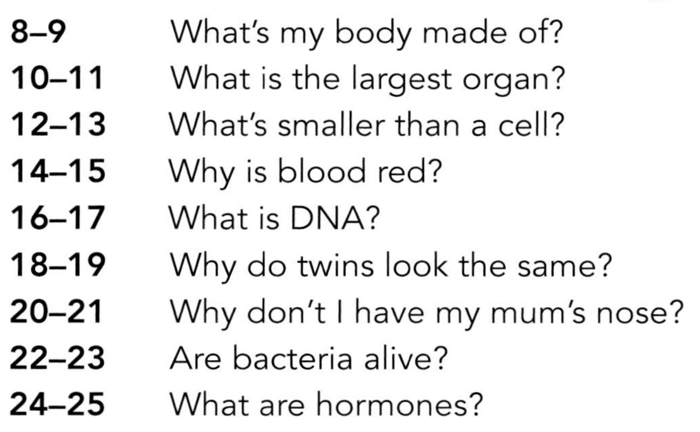

Piece by piece

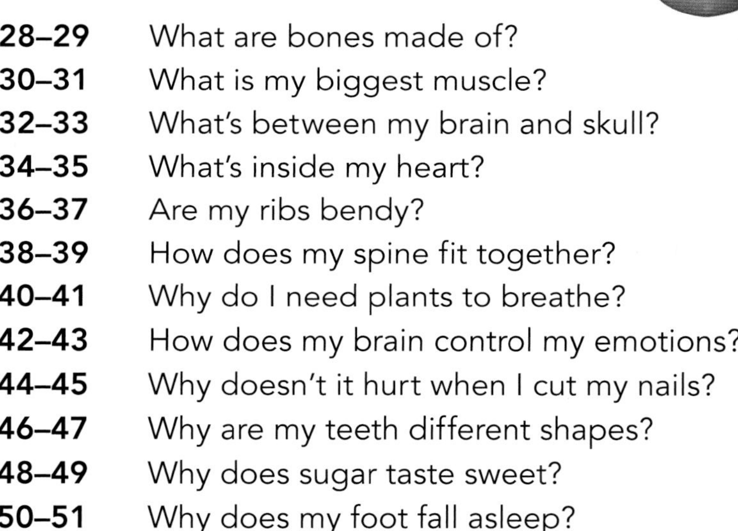

How it works

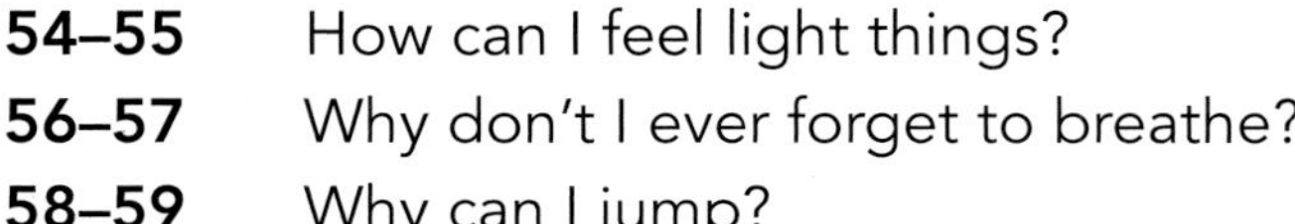

Find out how doctors can see inside your body on page 118.

Healthy habits

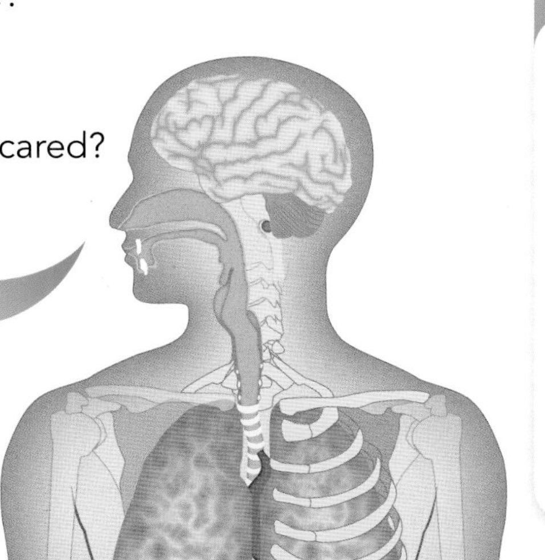

Find out how you breathe on page 56.

Medical marvels

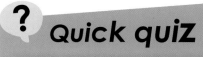

? Quick quiz

Test your knowledge! Look out for the "Quick quiz" box throughout this book to see how much you've learned. You'll find some of the answers on the pages, but you may have to look up or give your best guess for the others. Turn to pages 132–133 for the answers.

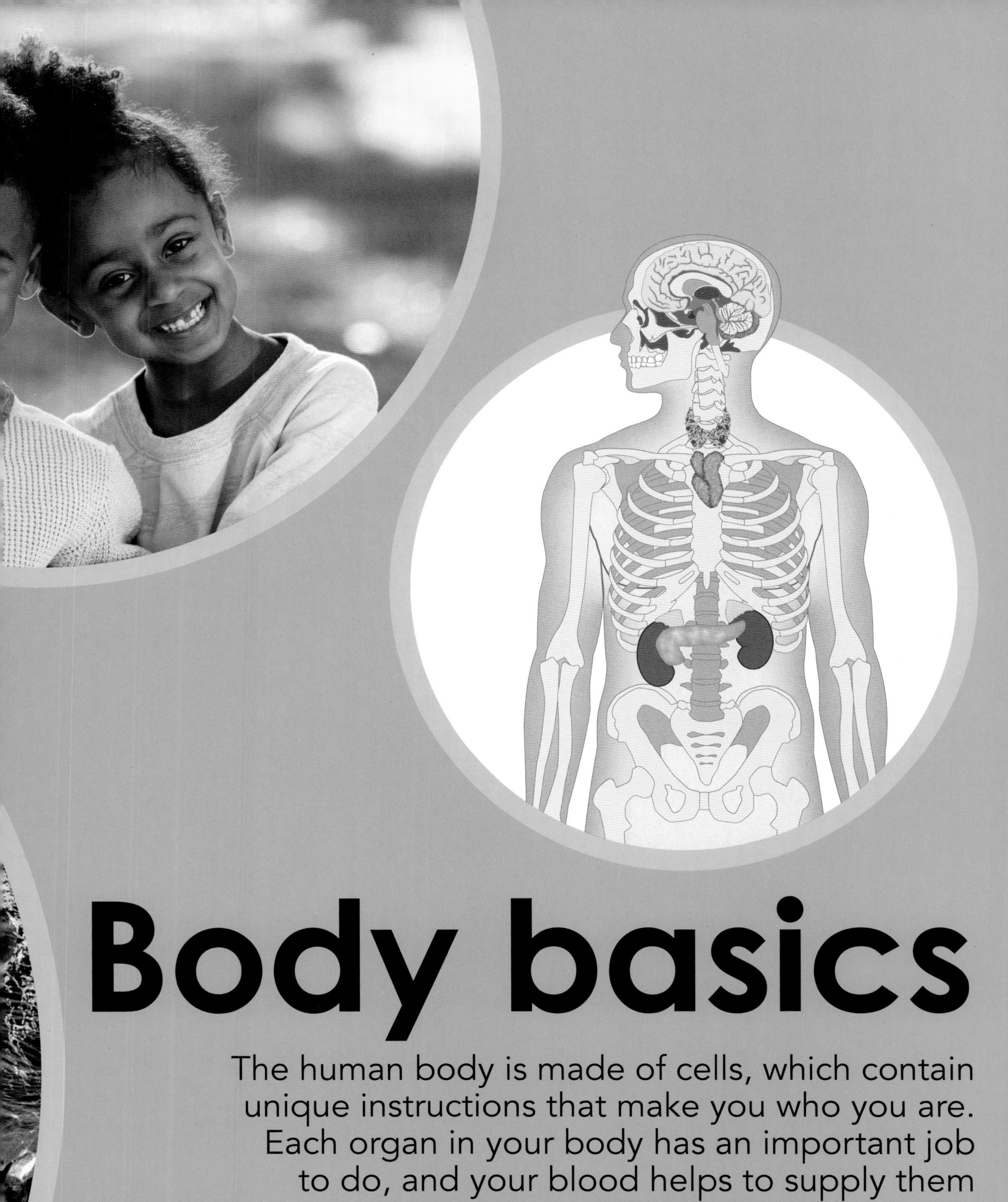

Body basics

The human body is made of cells, which contain unique instructions that make you who you are. Each organ in your body has an important job to do, and your blood helps to supply them with everything they need to work.

What's my body made of?

The smallest living building blocks in the body are cells. There are many different types of cell. The same cells join together to build tissue. Groups of tissues build organs, which work together in organ systems, such as the respiratory system.

Tissue

Tissue builds every part of the body. Some tissue creates strong structures, such as bone, while others make soft parts, such as nerves or muscle.

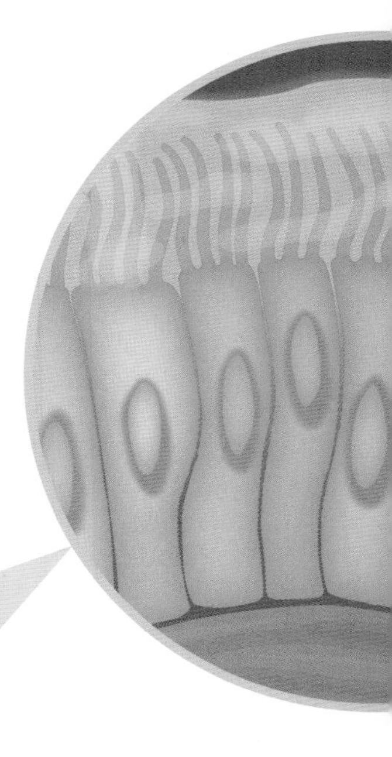

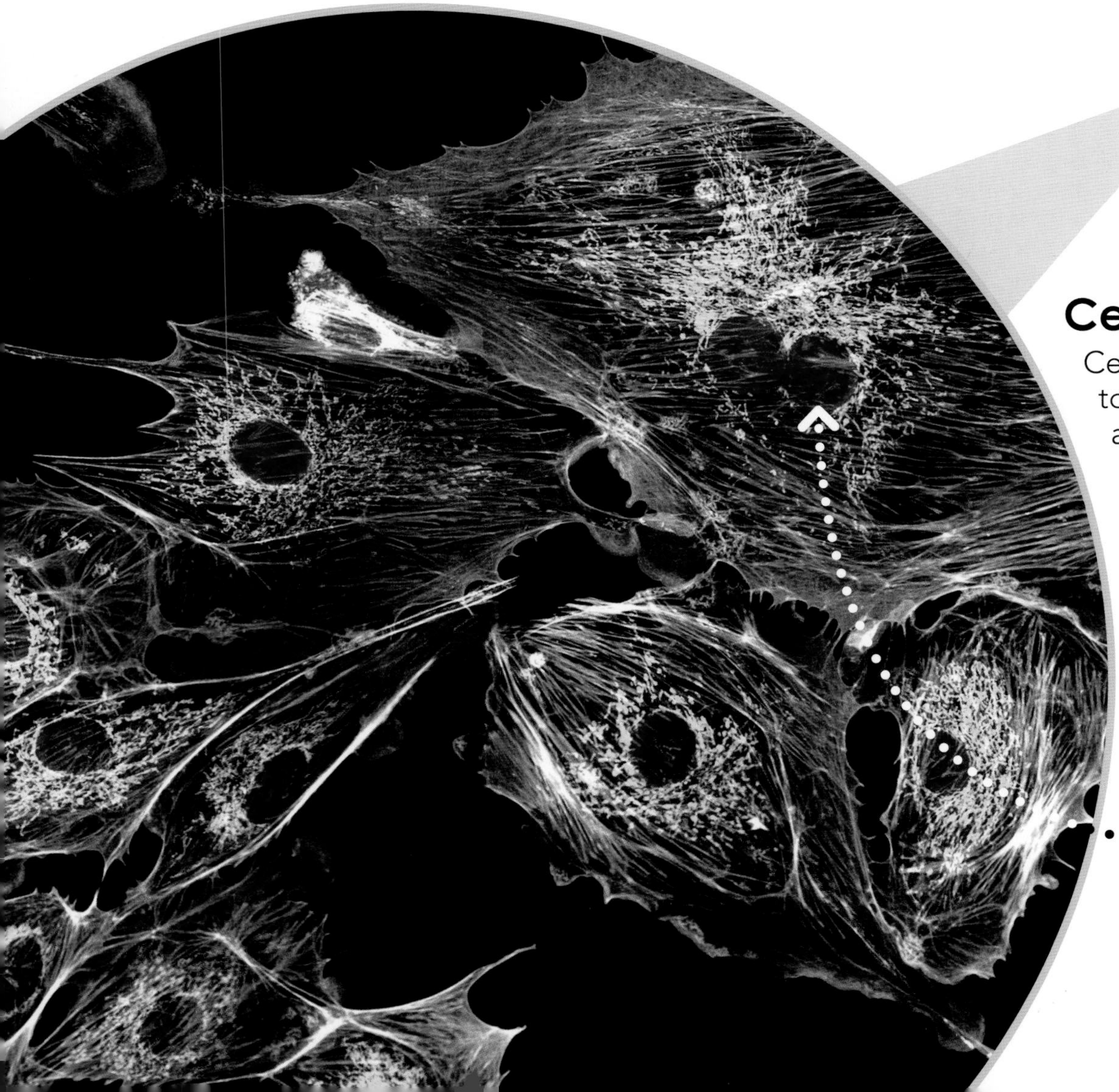

Cells

Cells hold the instructions to make a body, which are written in a coded sequence of chemicals called DNA. The DNA is kept in the nucleus – the centre of the cell.

This cell is about to divide into two cells. It has copied itself and made another nucleus.

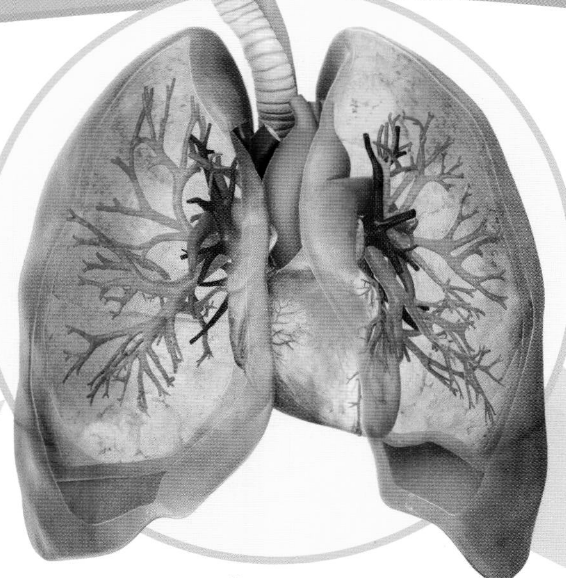

There are about 100 trillion cells in the body.

Organ

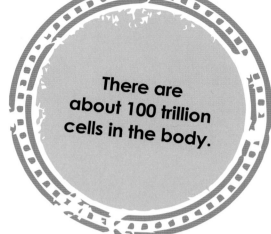

Organs are body parts that have a job to do. For example, the lungs take oxygen gas from the air and release it into the blood. They also remove carbon dioxide gas from the blood.

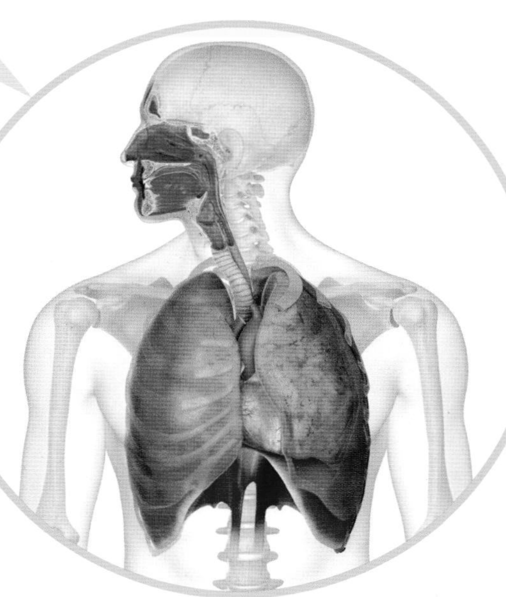

Organ system

Groups of organs work together in organ systems. The lungs are part of the respiratory system. This group of organs works together to help you breathe.

Where did all my cells come from?

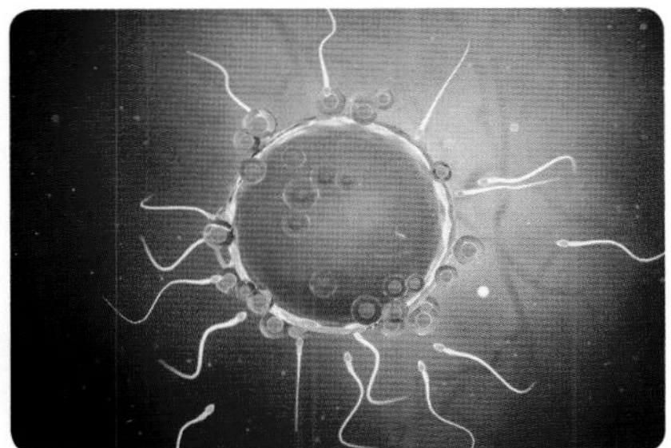

Egg
Half of the instructions to make your body came from an egg cell from your mother.

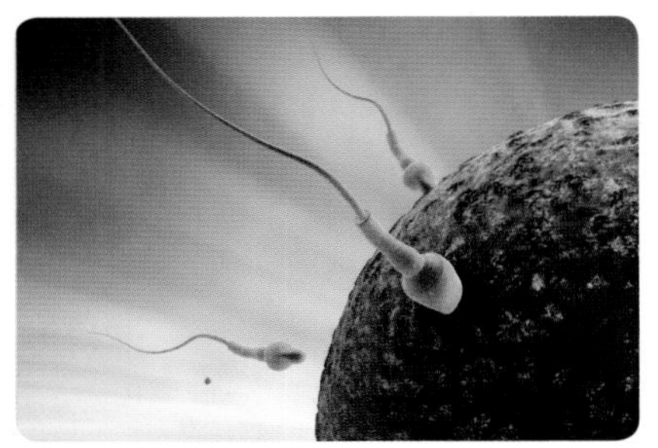

Sperm
Instructions to make the other half of your body came from your father's sperm cell.

? Quick quiz

1. What are the smallest living building blocks in the body called?
2. What is the centre of a cell called?
3. What do groups of tissues build?

See pages 132–133 for the answers

What is the largest organ?

The skin! It weighs about 4 kg (9 lb). Each organ in the body is a different shape and size, and each does a different job. The heart pumps blood, the eyes help you to see, and the brain controls everything you do.

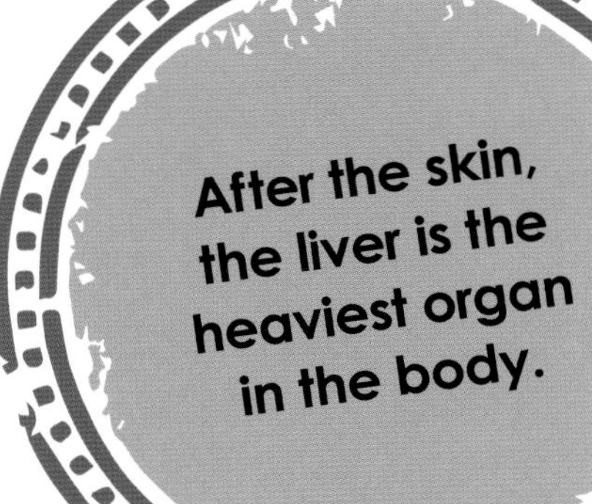

After the skin, the liver is the heaviest organ in the body.

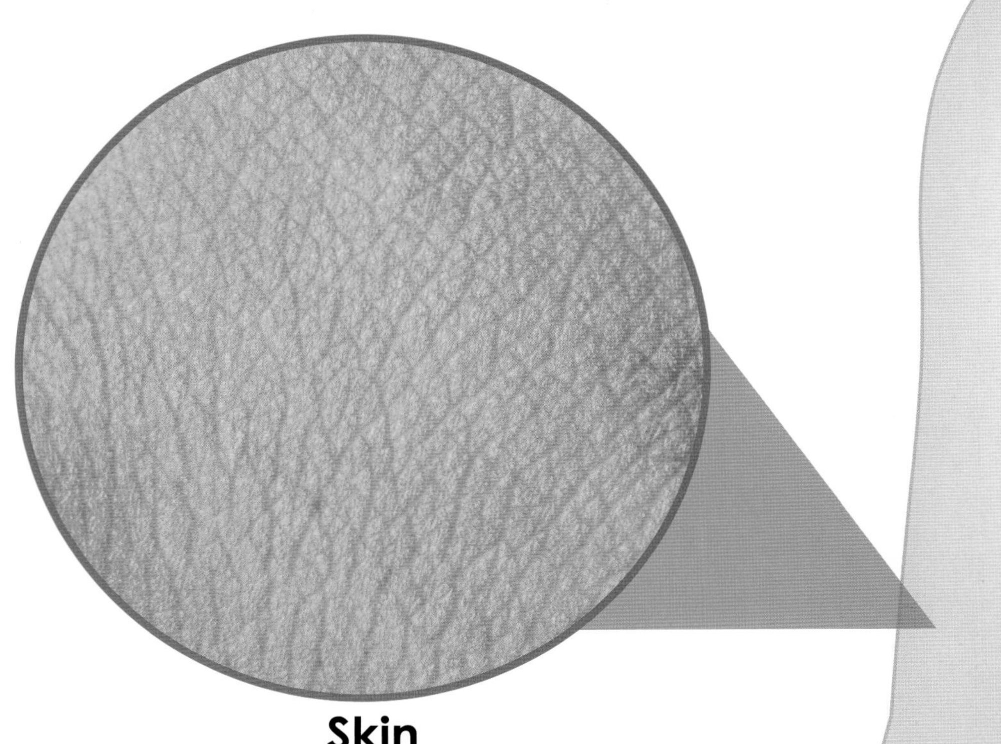

Skin

The skin keeps your body at a healthy temperature, and stops your insides from falling out. It protects you, too, by blocking out water, germs, and the Sun's rays.

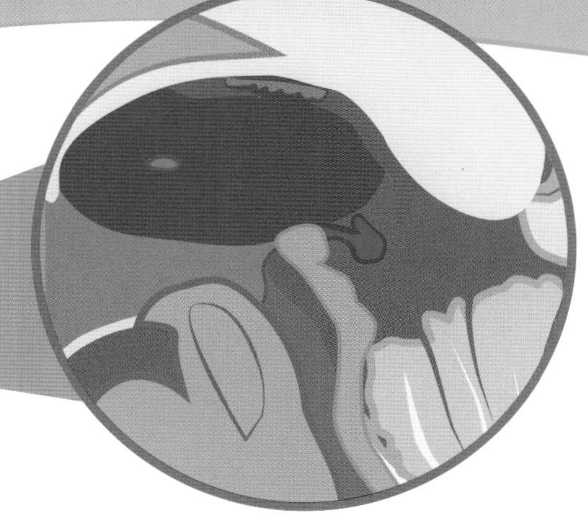

Pineal gland

The smallest organ in the body is the pineal gland (shown in red). It's in the brain and it releases a hormone, or chemical messenger, called melatonin into the blood when it gets dark. This helps your body relax so you can sleep.

? True or false?

1. The lungs are part of the circulatory system.
2. The brain is the largest organ in the body.
3. You need two kidneys to survive.

See pages 132–133 for the answers

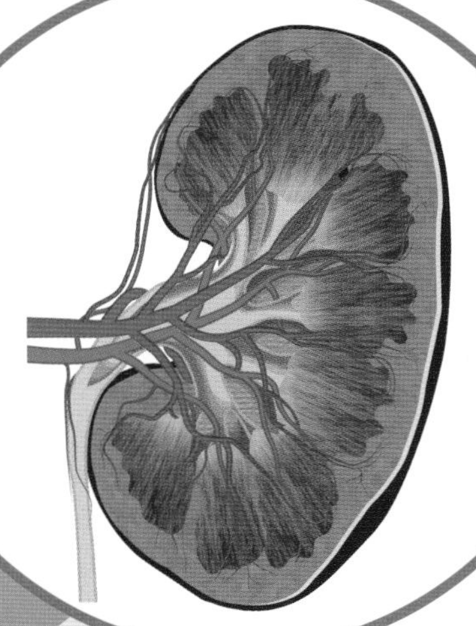

Kidney

The kidneys clean the blood and balance water in the body. They filter out waste from the blood and help the body remove this waste as urine, or pee. There are two kidneys in the body doing the same job, which means you can survive with just one!

Are there other organs we can live without?

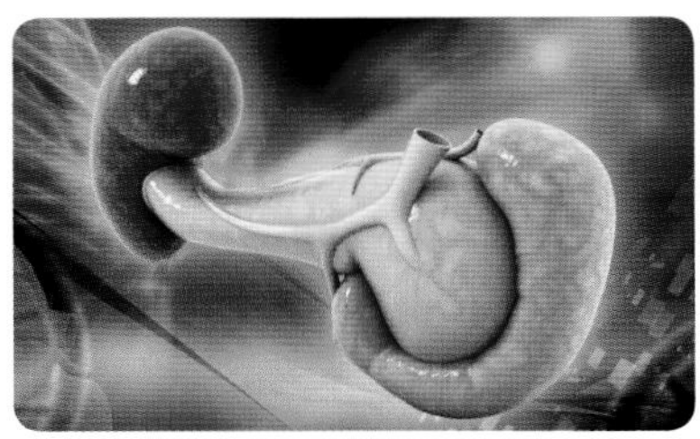

Spleen

The liver can take over if the spleen is removed. The spleen recycles red blood cells and contains white blood cells to fight sickness.

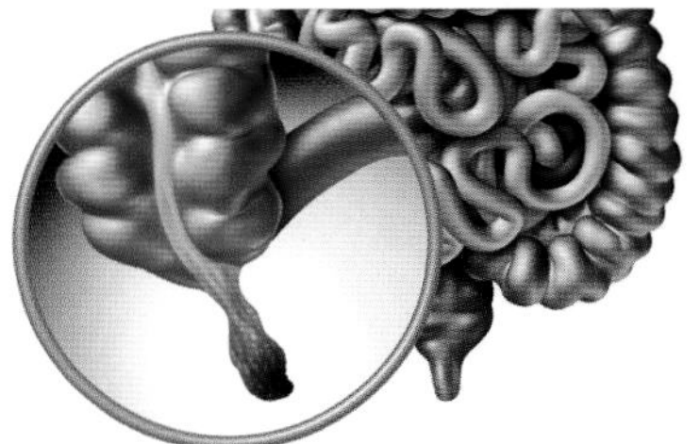

Appendix

Your appendix is removed if it becomes swollen and filled with bad bacteria. It usually stores good bacteria to help digestion.

What's smaller than a cell?

Cells are the smallest living parts of the body. Inside cells are small floating machines called organelles. Organelles do different jobs in the cell, such as turning food into energy.

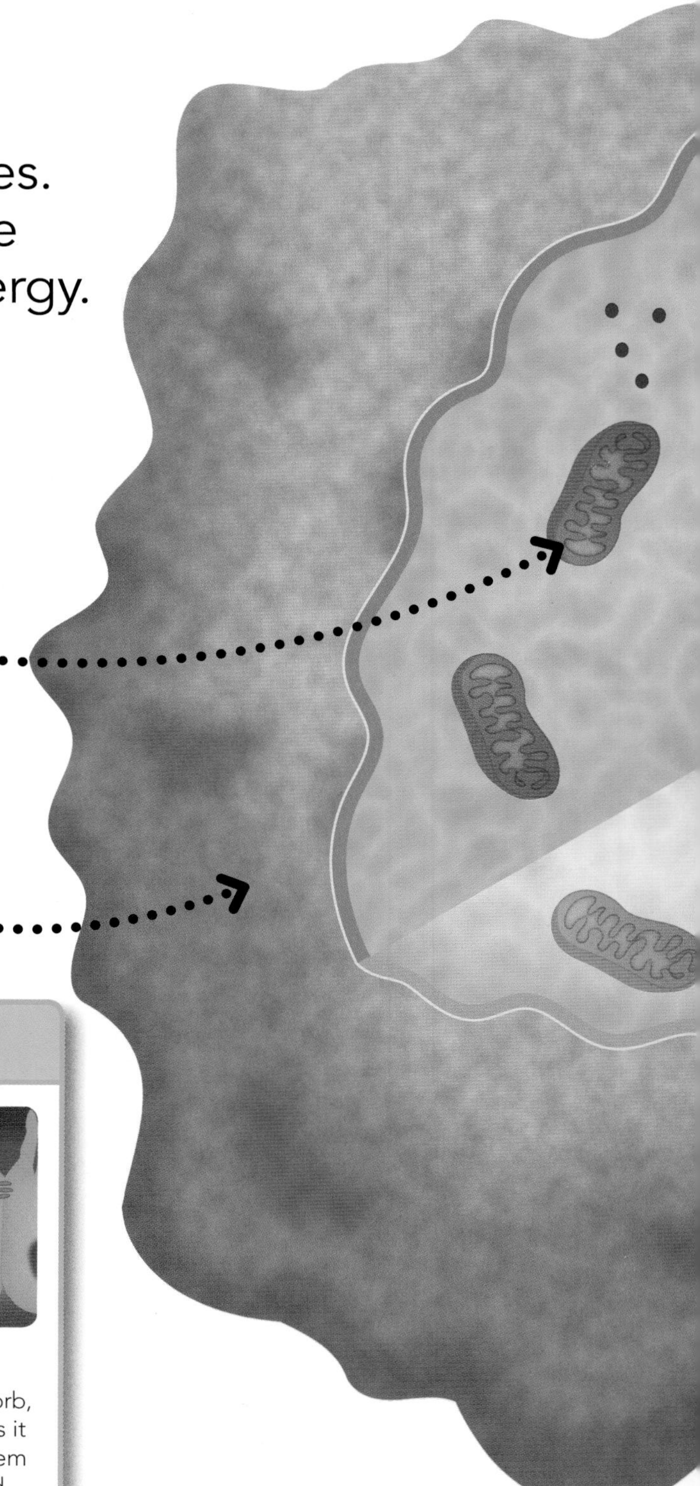

Organelles

Organs are parts of the body with important jobs to do. In cells, the parts with important jobs to do are called organelles. The nucleus and mitochondria are types of organelle.

Membrane

The membrane is the outer layer of the cell. It lets water and chemicals move in and out of the cell, depending on what the cell needs at any given time.

What shapes can cells be?

Stringy

Muscle cells are soft and stringy. They contract and slide over each other to shorten muscles, so they can move body parts.

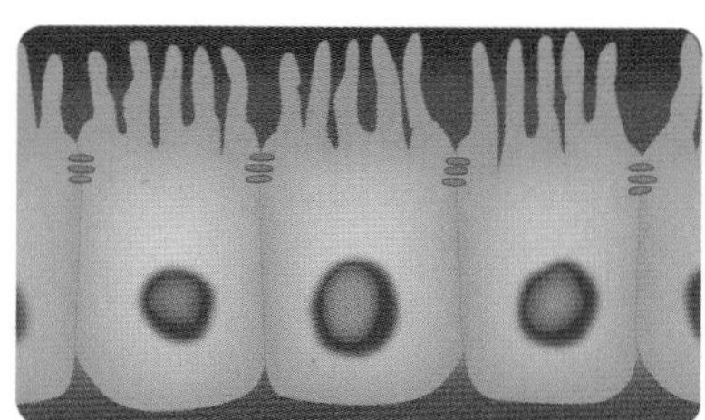

Frilly

Intestine cells are frilly. They absorb, or take in, nutrients from food as it goes through the digestive system and pass the nutrients into blood.

Cytoplasm

Organelles float around in a jelly-like fluid called cytoplasm. This fluid helps parts of the cell to pull things along smoothly from one side of the cell to the other, such as sugar.

Mitochondria

These organelles release energy to power the cell. The cell receives sugar from the food we eat and mitochondria break it down so the cell can use it as energy.

Nucleus

This is the control centre for everything in the cell. It contains the body's DNA and instructions that are needed to make every type of cell in the body.

Vacuoles

These are bubbles that can be used to store and transport food and chemicals. Vacuoles can also hold waste. When vacuoles eventually fuse, or join, to the cell membrane, this waste is ejected from the cell.

? Picture quiz

Which cell is shaped like a doughnut and carries oxygen?

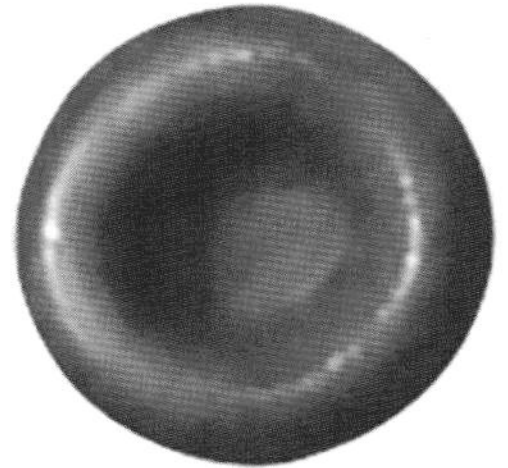

See pages 132–133 for the answers

The word "cell" means small room. The cells in the body are like tiny rooms!

Why is blood red?

Blood is red because half of it is made from red blood cells, which contain iron – an element with a red-brown colour. The rest is mainly made from water and other types of cell, such as broken-up cells called platelets. The cells in blood float along in a liquid called plasma.

Why do veins look blue?

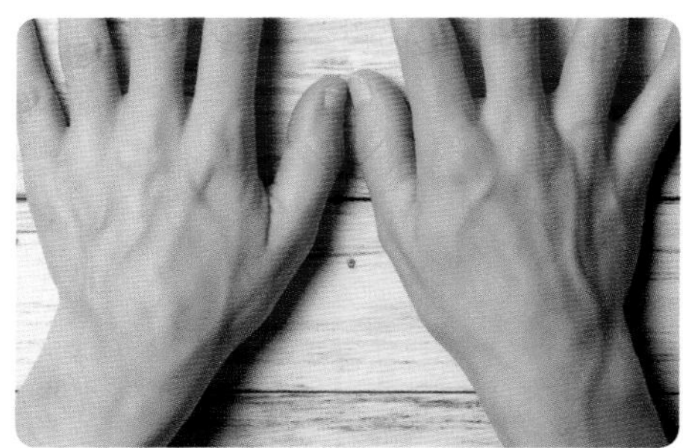

Veins carry blood back to the heart. This blood carries less oxygen gas, which makes it a dark-red colour. The dark-red blood flows inside light-coloured veins, which are covered by a layer of skin. This makes veins look blue.

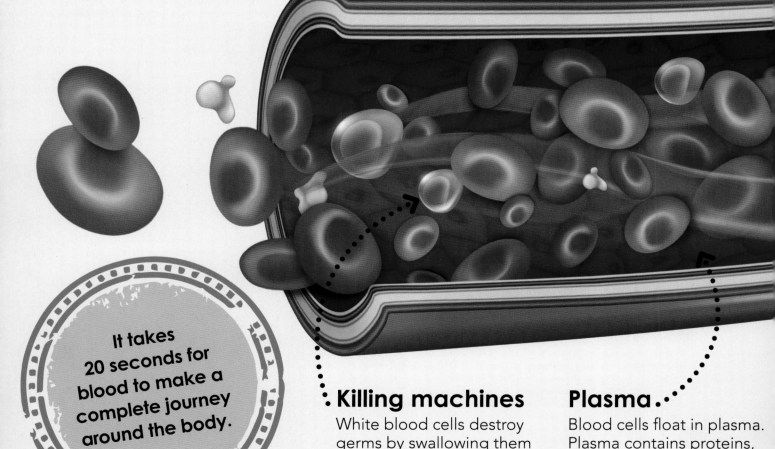

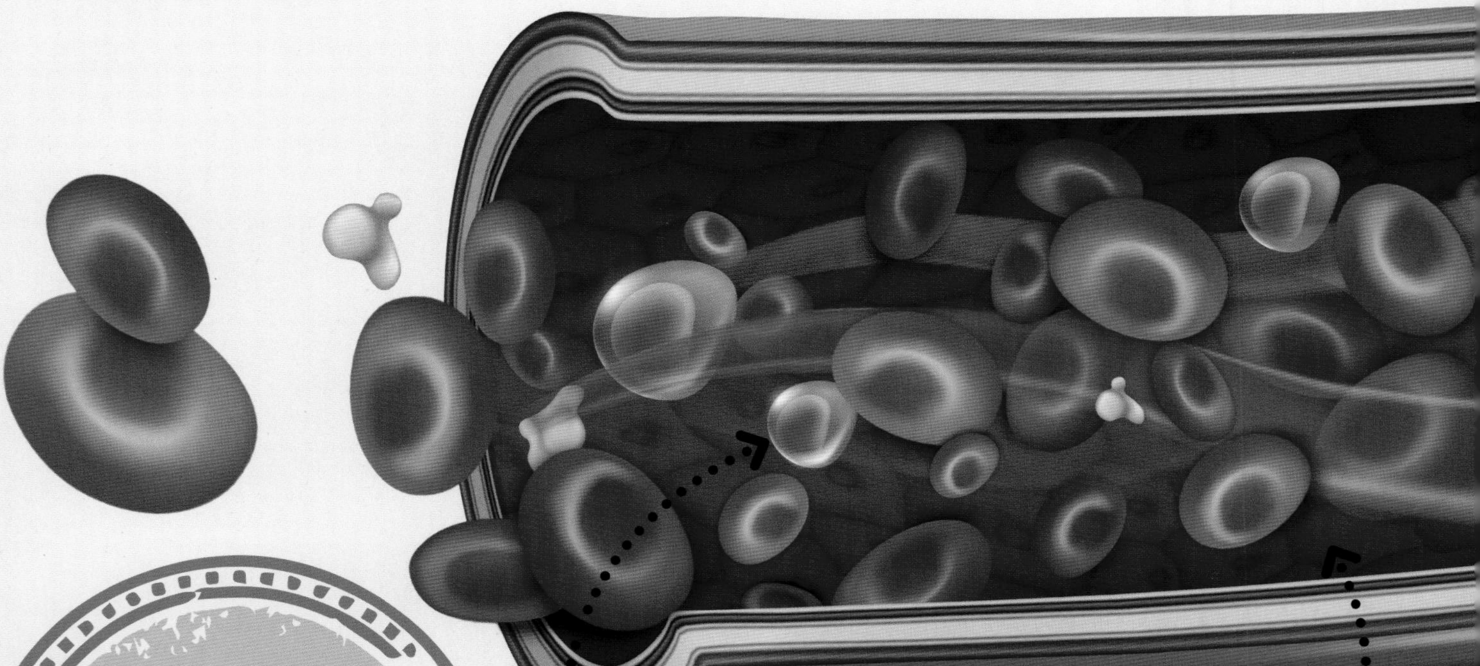

It takes 20 seconds for blood to make a complete journey around the body.

Killing machines

White blood cells destroy germs by swallowing them up, or by squirting killer chemicals at them.

Plasma

Blood cells float in plasma. Plasma contains proteins, sugars, salts, hormones, vitamins, and minerals mixed into lots of water.

Haemoglobin

Red blood cells get their colour from a protein called haemoglobin. This contains an element called iron, which is a red-brown colour. Haemoglobin grabs and holds onto oxygen. The blood cells then carry this oxygen around the body.

Repair team

Platelets are broken up cells that stick together when you get a wound. They make a scab and repair the damage.

Gas transporters

Red blood cells carry oxygen gas to wherever it is needed in the body. They drop oxygen off and then carry away a waste gas called carbon dioxide.

? True or false?

1. Veins carry blood away from the heart.
2. Iron makes blood red.
3. Red blood cells fight off germs.

See pages 132–133 for the answers

Switching on

Genes are similar to switches – they can be turned on and off. They can tell the cell what to be, such as a bone cell or part of an eyelash.

Chromosomes

DNA is curled up and wound into bundles, called chromosomes. These contain hundreds, and often thousands, of genes.

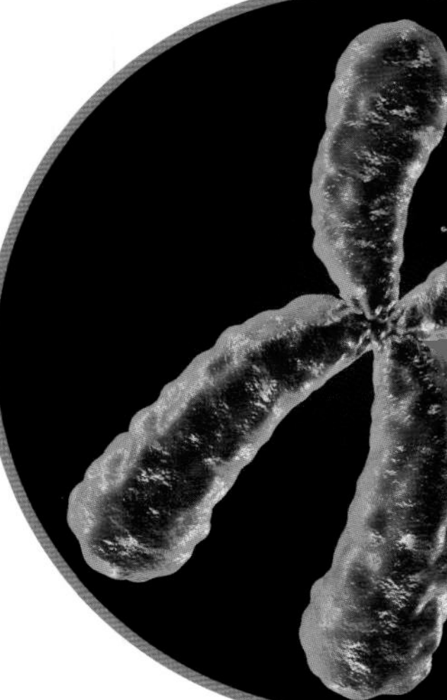

In the nucleus

Each cell in your body contains every single one of your genes. These are stored in chromosome pairs in the nucleus, which is the centre of the cell.

What is DNA?

The way the body works and looks is mostly controlled by genes. Bodies are built from tiny cells, which contain all of the instructions needed to make you who you are. These instructions are coded in sections of your DNA, which are called genes. DNA stands for **d**eoxyribo**n**ucleic **a**cid.

? Quick quiz

1. Where in the cell are chromosomes stored?
2. How does each cell in the body know what to do?
3. What is the name of the DNA's twisted ladder shape?

See pages 132–133 for the answers

Genes

These sections of DNA each contain the code to make a part of the body. We have 25,000 genes, which control everything from face shape to how many toenails you have.

DNA

This is a long chain of chemicals that are joined together in a double-helix shape. DNA makes use of four types of chemical to make a code for each part of the body.

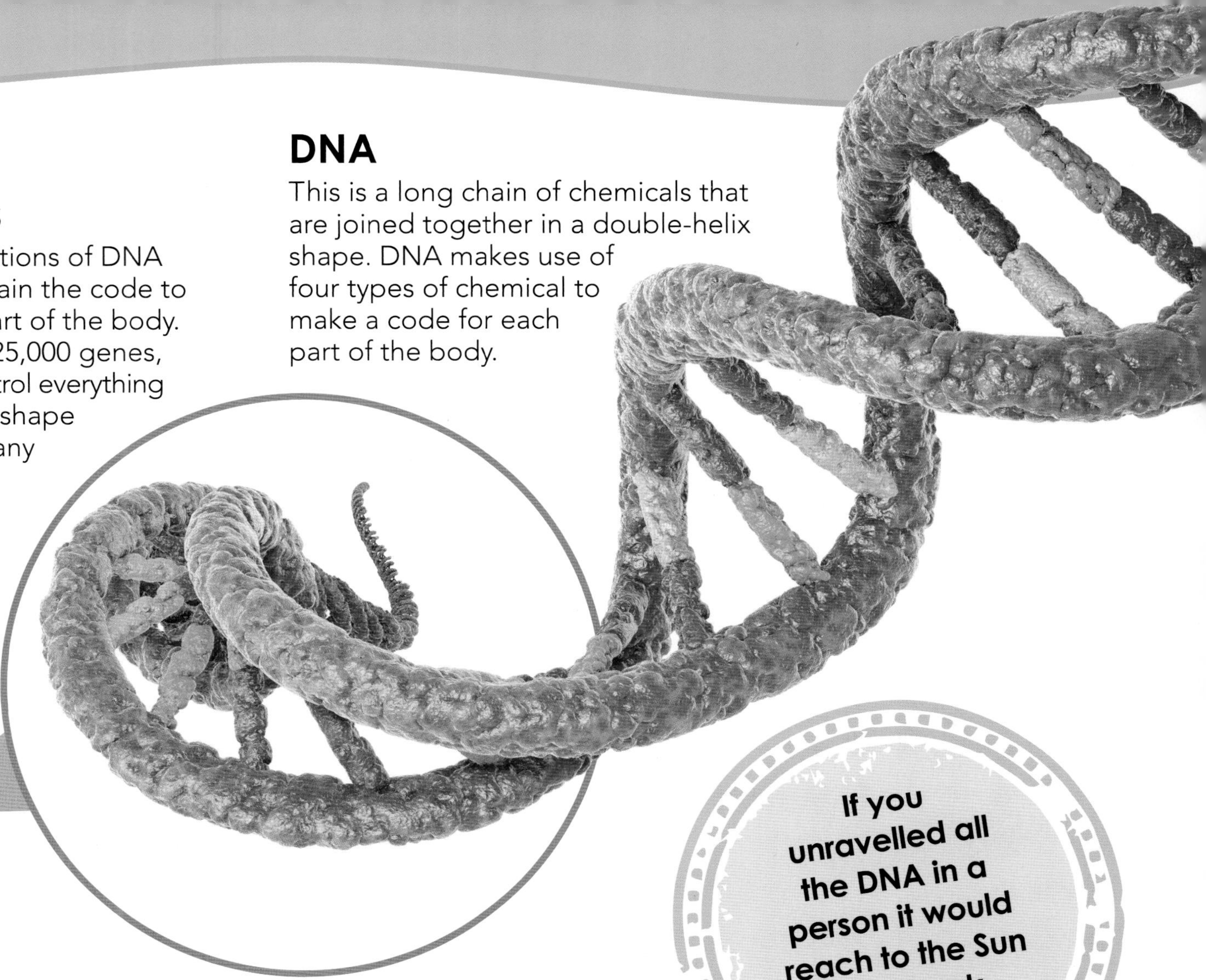

If you unravelled all the DNA in a person it would reach to the Sun and back 400 times!

Do genes control who I am?

Genes control many things, even parts of your personality, but your life experiences also shape who you are and your thoughts. What you eat and the exercise you do also changes your body shape.

Chromosome pairs

Chromosomes come in pairs and the body has 23 chromosome pairs in total. Each pair contains a set of genes from your mother and a set of genes from your father.

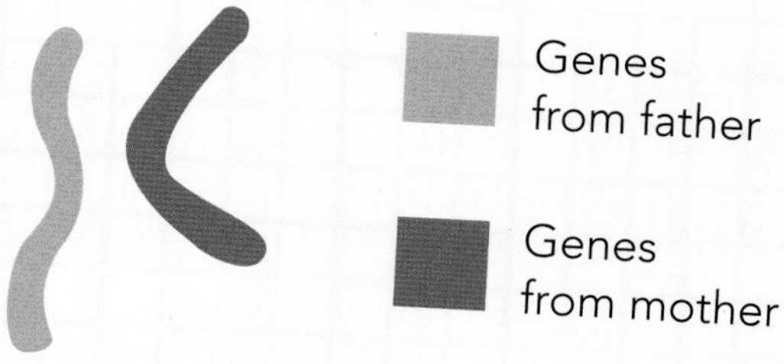

Pair of chromosomes

Are all twins identical?

Non-identical twins have different genes to each other. Each child gets a copy of genes from each parent, but these copies are not the same for each twin. Non-identical twins have some similarities and differences, like any other set of siblings.

Why do twins look the same?

Identical twins share the same genes, that's why they look the same. All of the instructions that make people unique are in each cell of the body. These tiny instructions are put into a code in molecules called DNA. Identical twins have the same coded sequence of DNA.

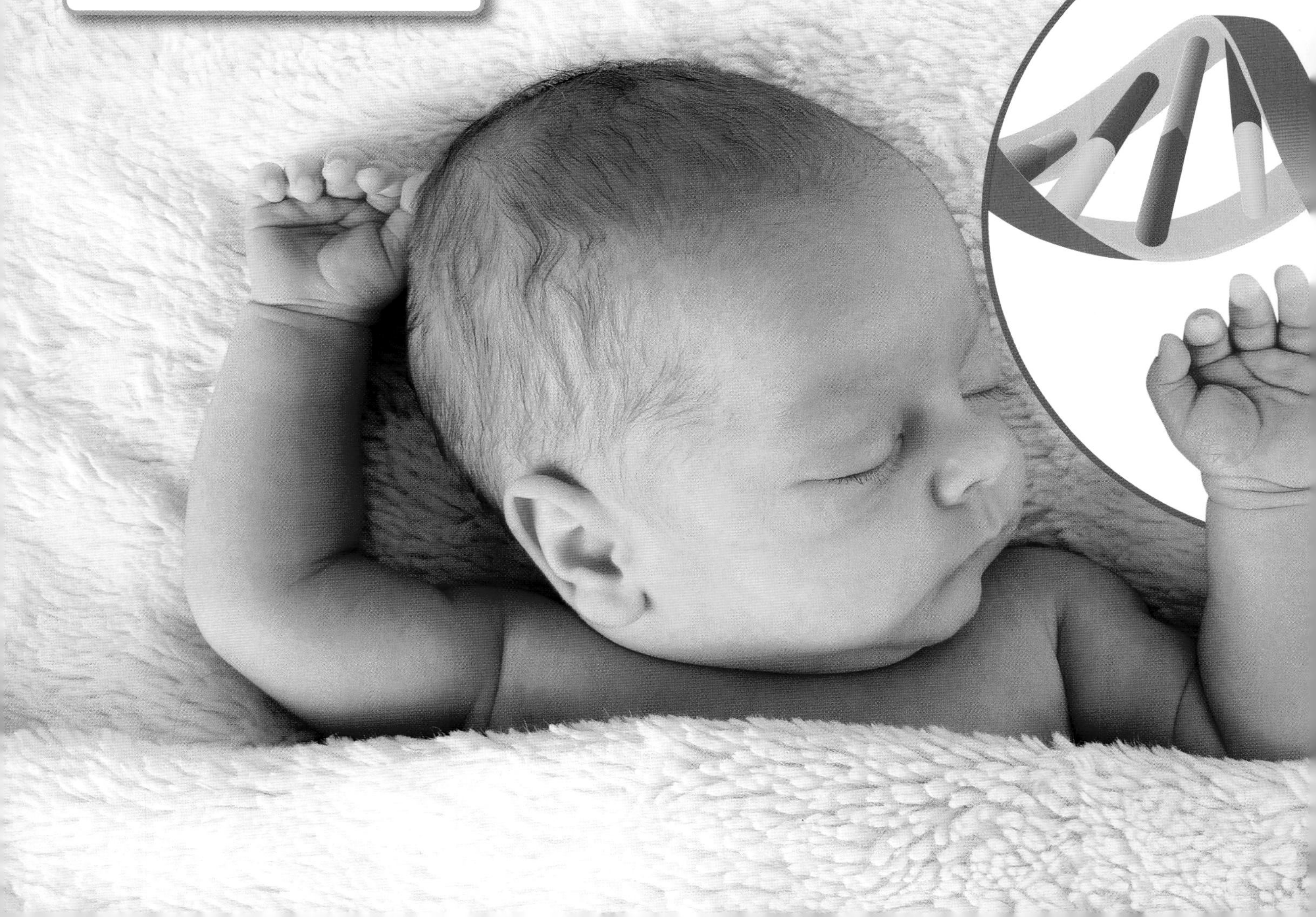

Coded sequence

The four chemicals that make up a coded sequence of DNA are Adenine (A), Thymine (T), Guanine (G), and Cytosine (C). Their letters spell out body-making instructions in sequences called genes.

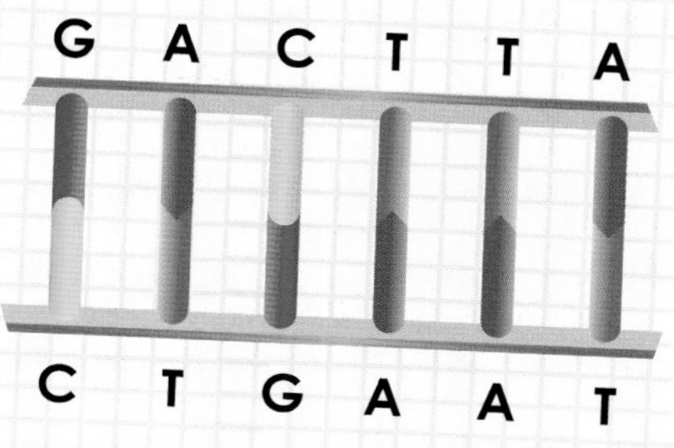

? Quick quiz

1. How does so much DNA fit inside a tiny cell?
2. What does most of your DNA do?
3. Where does your DNA come from?

See pages 132–133 for the answers

DNA

Every cell in the body contains 2 m (6.6 ft) of thin, wound-up DNA. However, we only know what about 4 cm (1.6 in) of it does, the rest is still a mystery to us.

Differences

Even though they share the same genes, identical twins can grow to different heights if one has a different diet or does more exercise. They also develop different personalities.

All humans share 99.9 per cent of their DNA with each other.

Why don't I have my mum's nose?

Genes

Your DNA is inside groups of instructions called genes. The genes you have decide your characteristics, such as the shape of your nose.

The shape of your nose depends on the genes that were passed on to you from your parents. It will stop changing shape when you're about 10 years old, but it will keep growing slowly.

Genetic family tree

Here's an example of how you might inherit the shape of your nose from your parents.

Key:
In this example, there are two gene variants, or alleles.

N = long nose
n = short nose

The father and the mother pass on one of their alleles to each child at random.

The N (long nose) allele is dominant. That means that when a person has both alleles, the N allele overrides the n allele – and the person has a long nose.

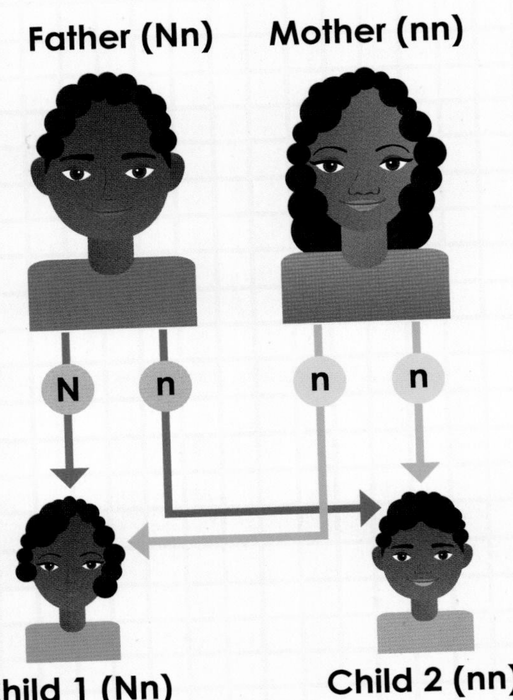

Each child receives a mixture of alleles from their parents.

Inheritance

You get one set of genes from each of your parents, for each of your characteristics. Some genes are stronger than others, so most people end up looking like a mixture of both parents.

What affects the colour of my teeth?

Genes

Genes decide the thickness of enamel – a hard, white tooth coating. Under this layer, teeth are yellow. People with yellow teeth have a thin layer of enamel.

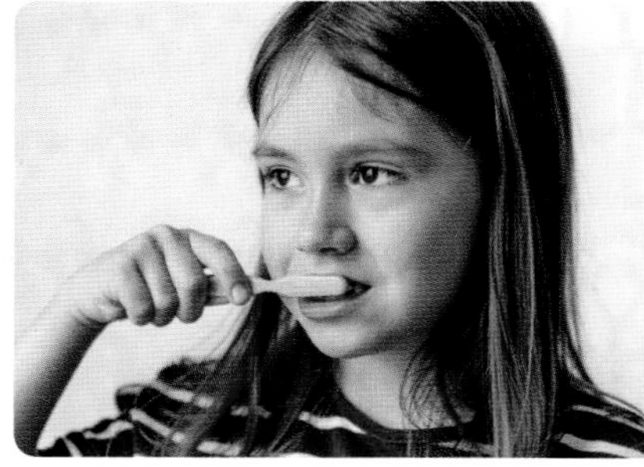

Lifestyle

What you eat and drink, and how often you brush your teeth can affect the colour and strength of teeth. For example, too much orange juice can rot teeth because it is acidic.

? Quick quiz

1. Where do your genes come from?
2. What word describes something passed on from your parents?

See pages 132–133 for the answers

Are bacteria alive?

Yes! Bacteria are tiny, one-celled organisms (living things). Bacteria play an important role in your body. Some help your digestive system break down food and produce important vitamins. Other bacteria can produce poisonous substances, called toxins, that can make you sick. We sometimes use another name for these bacteria: germs.

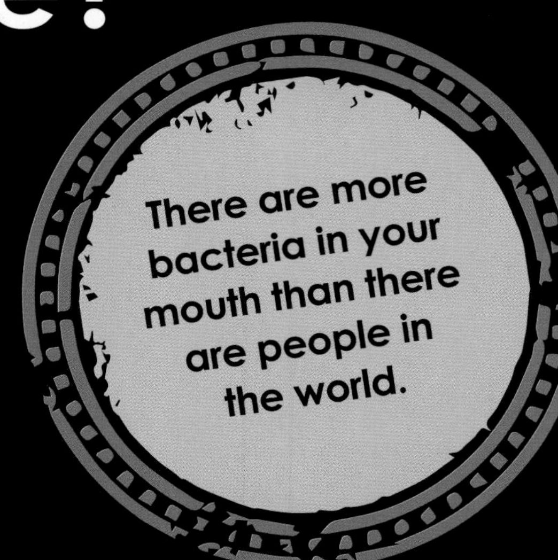

There are more bacteria in your mouth than there are people in the world.

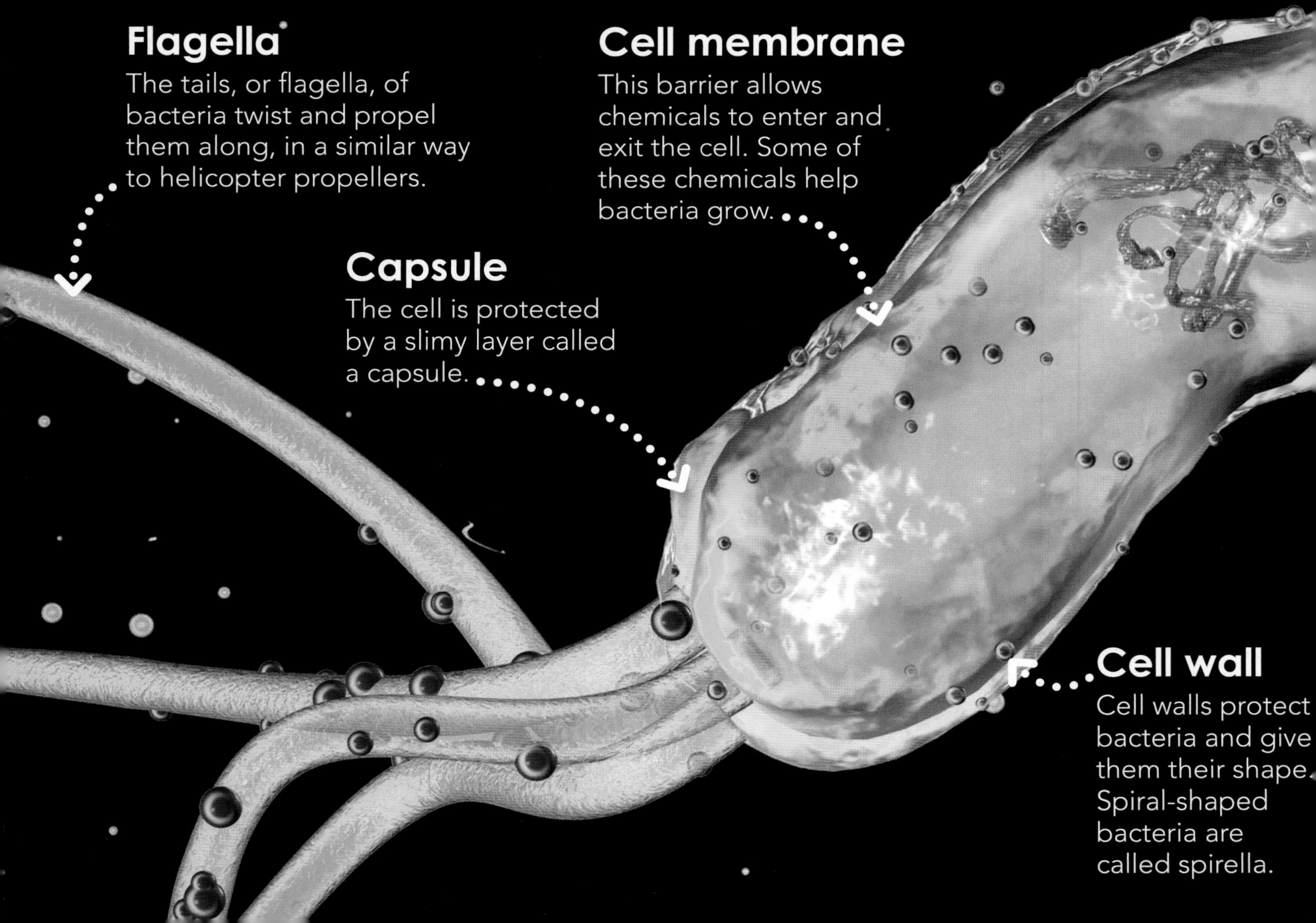

Flagella

The tails, or flagella, of bacteria twist and propel them along, in a similar way to helicopter propellers.

Cell membrane

This barrier allows chemicals to enter and exit the cell. Some of these chemicals help bacteria grow.

Capsule

The cell is protected by a slimy layer called a capsule.

Cell wall

Cell walls protect bacteria and give them their shape. Spiral-shaped bacteria are called spirella.

Ribosomes

Bacteria reproduce by splitting in two. Ribosomes make proteins that help build bacteria.

Chromosome

The DNA in the cell is in one big circular loop called a chromosome. DNA contains information about what the cell is and how it works.

Cytoplasm

The fluid inside the cell is called cytoplasm. It contains substances that make the bacteria in your body work.

True or false?

1. Half of your poo is made of bacteria.
2. Bacteria and viruses are different things.

See pages 132–133 for the answers

What other shapes do bacteria have?

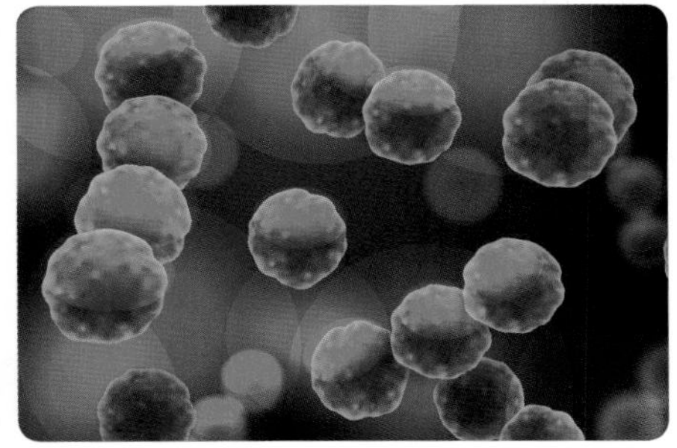

Coccus bacteria

Types of bacteria that have spherical, or round, shapes are known as coccus bacteria.

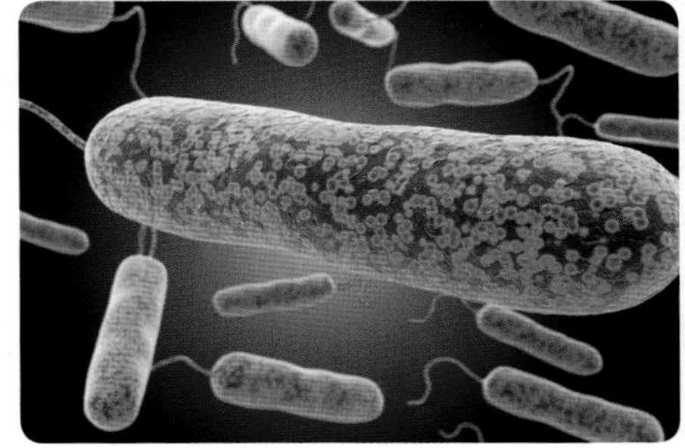

Bacillus bacteria

Any types of bacteria that have rod shapes are called bacillus bacteria.

What are hormones?

Hormones are chemical signals that travel in your blood. They are made in many organs of the body, including glands, and they do different jobs. Hormones help you to regulate and control many things, such as your energy levels, mood, and growth. Hormones are slower to act than the electrical signals of nerves, but their effects usually last longer.

How do your hormones work?

Your brain monitors your body and signals the release of hormones when something needs to change. For example, when it is dark, your brain tells your pineal gland to release melatonin to relax the body.

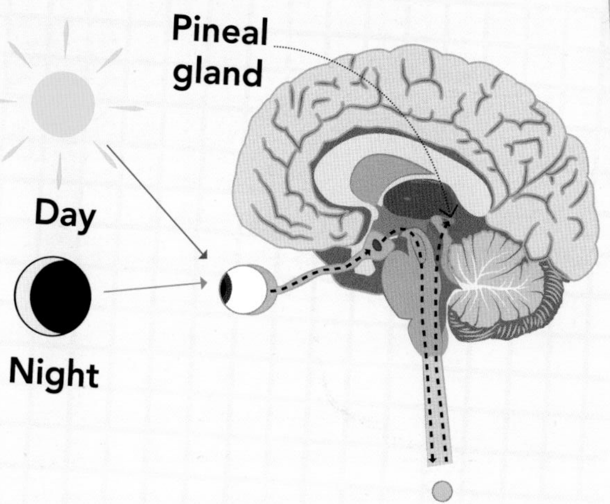

Pituitary gland

This gland releases nine different chemical signals, including one that helps you to grow. The pituitary gland produces hormones that control many of the other glands.

Thymus gland

The thymus gland makes hormones that tell the body to produce white blood cells to fight off sickness. This gland lies behind your sternum, or breastbone. It is a large gland in children, but it shrinks as you get older.

Thyroid gland

This produces many hormones in your body. Some of these signals help to control your body weight and temperature.

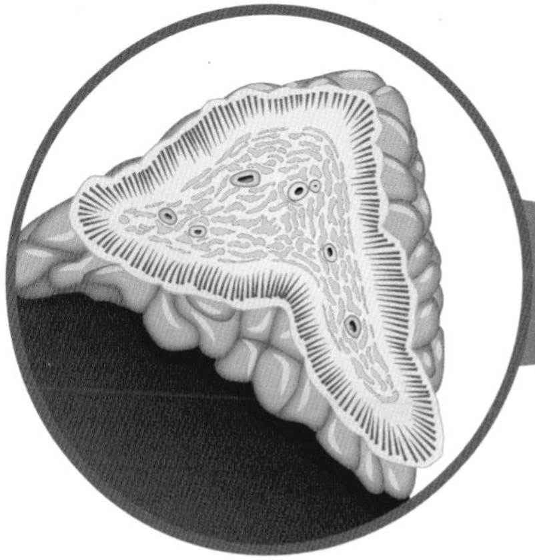

Adrenal glands

These glands produce many hormones that help your body work, such as adrenaline – a hormone that is released when you are cold or scared.

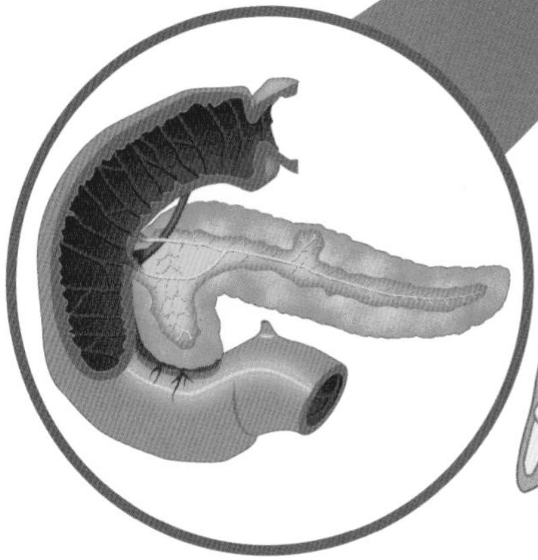

Pancreas

The main job of the pancreas is to release a hormone that controls the level of sugar in your blood. It also sends signals to the stomach to make acid to digest your food.

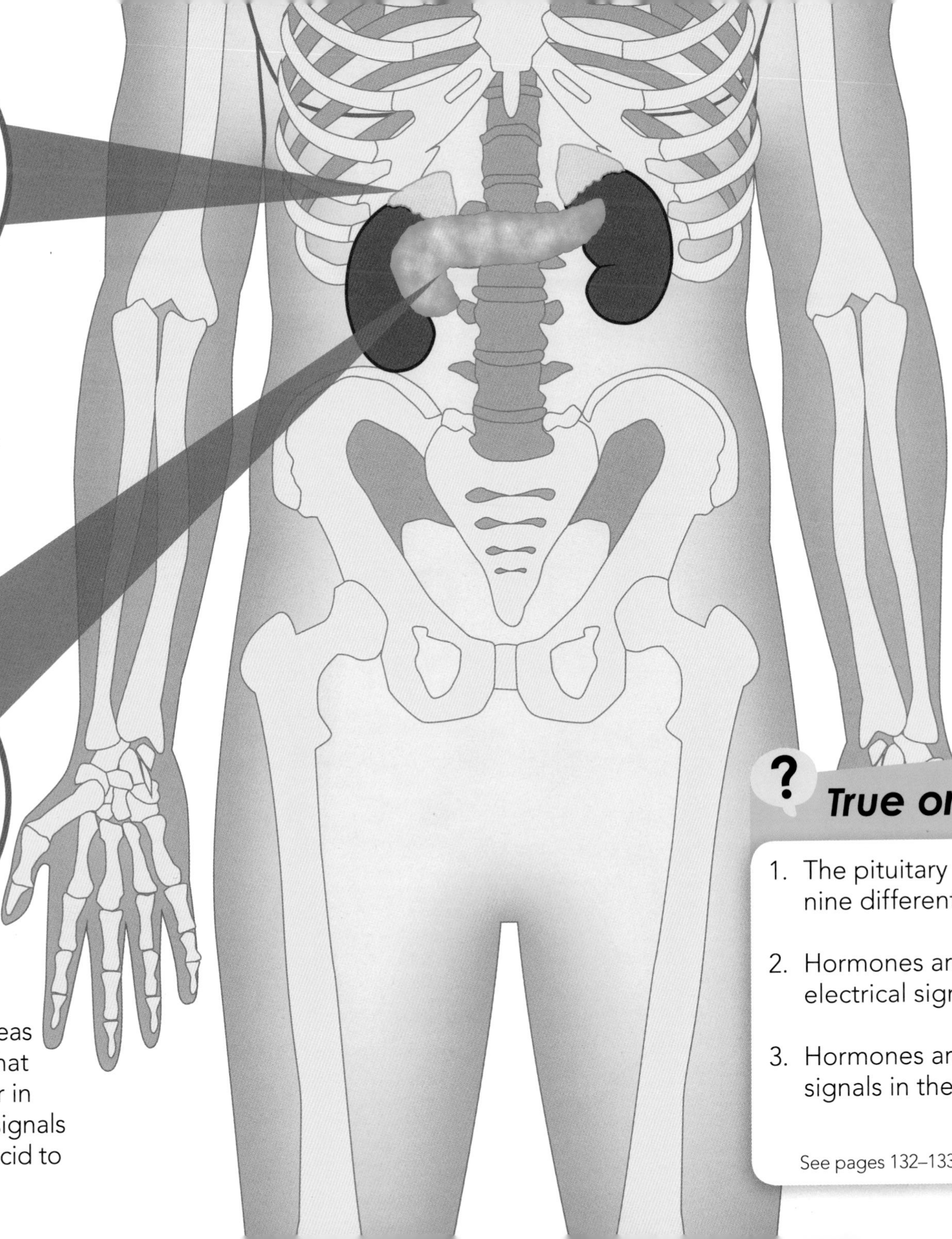

True or false?

1. The pituitary gland makes nine different hormones.
2. Hormones are electrical signals.
3. Hormones are the fastest signals in the body.

See pages 132–133 for the answers

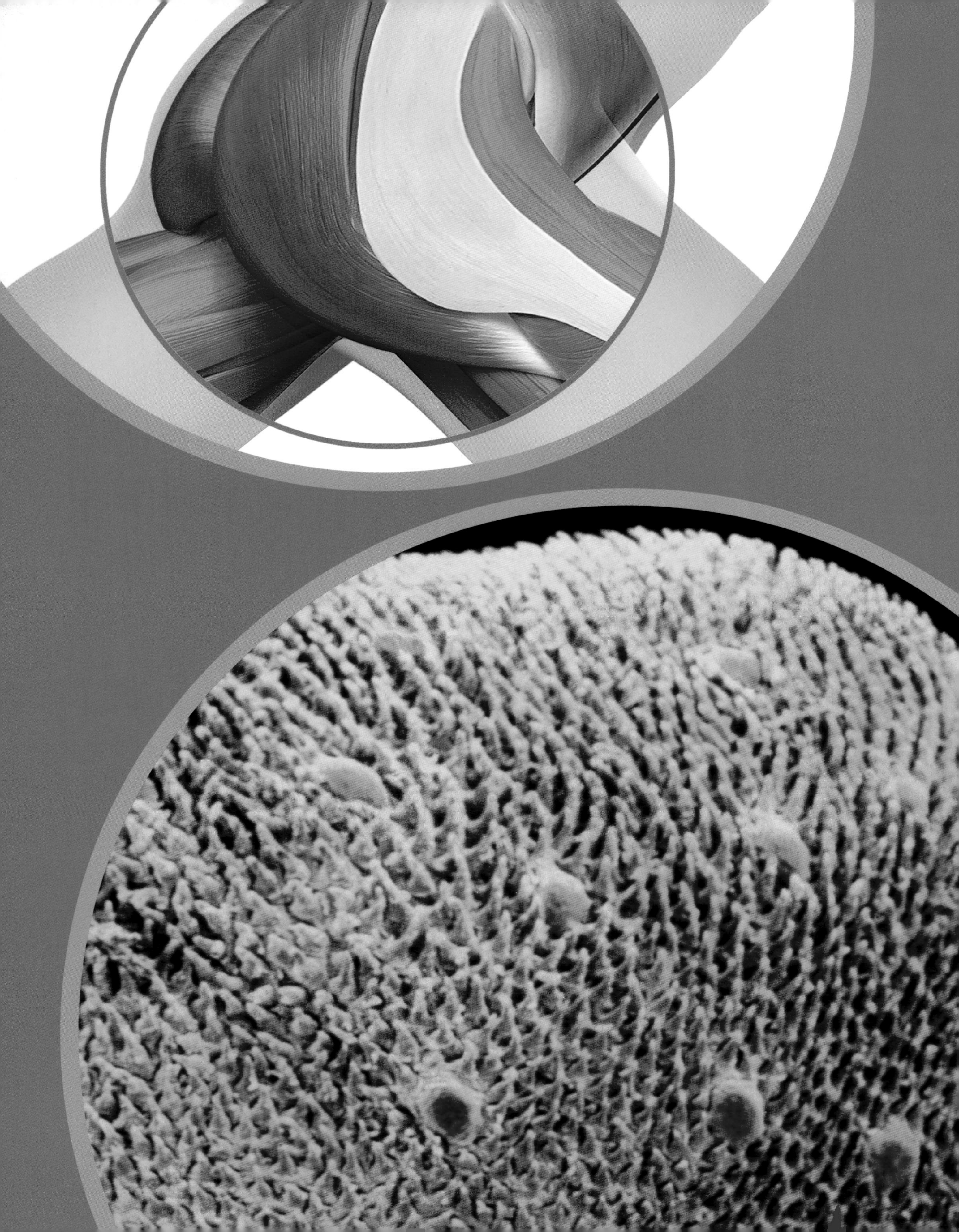

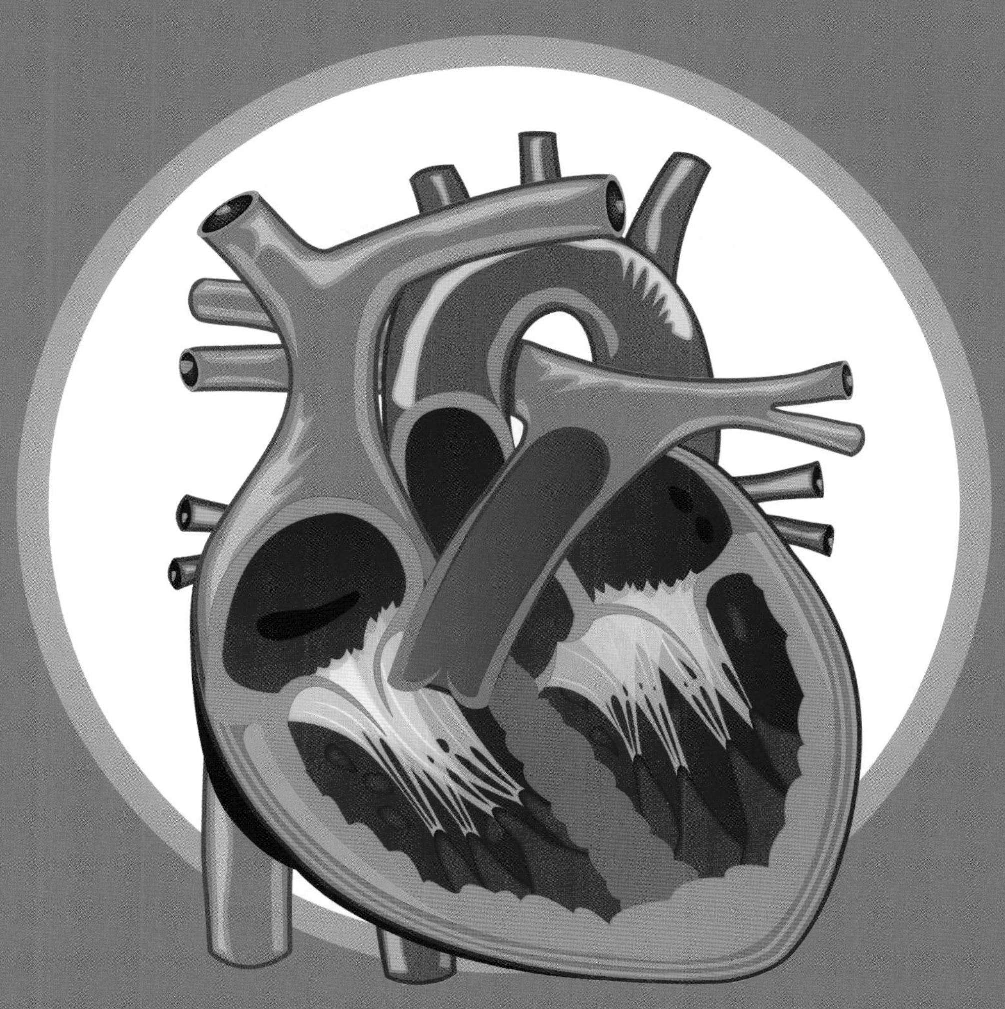

Piece by piece

All of the different parts of your body have important jobs to do – they work together to keep you working. Your bones make blood cells, your spine bends with flexible joints, and your lungs take in air for you to breathe.

What are bones made of?

Bones give your body strength and structure. They are organs with a blood supply, nerves, and several layers of tissue. The outer shell is solid, but inside there is a jelly-like substance called bone marrow. Here is a thigh bone, or femur. It's the largest bone in your body.

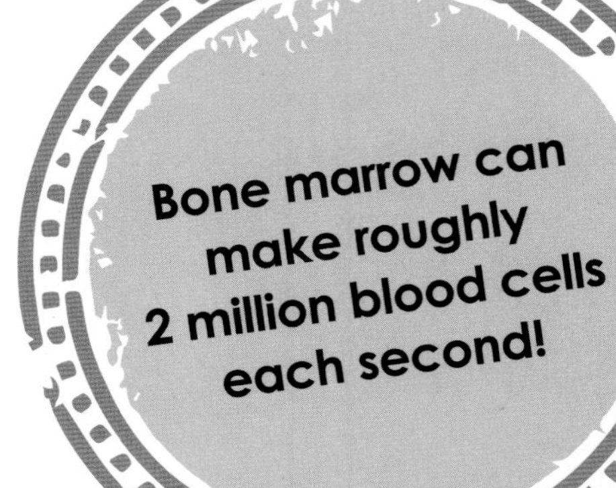

Bone marrow can make roughly 2 million blood cells each second!

Compact bone

The outer layer of bone is hard and heavy. It is made up of tightly packed tubes of strong bone tissue called osteons.

Periosteum

Bones are covered in a smooth coating called the periosteum. This protects the bone and helps connect it to the muscles around it.

Steel beams

Strong and light

Human bones are six times lighter than steel, but they are just as strong.

How many bones are in the body?

Babies are born with about 300 bones, which are made from cartilage, a flexible tissue. These fuse (join together) and harden as the baby grows. A baby's skull, for example, has separate bones, which fuse together over time. By the age of about 18, an adult human has just 206 bones.

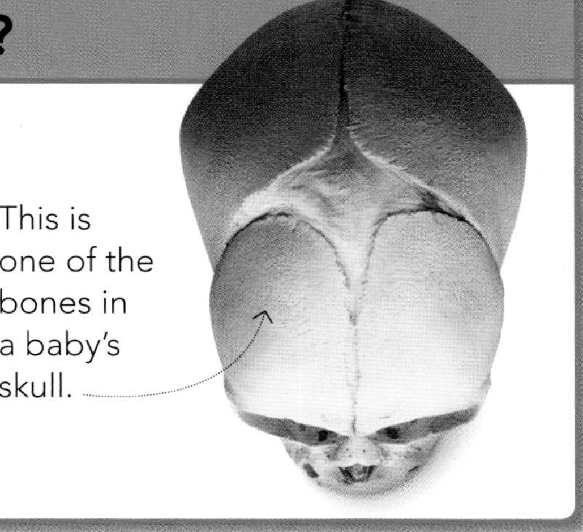

This is one of the bones in a baby's skull.

Quick quiz

1. What does yellow bone marrow store?
2. What makes bones so strong?
3. What are babies' skeletons mostly made of?

See pages 132–133 for the answers

Bone marrow

There are two types of bone marrow. Red marrow makes blood cells, while yellow marrow stores fat, which gives you energy.

Spongy bone

A light, but strong layer of spongy bone sits under the compact bone. It is filled with bone marrow, and the holes hold blood vessels and nerves.

Head

The head of the femur is round so it fits in the socket of the hip bone, to make the hip joint. The head has both spongy bone and compact bone.

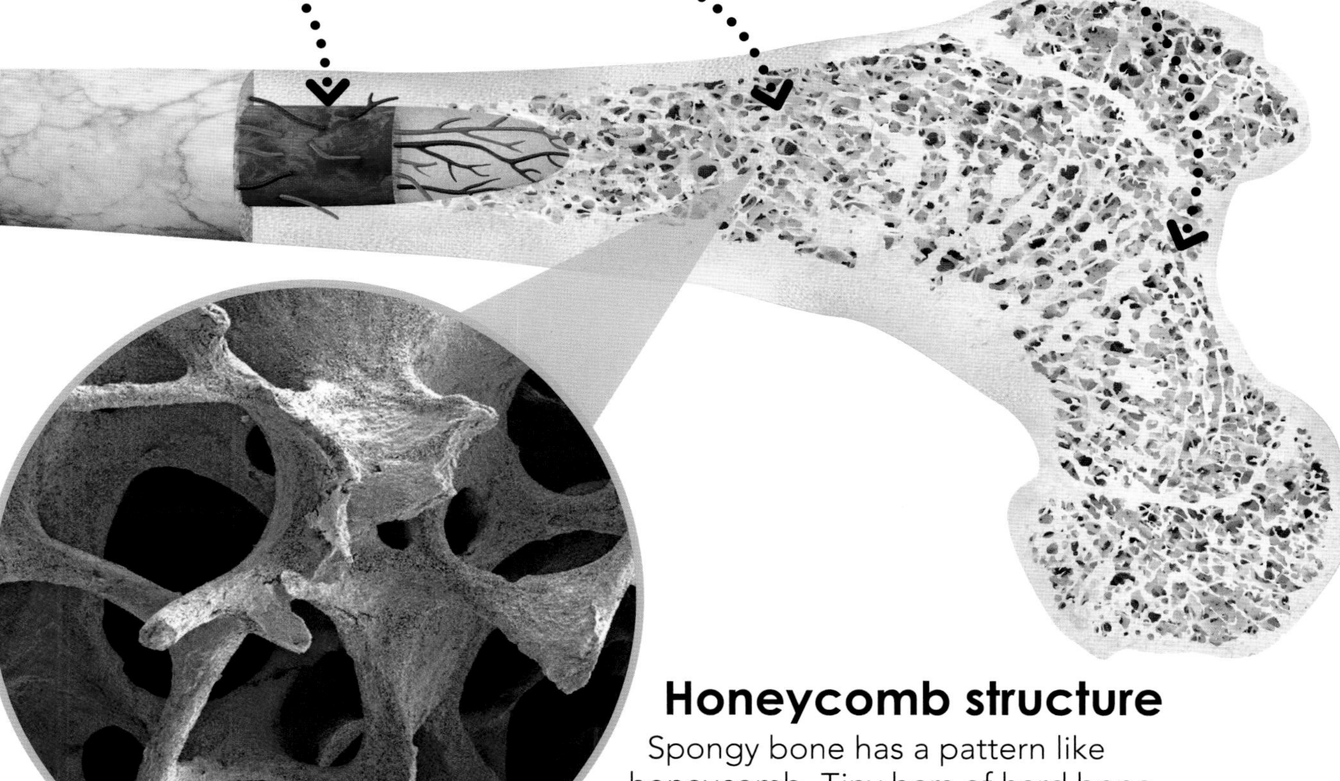

Honeycomb structure

Spongy bone has a pattern like honeycomb. Tiny bars of hard bone cross over each other with spaces in between. The spaces keep bones light, while the bars make them strong.

You use 300 different muscles just to stand up!

Quick quiz

1. Of the three main types of muscle, which type moves bones?
2. Which muscles raise the forearm?

See pages 132–133 for the answers

Tendons

Muscles are attached to bones by tendons. These can be thick or thin, flat or round. Tendons can also join muscles to moving objects, such as eyeballs!

Tendons

Muscle cells

Muscle cells are sometimes called muscle fibres because they are long and thin. When muscle fibres contract, they glide past one another. This shortens the muscle and pulls your body into a different shape. If you lift up your leg, you use your gluteus maximus to pull your leg back into a straight position.

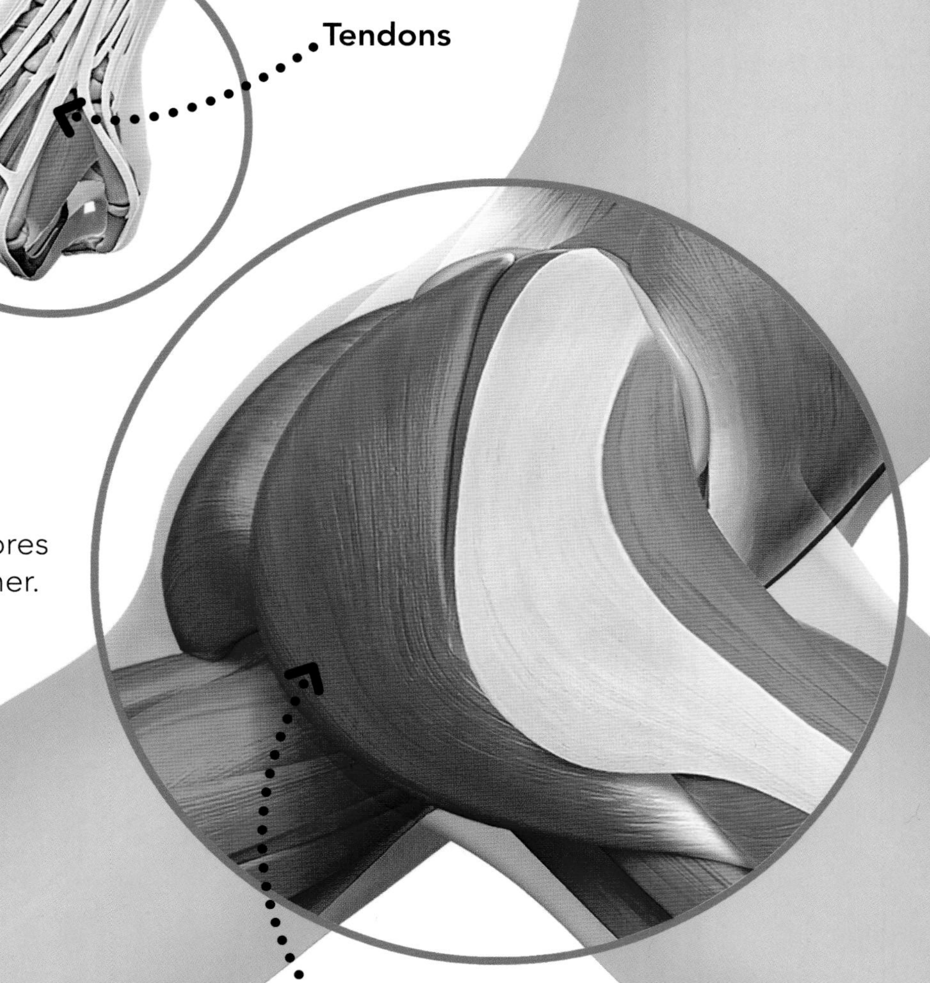

How do muscles move my body?

Skeletal muscles work in pairs to move bones. To raise your arm, the bicep muscle contracts and pulls the arm bones up while the tricep muscle relaxes. To straighten your arm, the tricep contracts and the bicep relaxes.

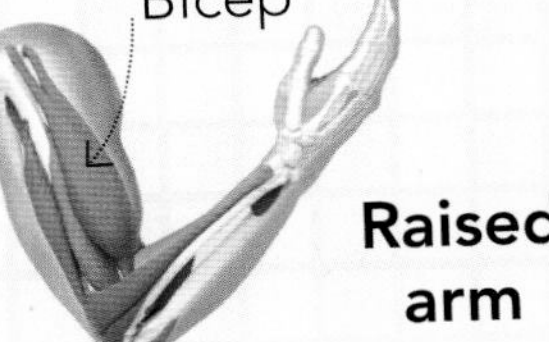

Skeletal muscles

Skeletal muscles are one type of muscle. Most are attached to your bones by tendons. This type of muscle helps to shape and move your body.

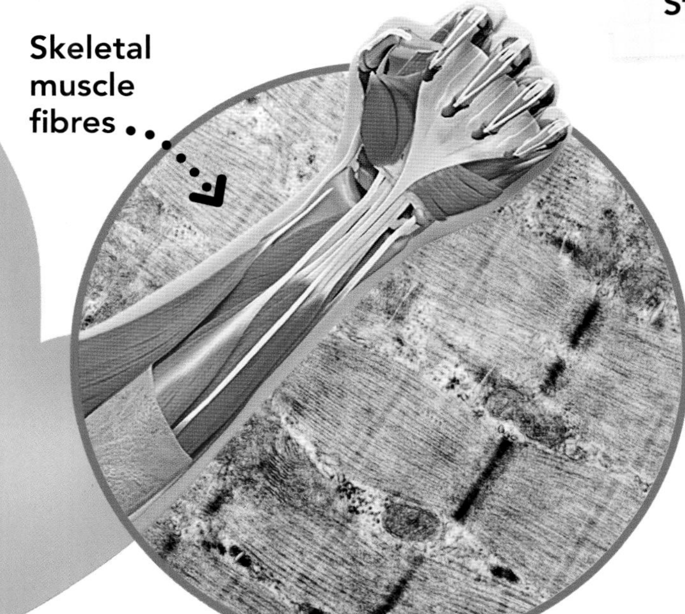

What other muscle types do I have?

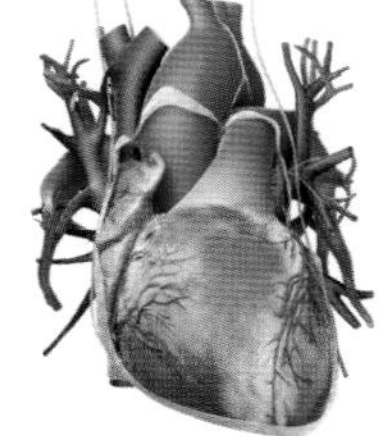

Cardiac muscles
Your heart is made from cardiac muscles. These make your heart beat to pump blood. Cardiac muscles work continuously.

Smooth muscles
These muscles are found within the walls of hollow organs, such as the bladder. Smooth muscles contract to squeeze the organ.

What is my biggest muscle?

The gluteus maximus is the biggest muscle in your body. It is located in your bottom. This muscle helps you to run, jump, and climb. Groups of muscles work in teams to move different parts of the body. Electrical signals sent from the brain control muscle movement.

What helps keep my brain healthy?

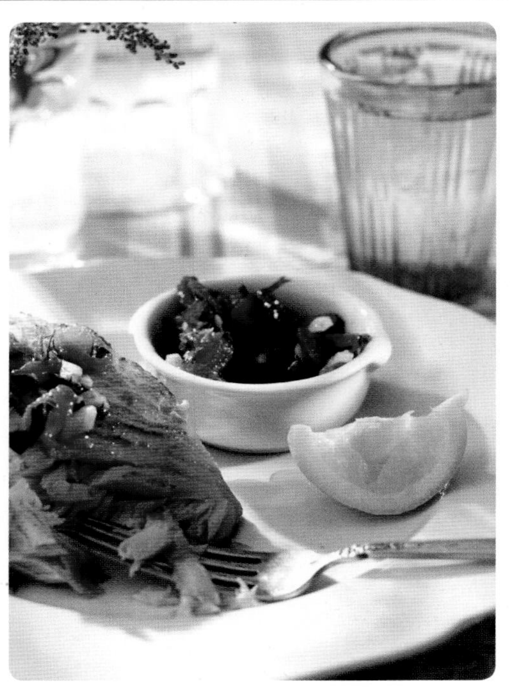

Food and water
A healthy diet supplies your brain with nutrients. Water helps make the fluid that surrounds the brain. This fluid delivers nutrients and takes away waste.

Cushioning fluid

The brain floats in one type of fluid called cerebrospinal fluid (CSF). It keeps the brain afloat and helps cushion it if you bang your head. It also supplies the brain with nutrients.

Membranes

These three sheet-like layers of tissue surround and protect your brain. Together, they are called the meninges.

Moving fluid

CSF flows around your brain. It follows the arrows on this diagram as it moves around your brain and spinal cord.

What's between my brain and skull?

Clear fluid flows around between your brain and your skull, and there are three flat layers of tissue, called meninges. One layer wraps around your brain, your skull is lined with another layer, and the third layer floats between the two.

Blood vessels

These supply blood to the brain. They are different to the blood vessels in the rest of your body as they do not allow viruses or germs to enter the brain. These are filtered out from the blood by cells in the ventricles.

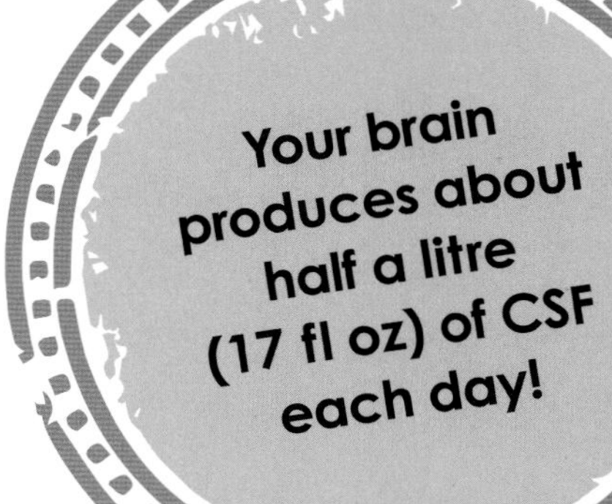

Your brain produces about half a litre (17 fl oz) of CSF each day!

Making fluid

Cavities in the brain called ventricles are lined with cells that make CSF. It flows around and inside the brain and down the spinal cord. CSF has white blood cells, sugar, and proteins in it to help the brain to work.

Skull

Your skull helps to protect your brain. It is made of several bones, and encases your brain and other organs in your head, such as your eyes.

Spinal cord

Your spinal cord is also cushioned by CSF. It flows down the back of your spinal cord and then back up the front to reach the brain again.

? Quick quiz

1. How many membrane layers are there between your brain and skull?
2. What does the fluid around your brain do?
3. Apart from your brain, where would you find CSF?

See pages 132–133 for the answers

What's inside my heart?

Your heart contains four compartments, called chambers. There are two atria and two ventricles. Their muscular walls relax and contract, pushing blood to the next compartment or out to the body and lungs.

Your aorta is the largest artery in your body. It looks like a hosepipe!

? Quick quiz

1. What makes the sound of your heart beating?
2. What does blood collect from the lungs?
3. What takes blood out of the heart?

See pages 132–133 for the answers

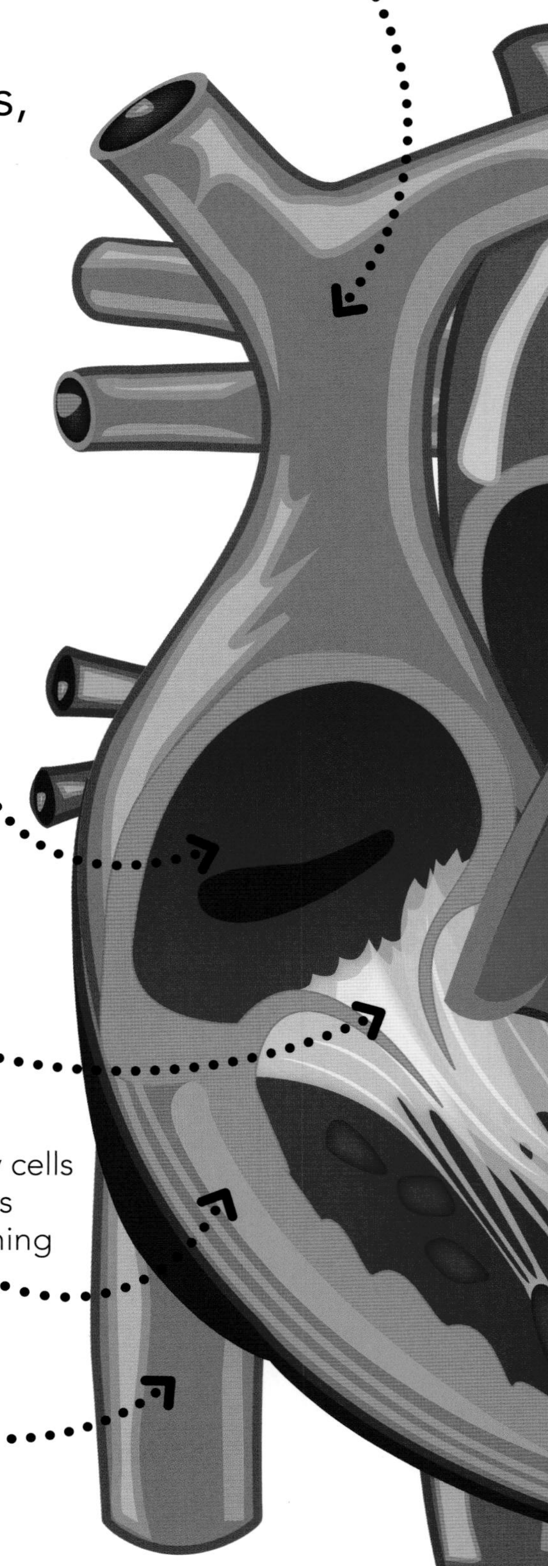

Superior vena cava

This vein returns blood from the head and upper body to the right atrium.

Atrium

Blood flows into the smaller chambers of the heart – the left and the right atrium.

Valves

Doors in the heart called valves only open one way, so blood flows in one direction. The sound of a heart beating is the valves shutting.

Heart walls

Electrical signals made by cells in the heart walls cause its muscles to contract, pushing blood through the heart.

Inferior vena cava

This is the largest vein in your body. Blood enters the right atrium from the lower body.

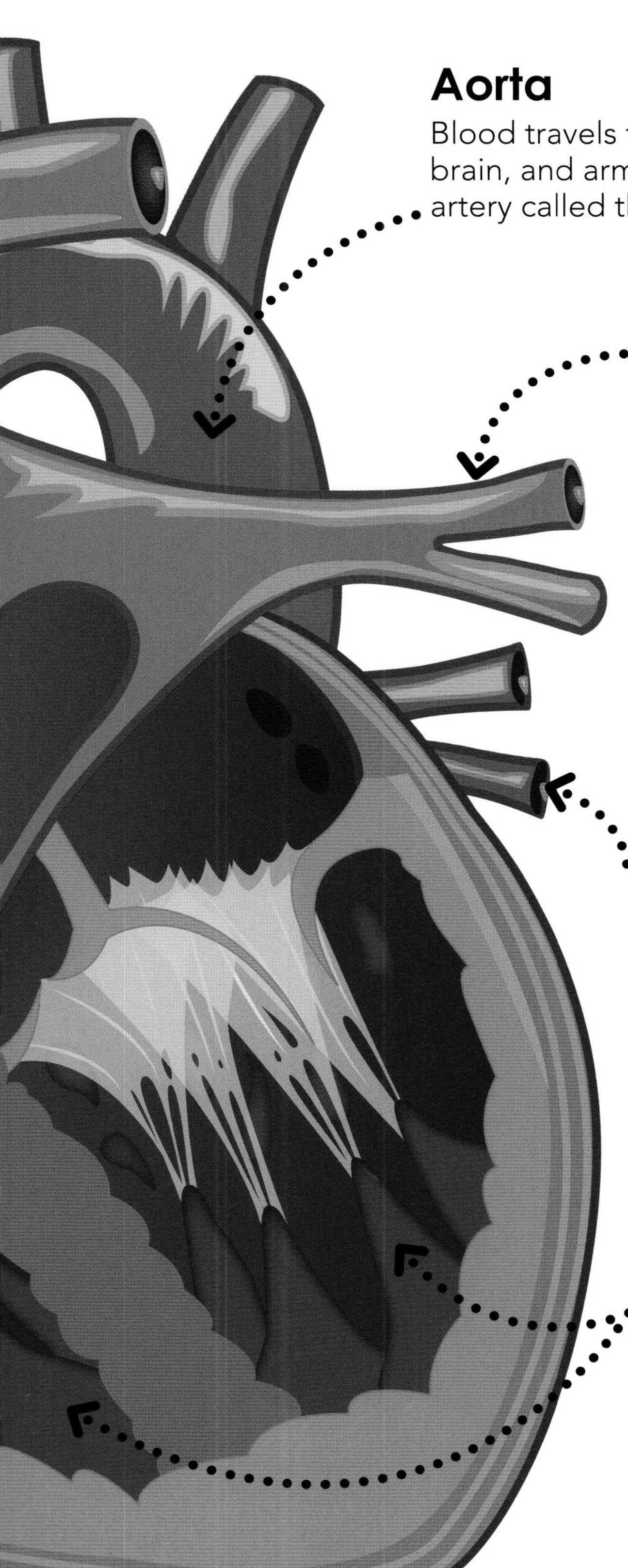

Aorta

Blood travels to the head, brain, and arms through an artery called the aorta.

Pulmonary artery

Most arteries carry oxygen-rich blood, but the pulmonary artery carries oxygen-poor blood to the lungs, where it can collect more oxygen.

Pulmonary vein

Oxygen-rich blood returns from the lungs in pulmonary veins on either side of the heart.

Ventricles

Blood is continually pushed in and out of the ventricles when the heart squeezes.

How does blood move around the body?

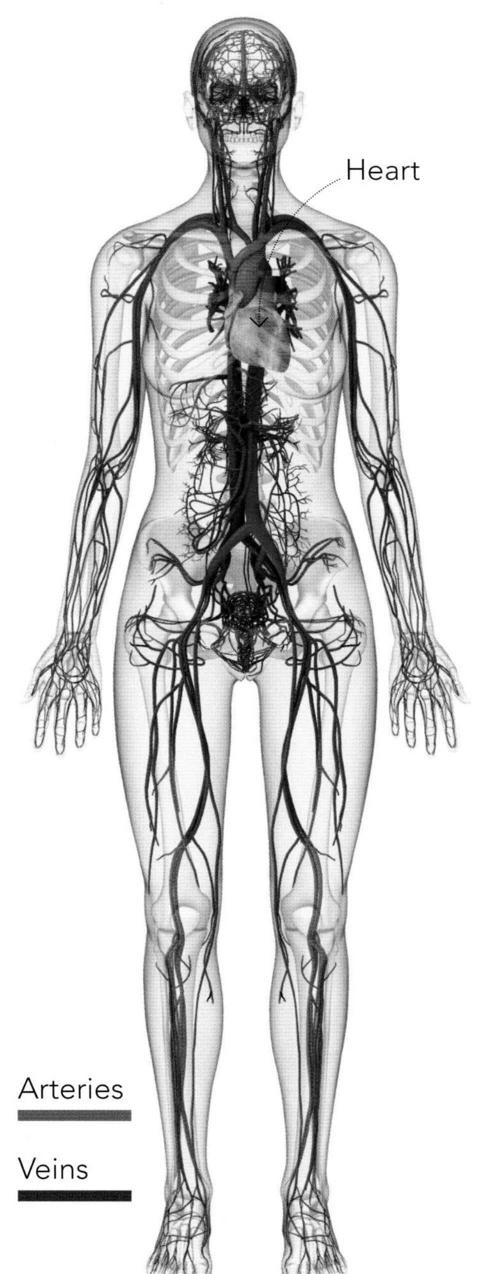

Blood vessels

Blood travels in a network of tubes called blood vessels. Vessels that carry blood away from the heart are called arteries. Vessels that carry blood to the heart are called veins.

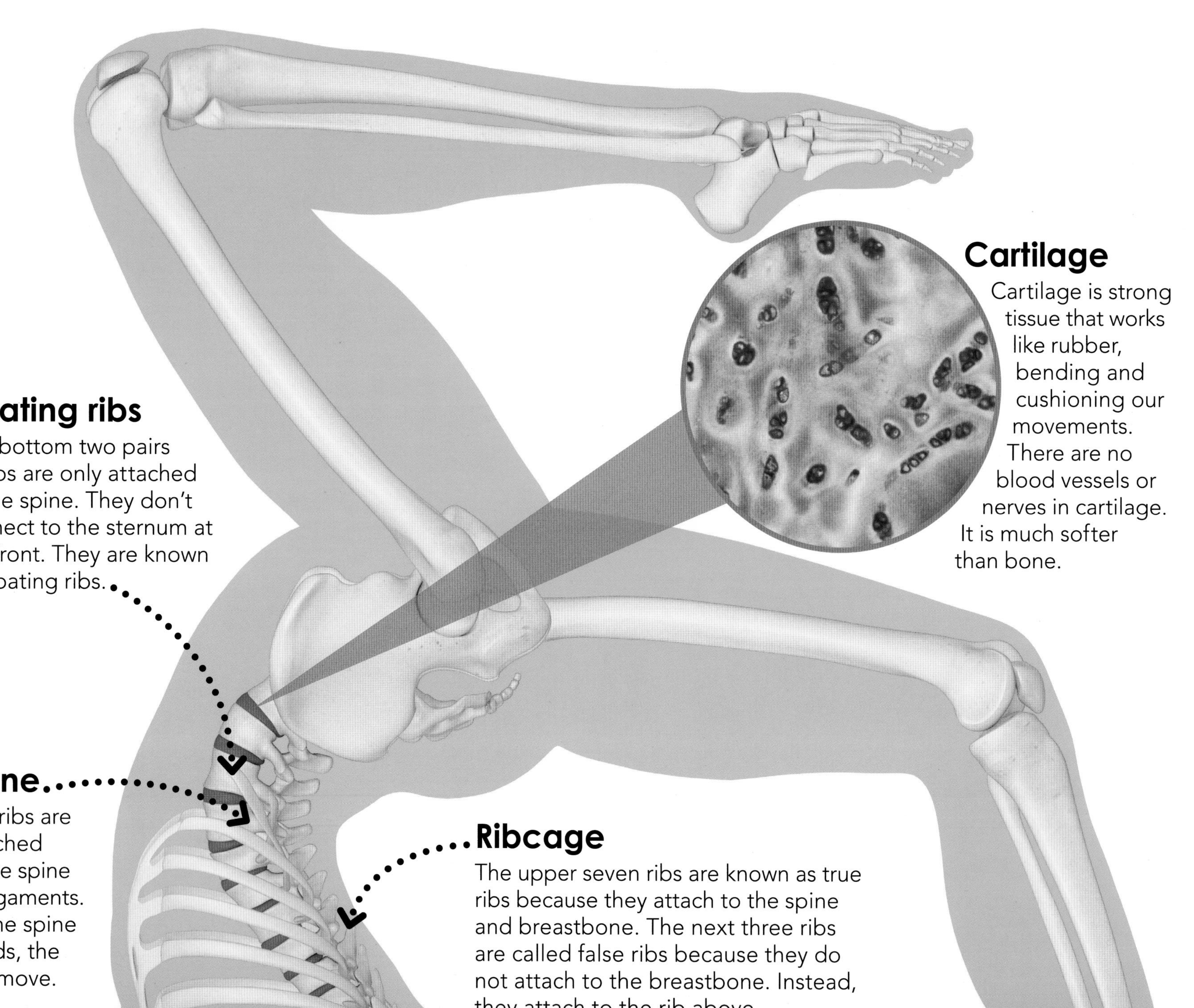

Cartilage

Cartilage is strong tissue that works like rubber, bending and cushioning our movements. There are no blood vessels or nerves in cartilage. It is much softer than bone.

Floating ribs

The bottom two pairs of ribs are only attached to the spine. They don't connect to the sternum at the front. They are known as floating ribs.

Spine

The ribs are attached to the spine by ligaments. As the spine bends, the ribs move.

Ribcage

The upper seven ribs are known as true ribs because they attach to the spine and breastbone. The next three ribs are called false ribs because they do not attach to the breastbone. Instead, they attach to the rib above.

Sternum

The sternum is also known as the breastbone. The top 10 pairs of ribs are attached to it by cartilage.

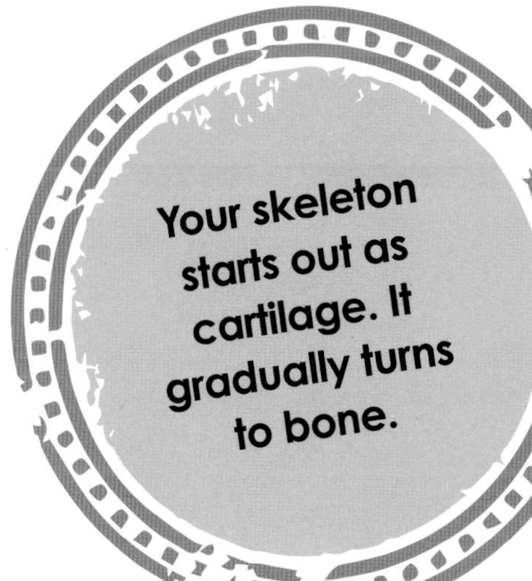

Your skeleton starts out as cartilage. It gradually turns to bone.

True or false?

1. Cartilage is harder than bone.
2. Teeth are made from cartilage.

See pages 132–133 for the answers

Are my ribs bendy?

No. Your ribs are not bendy, but they are attached to sections of strong, flexible cartilage, which let your ribcage move up and out to help inflate the lungs as you breathe. Your ribcage is made from 12 pairs of bones. It forms a protective cage around the heart and lungs.

Where else do I have bendy cartilage?

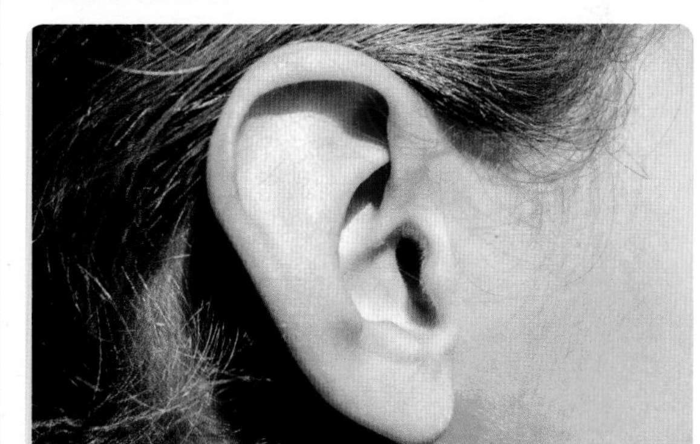

Your outer ear flaps and nose are made of cartilage. Both your ears and your nose keep their shape, but you can wiggle and bend them.

How does my spine fit together?

Your spine is made of circles of bone, or vertebrae. These are joined together by ligaments – a flexible tissue. Vertebrae have cushions between them called discs, which are made from a tough but bendy tissue called cartilage.

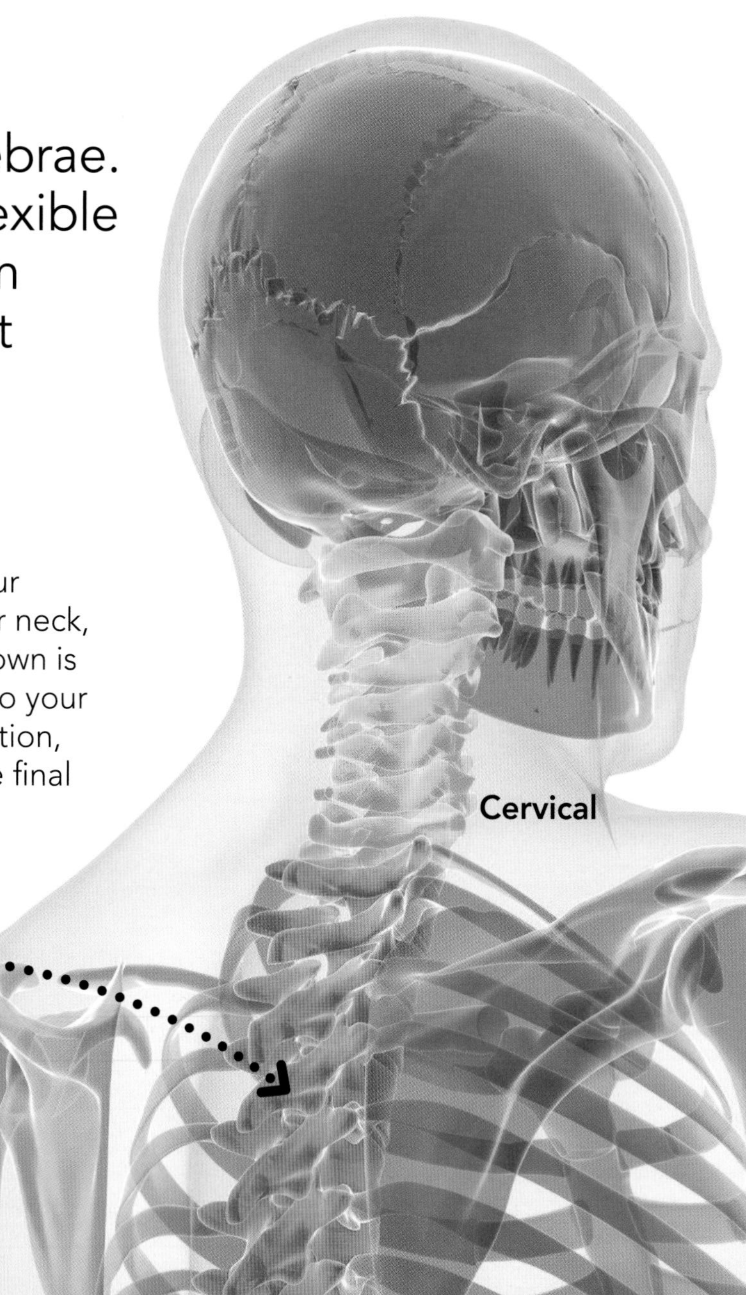

How thick is my spinal cord?

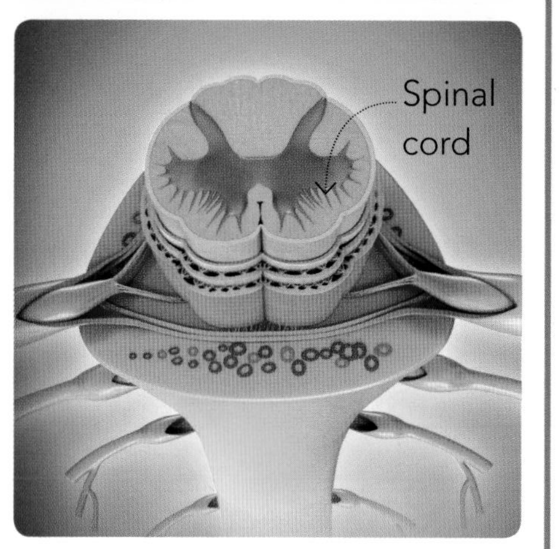

Your spinal cord is about the same width as one of your fingers, and it fits snugly into the vertebrae in your spine. It contains billions of nerves, and also layers of membrane and fluid, which protect it.

Four sections

There are four sections that make your spine. The cervical section forms your neck, which supports your head. Further down is the thoracic section, which is joined to your ribcage. Then, there's the lumbar section, which bears most of your weight. The final section is the sacrum and coccyx.

Spinal cord

The spinal cord lies in a tunnel formed by the vertebrae. It connects the brain to the rest of the body by using nerves. These carry electrical signals, and enter and exit the spinal cord through

Spinal nerves

Some electrical signals never reach the brain, and only get as far as the spinal cord. These enter the spinal cord through spinal nerves, which travel to and from some parts of the body.

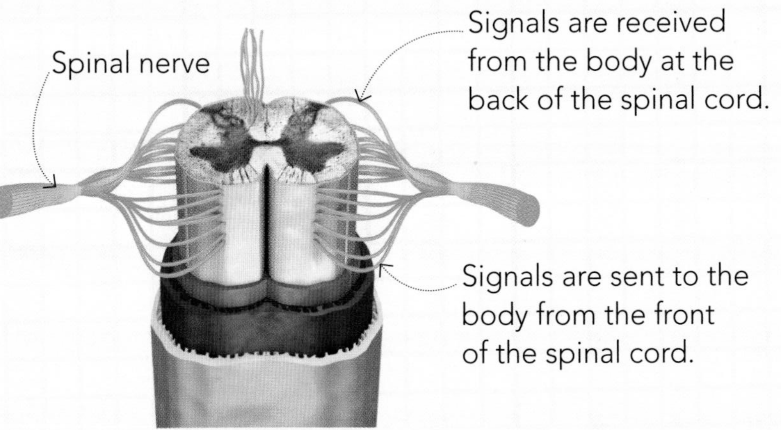

Spinal nerve
Signals are received from the body at the back of the spinal cord.
Signals are sent to the body from the front of the spinal cord.

Lumbar
Sacrum
Coccyx

Flexible joints

You can bend your back because of joints between your vertebrae. Ligaments here hold everything in place, and discs act as cushions between each vertebra.

Quick quiz

1. What is between each vertebra in the spine?
2. How is the spinal cord protected?

See pages 132–133 for the answers

Vertebrae

Most of your vertebrae move when you move your body. However, there are 10 vertebrae at the base of your spine that cannot move, including your tail-like coccyx bone.

Plant respiration

Like every living thing, a plant needs energy to live. Plants get it by breaking down sugar during respiration when they take in oxygen. Plants also make their own food through photosynthesis.

Stomata

Tiny holes, called stomata, are on a plant's leaves, stem, roots, and flowers. When open, the stomata let gas flow in and out during both respiration and photosynthesis.

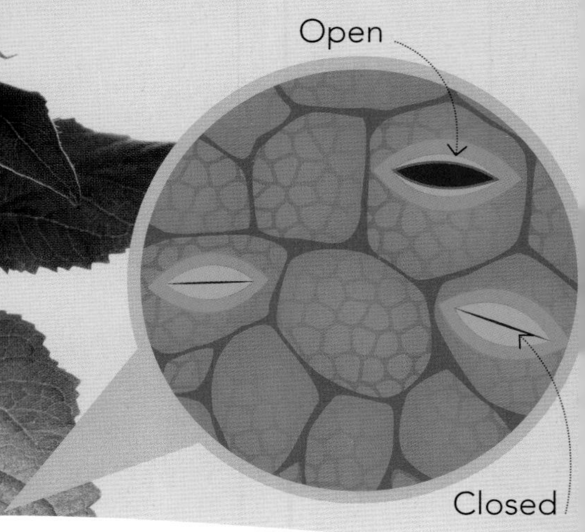

Open

Closed

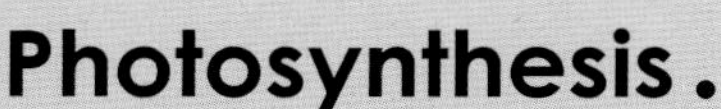

Photosynthesis

Plants use sunlight to make sugar from carbon dioxide in the air. They can only do this in the daytime, when the Sun is out. Plants need water from the ground, too. Photosynthesis releases oxygen from the plant, which you need to breathe.

Why do I need plants to breathe?

When you breathe, you take in a gas called oxygen and release a gas called carbon dioxide. Plants produce the oxygen you breathe in a process called photosynthesis. Plants and animals use oxygen to generate energy during a process called respiration.

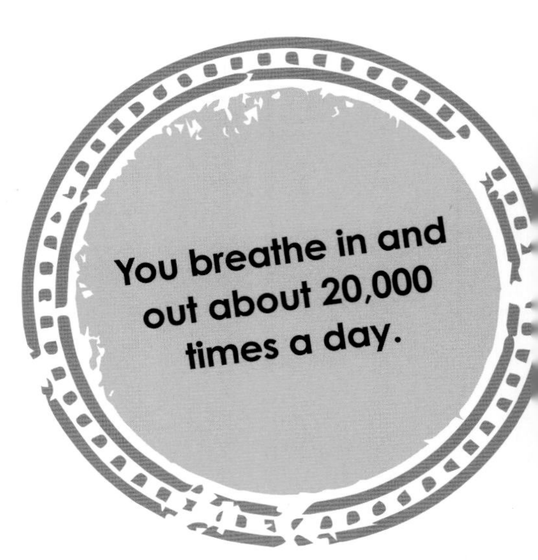

You breathe in and out about 20,000 times a day.

Human respiration

Respiration in humans is very similar to respiration in plants. However, humans take in oxygen with their lungs and can't make sugar from sunlight. Instead, sugar comes from the food we eat. We mix oxygen with sugar to release energy to power the body.

Trachea, or windpipe

Nose and mouth

You take air in and out through two holes – your nose and mouth.

Lungs

You breathe in and out by inflating and deflating your lungs. Air travels down your trachea and into your lungs, where it ends up in air sacs called alveoli.

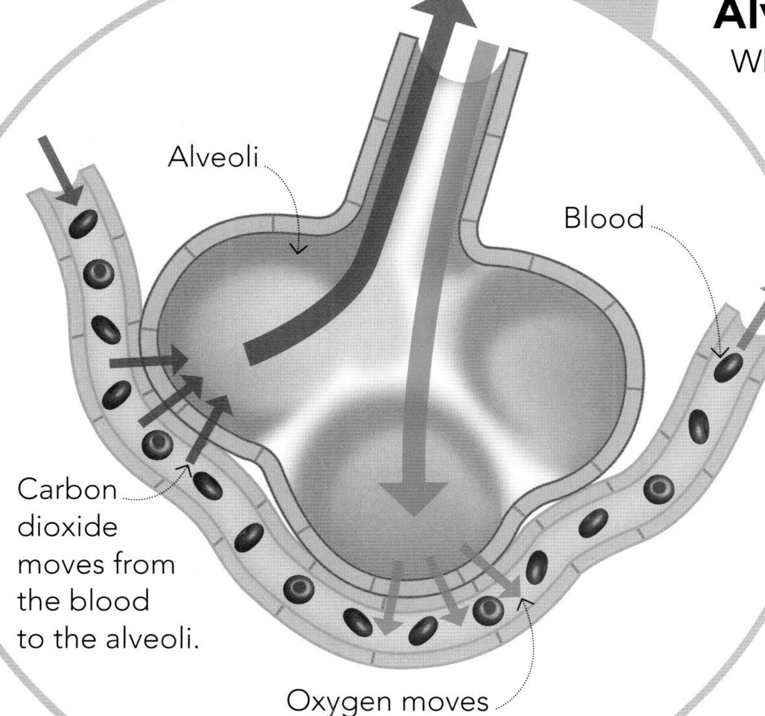

Alveoli
Blood
Carbon dioxide moves from the blood to the alveoli.
Oxygen moves from the alveoli to the blood.

Alveoli

When you breathe in, oxygen fills the alveoli in your lungs. The blood takes this oxygen and sends it around your body. Carbon dioxide is passed into the blood and back to the alveoli, to be released when you breathe out.

? True or false?

1. Plants take in oxygen and release carbon dioxide during photosynthesis.
2. Alveoli are located in the small intestine.
3. Humans breathe in order to take in oxygen and remove carbon dioxide.

See pages 132–133 for the answers

How does my brain control my emotions?

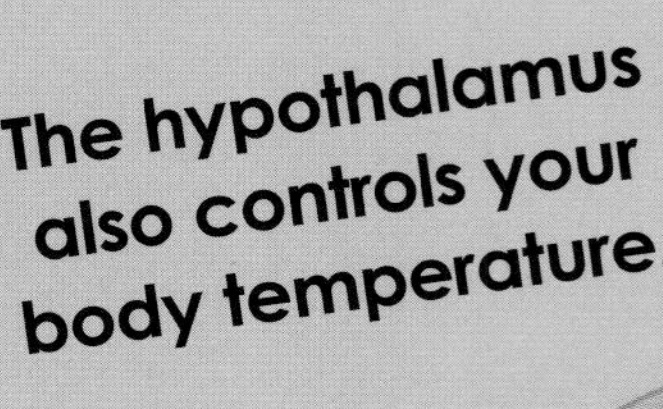
The hypothalamus
also controls your
body temperature.

Your brain has four main areas that control your emotions. These work together to help your brain figure out what is going on around you and to produce emotions. Your emotions help you to respond to situations.

Prefrontal cortex
Located at the front of your brain, the prefrontal cortex is where thinking, problem-solving, and learning takes place. It helps you to judge what is happening around you so you can make plans to respond.

What are reflexes?

Some body movements, such as blinking, happen automatically to protect you. These automatic movements are called reflexes. The signal to move goes straight to the brain and back out to your muscles without you realizing!

Hypothalamus
This tiny part of the brain controls many things. It can produce emotional responses, slow down emotions, and also release the chemical signals that prepare your body to respond to something.

Amygdala
Your amygdala allows you to feel emotions that signal danger – fear and anger. These emotions are useful as you can recognize that you are in danger, but they can also be produced when something is not as dangerous as it seems.

Personal responses

The emotions you have when you sense different things depend on your own memories and how you respond to an event. For example, you might feel happy when you see a dog, but someone else might feel scared.

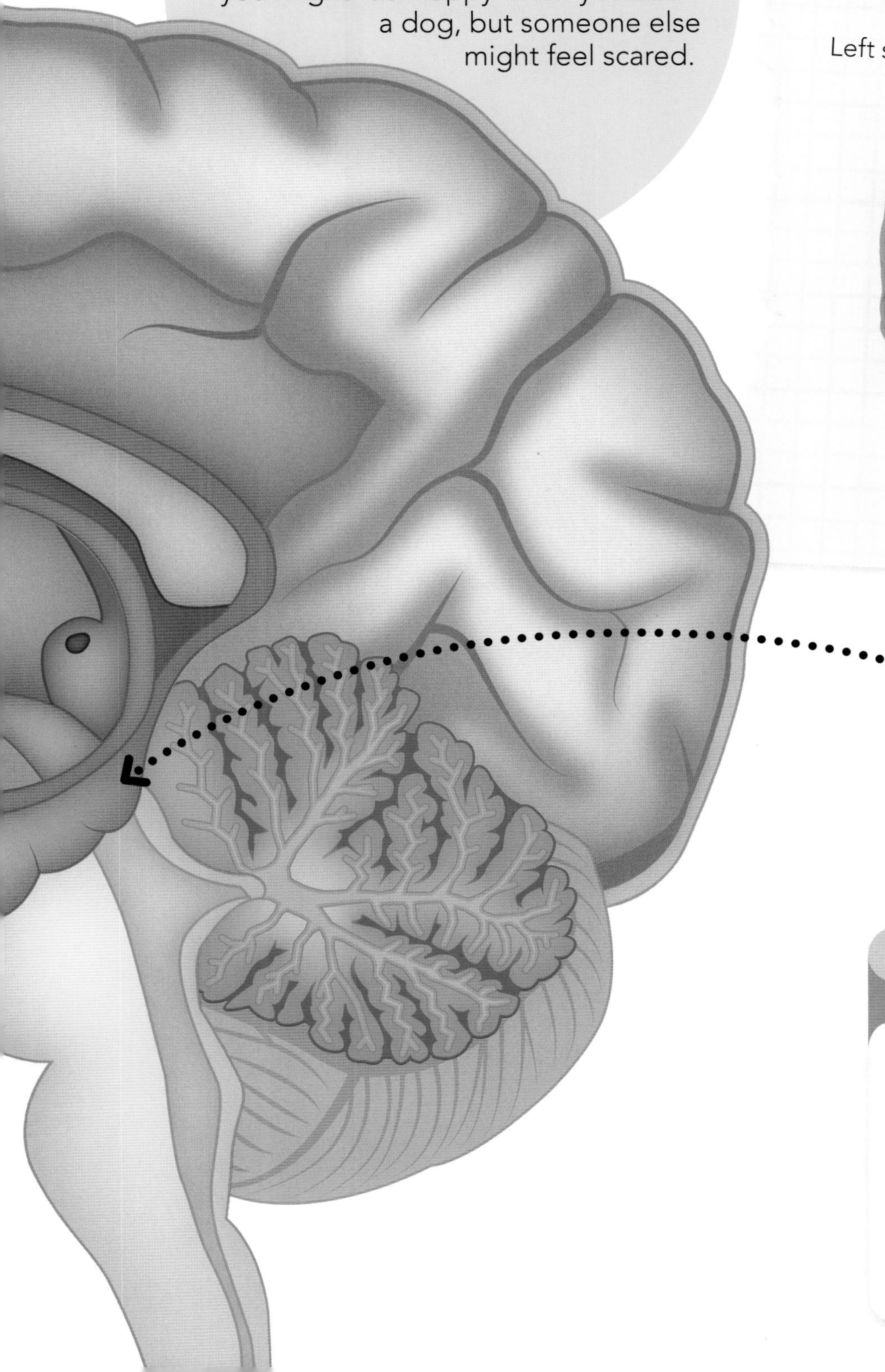

Controlling the body

The left side of your brain controls the right side of your body, and the right side of your brain controls the left side of your body. Different areas of the brain control the movement of different body parts.

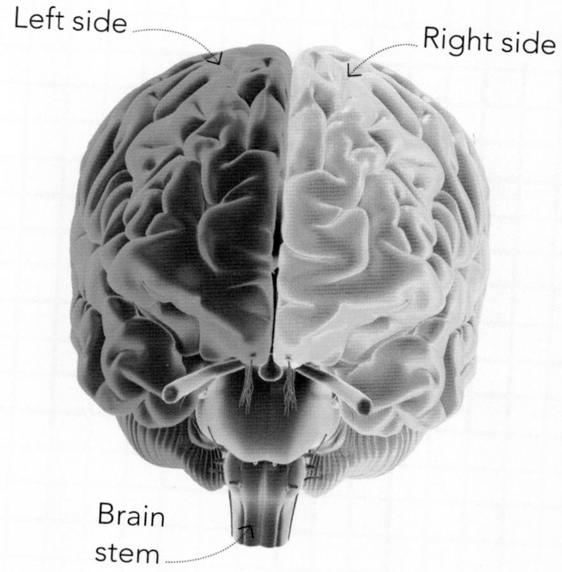

Hippocampus

This area helps you to find memories when you need them. Your memories make up a large part of your emotional response to something.

? Quick quiz

1. Which area of the brain helps you to find memories?

2. How many areas of the brain work together to control your emotions?

See pages 132–133 for the answers

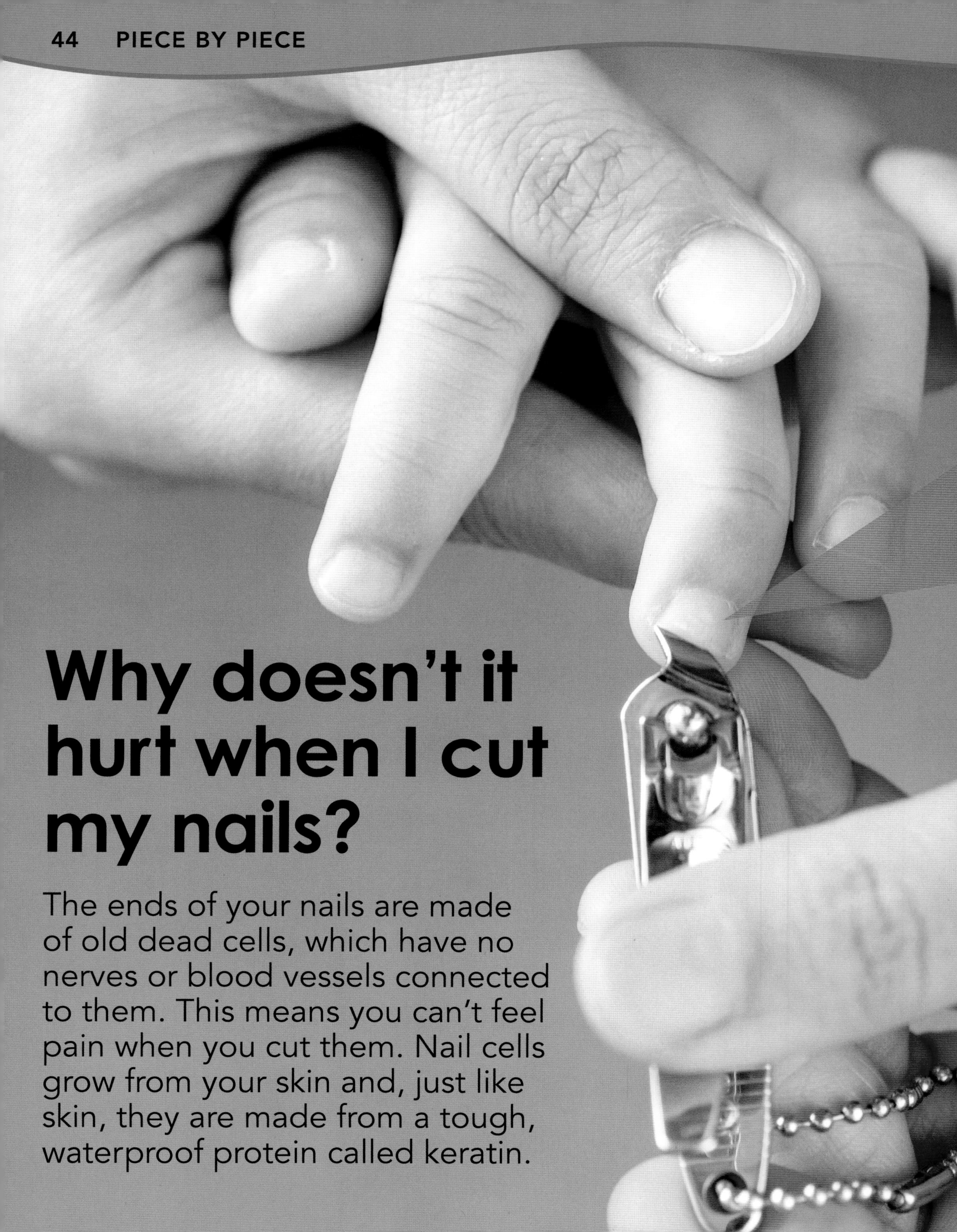

Why doesn't it hurt when I cut my nails?

The ends of your nails are made of old dead cells, which have no nerves or blood vessels connected to them. This means you can't feel pain when you cut them. Nail cells grow from your skin and, just like skin, they are made from a tough, waterproof protein called keratin.

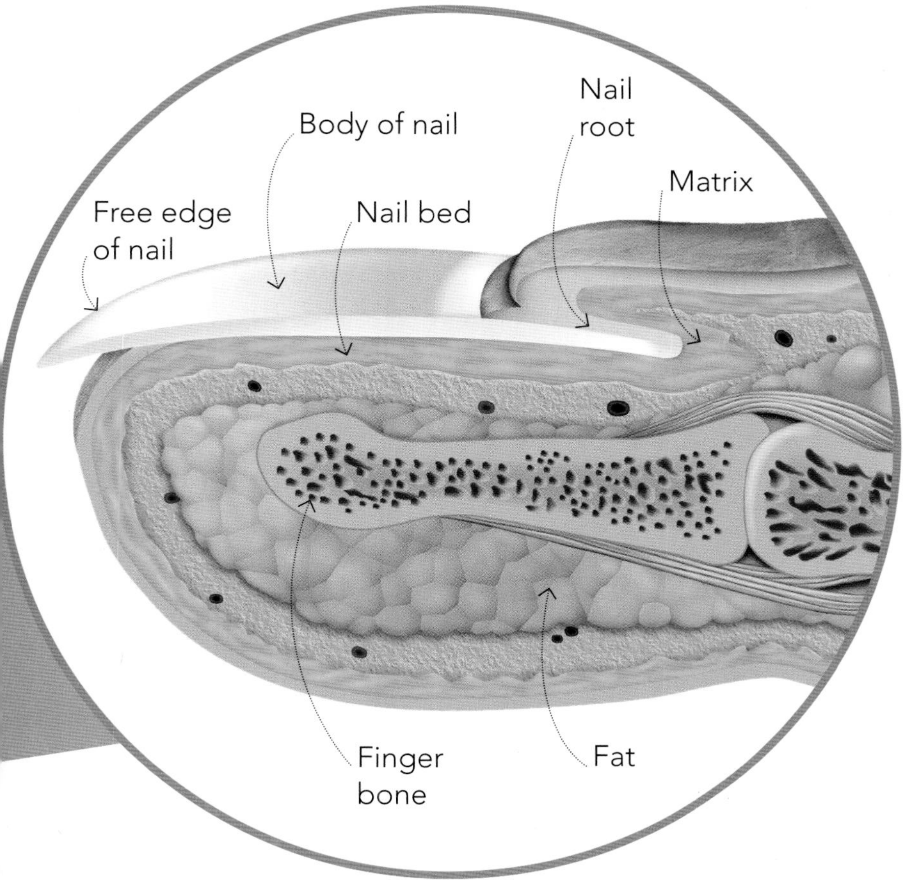

Parts of a nail

Nails have a root, body, and free edge. Behind the root is an area called the nail matrix, from which new living cells grow. The old cells are pushed forwards over the nail bed, which is made of skin. As the nail grows, the old cells flatten and die.

Where else do we find keratin?

Hair

Like nails, hair grows from the skin. Living cells in the hair follicle, or root, are filled with keratin and push the hair upwards. As the hair grows, the cells die as more new cells are made in the root.

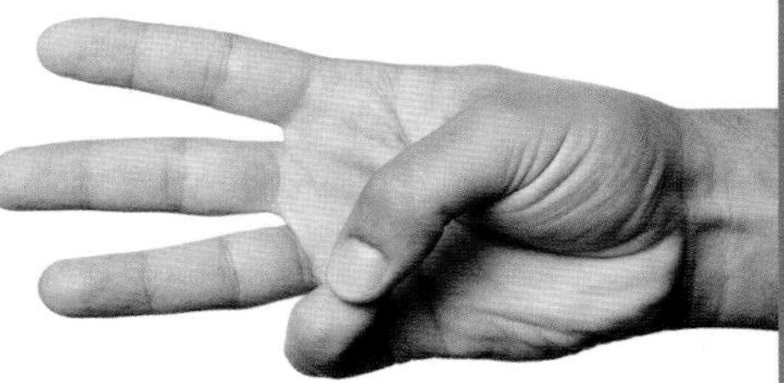

Skin

Skin cells stick together in layers. At the top is a layer of flattened, dead cells filled with keratin. These cells are shed when skin flakes off and new cells are continually made underneath.

Keratin

Nails are made of flattened, dead cells filled with keratin. As the nail grows, the cells form thin plates that lock together in overlapping layers. This makes nails hard and strong.

Keratin cells

? Quick quiz

1. What are your nails made from?
2. What part of the nail is behind the nail root?
3. Do your fingernails grow faster in summer or winter?

See pages 132–133 for the answers

Why are my teeth different shapes?

You have three types of teeth, each a different shape to help you eat different foods. Your milk teeth appear when you are about six months old. Your adult teeth grow and push the milk teeth out when you are about six years old. When you are fully grown, you have 32 adult teeth.

Canine

Third molar

Molars and premolars

Adults have eight premolars and twelve molars at the back of each jaw. These teeth squash and grind up food for swallowing.

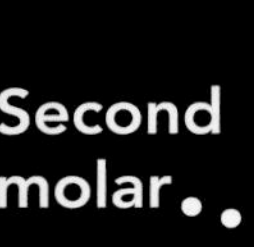
Second molar

First molar

Canines

You have four canine teeth – two in each jaw. They are at either end of your incisors. Canines are pointy to grip and tear away chunks of food.

? *True or false?*

1. Molars have the widest roots.
2. Enamel makes your teeth look white.
3. You are born with 32 teeth.

See pages 132–133 for the answers

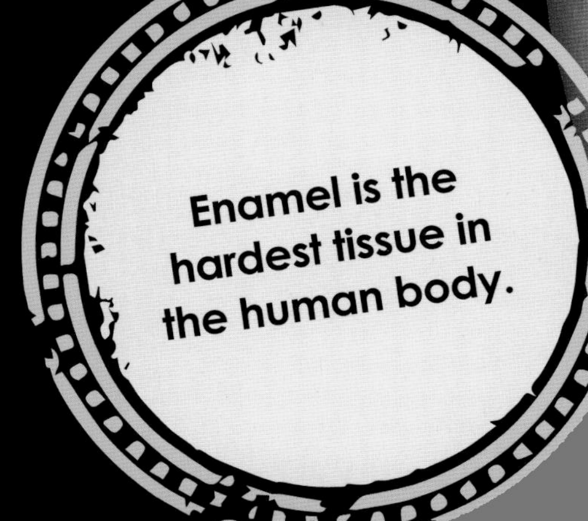

Enamel is the hardest tissue in the human body.

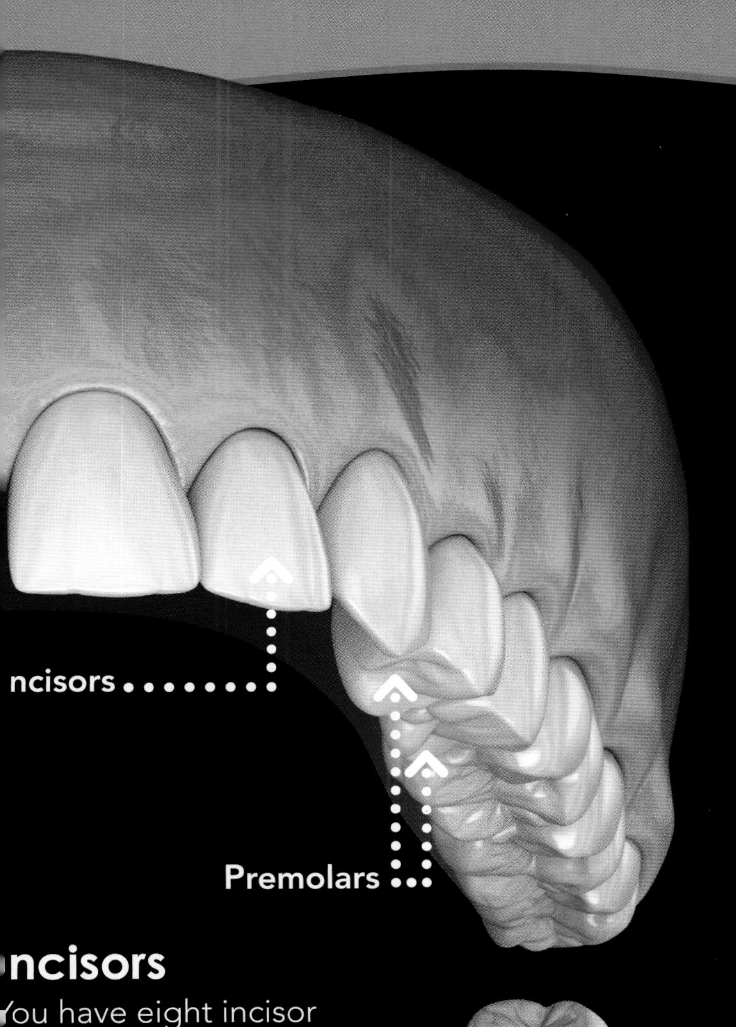

ncisors

You have eight incisor teeth – four in the upper jaw and four in the lower jaw. They are at the front of your mouth and cut and slice food. When you take a bite of something large, such as an apple, the incisors slice a section off.

What's inside a tooth?

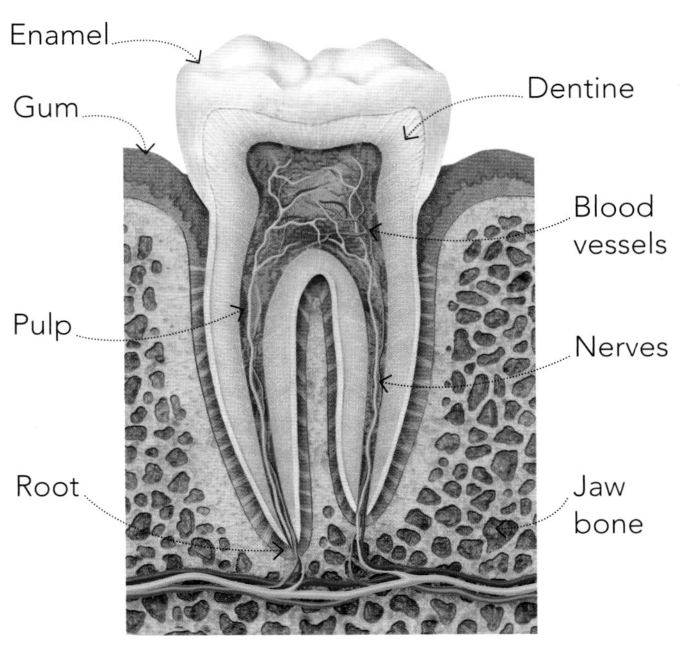

Your teeth are protected by a hard outer layer of enamel. Under this coating is a tissue called dentine, which makes up most of the tooth. Inside this is a living tissue called pulp, which contains blood vessels and nerves. Nerves help the tooth to detect pain.

Under the gum

Each tooth has a crown and a root. The crown is the top of the tooth, which can be seen in the mouth. The root is under the gum and anchors the tooth into the jawbone. The root is covered in a bone-like tissue called cementum.

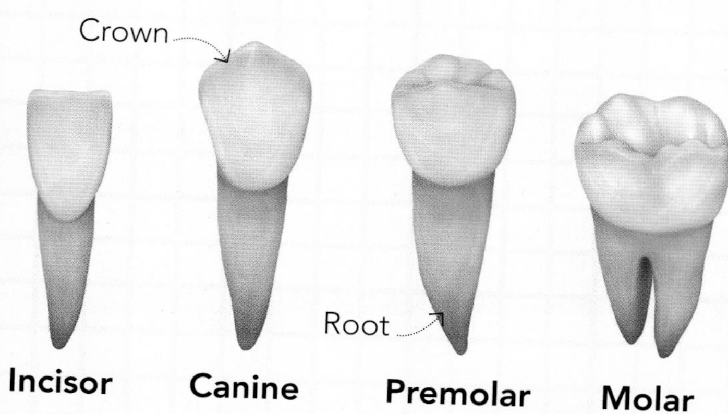

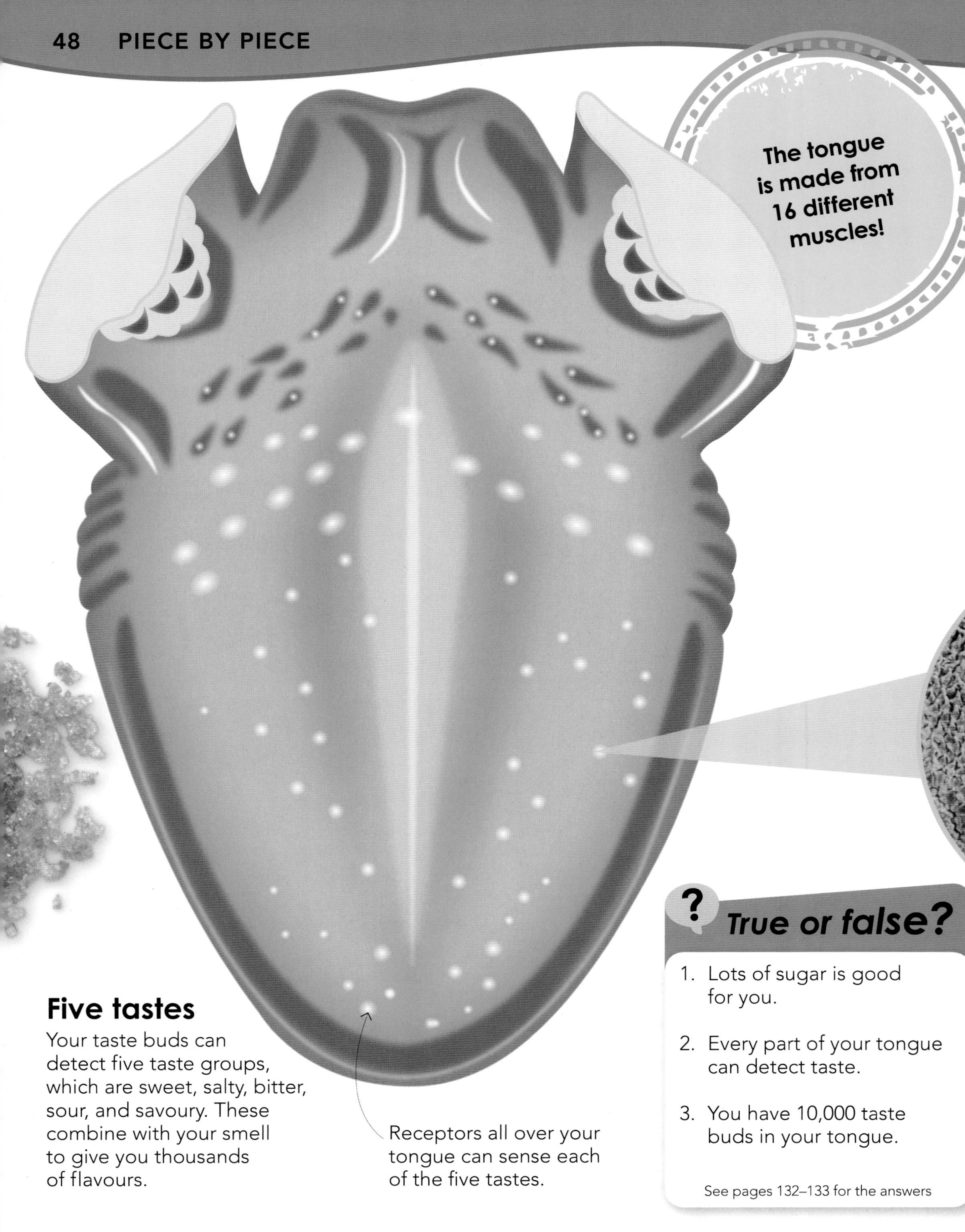

The tongue is made from 16 different muscles!

Five tastes

Your taste buds can detect five taste groups, which are sweet, salty, bitter, sour, and savoury. These combine with your smell to give you thousands of flavours.

Receptors all over your tongue can sense each of the five tastes.

? True or false?

1. Lots of sugar is good for you.
2. Every part of your tongue can detect taste.
3. You have 10,000 taste buds in your tongue.

See pages 132–133 for the answers

Why does sugar taste sweet?

Sensors in the tongue, called taste buds, detect sugar in your food when it dissolves in saliva in your mouth. Your brain recognizes the taste of sugar as sweet, and releases chemicals that make you feel good in response. However, too much sugar is bad for you.

Are smell and taste linked?

Nose takes in smells from food

Tongue detects how food tastes

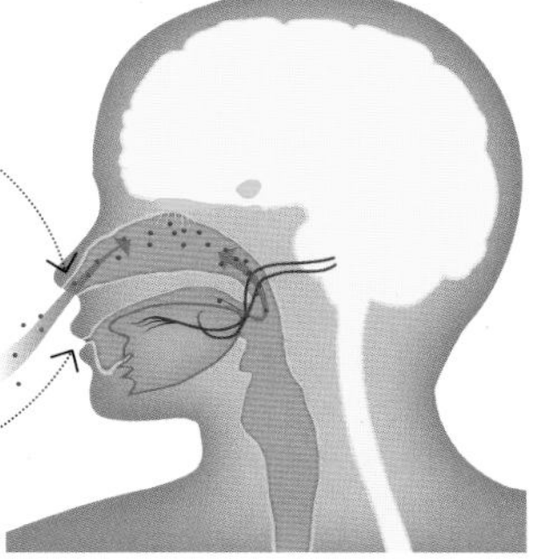

Smell particles travel into the nose from the air and from the back of your mouth when chewing food. They dissolve in mucus, and sensors in the nose send the information to the brain. This, together with information sent to the brain by the taste buds, allows you to make out different tastes.

Tip of the tongue

The tongue is covered with tiny bumps, called papillae. There are three types of papillae. The big ones are full of taste buds that detect different tastes. The two smaller ones grip food and move it around.

Most of the papillae on the tongue are small and pointy. They help the tongue grip food, and can also sense the temperature and texture of food.

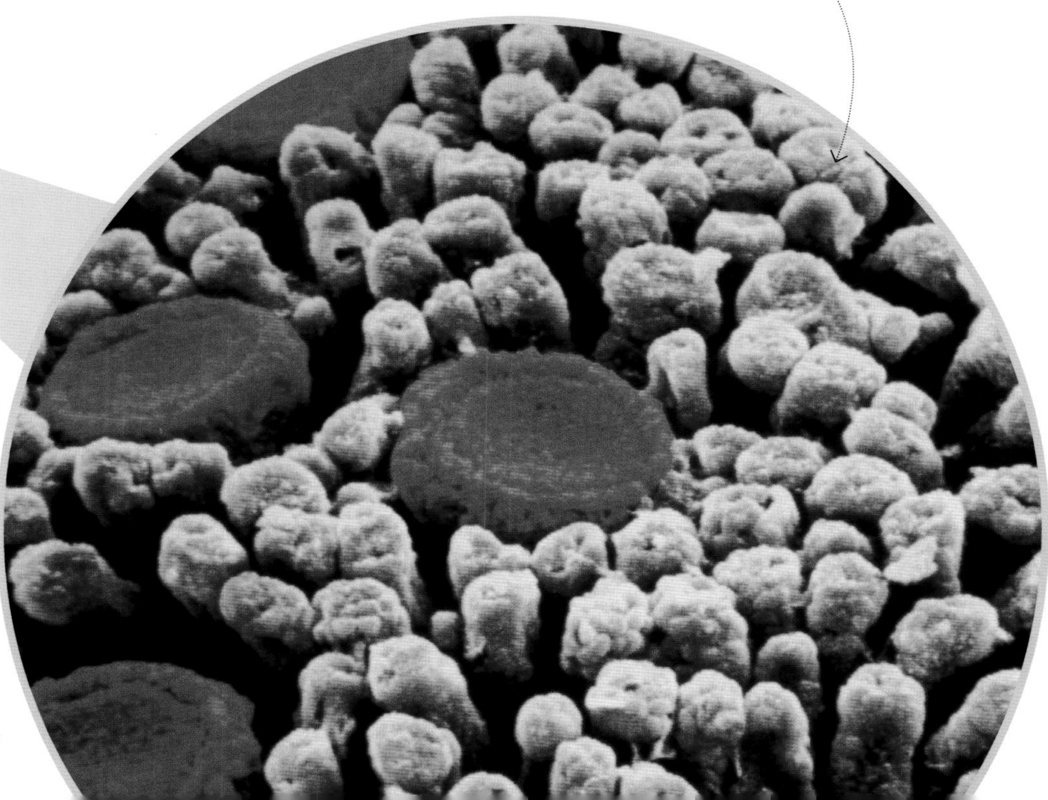

Papillae

Food mixes with your saliva when you eat, and washes over your papillae. Tiny holes allow the food in, and sensors called taste buds send information to the brain through nerve cells.

Sensitive skin

Sensors in your skin feel heat, pain, touch, and pressure. Nerve cells in your skin carry signals from these sensors to the brain. When there is pressure on your skin for a long time, it becomes squashed, and that area goes numb.

Numbness

If you kneel or cross your legs, you squash the nerves of your foot. The nerves cannot send messages to the brain, which means that your foot can't feel things properly. This is called being numb.

Why does my foot fall asleep?

When the nerves carrying signals from the skin of your foot are squashed, they are unable to send signals to your brain. This makes your foot go numb. When your foot is released, it takes time for the nerves to send signals to the brain again, and for you to regain feeling in your foot.

Picture quiz

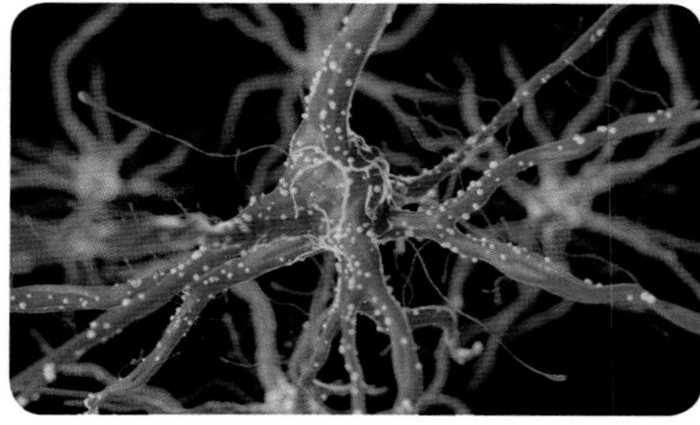

What type of cell is this?

See pages 132–133 for the answers

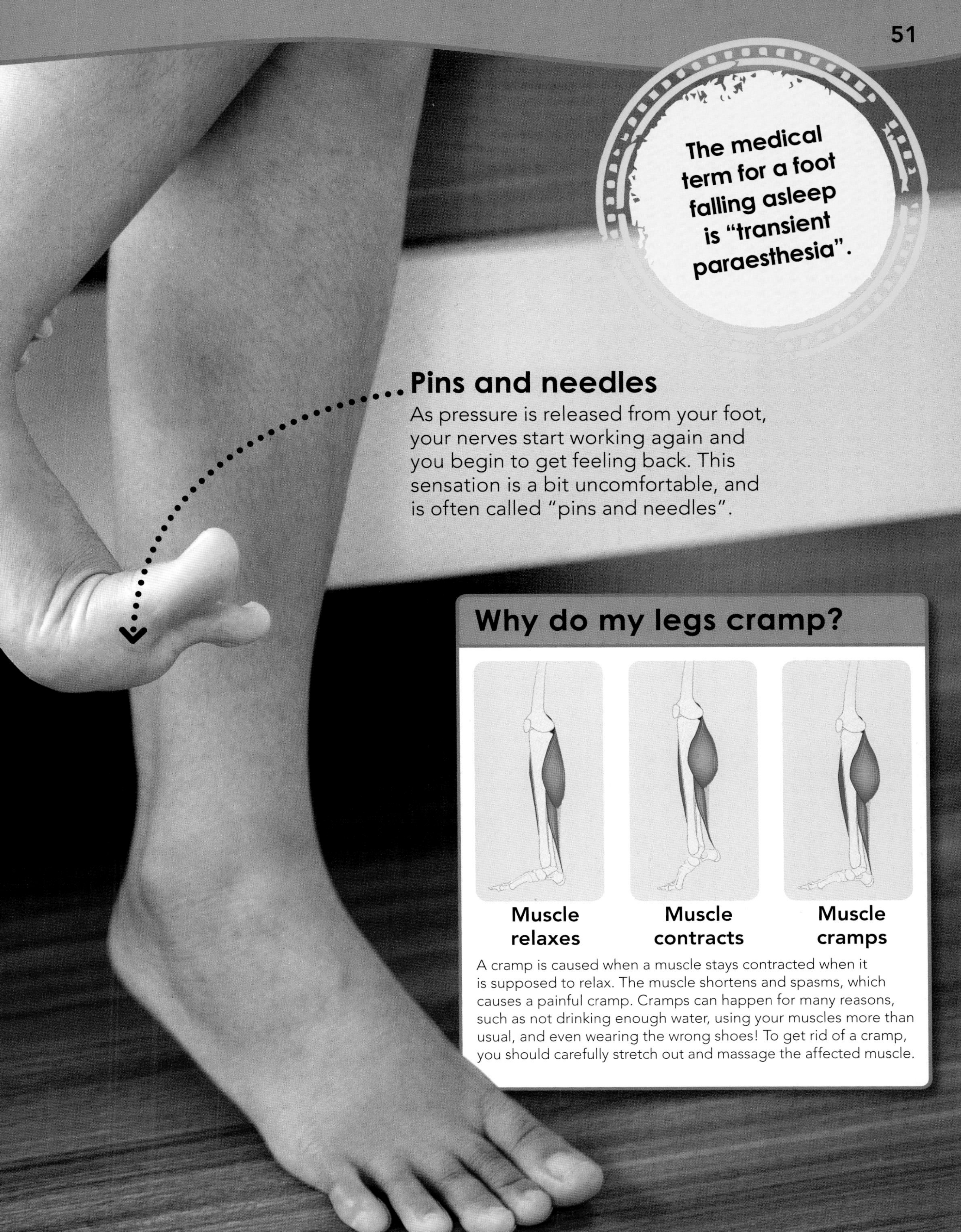

The medical term for a foot falling asleep is "transient paraesthesia".

Pins and needles

As pressure is released from your foot, your nerves start working again and you begin to get feeling back. This sensation is a bit uncomfortable, and is often called "pins and needles".

Why do my legs cramp?

A cramp is caused when a muscle stays contracted when it is supposed to relax. The muscle shortens and spasms, which causes a painful cramp. Cramps can happen for many reasons, such as not drinking enough water, using your muscles more than usual, and even wearing the wrong shoes! To get rid of a cramp, you should carefully stretch out and massage the affected muscle.

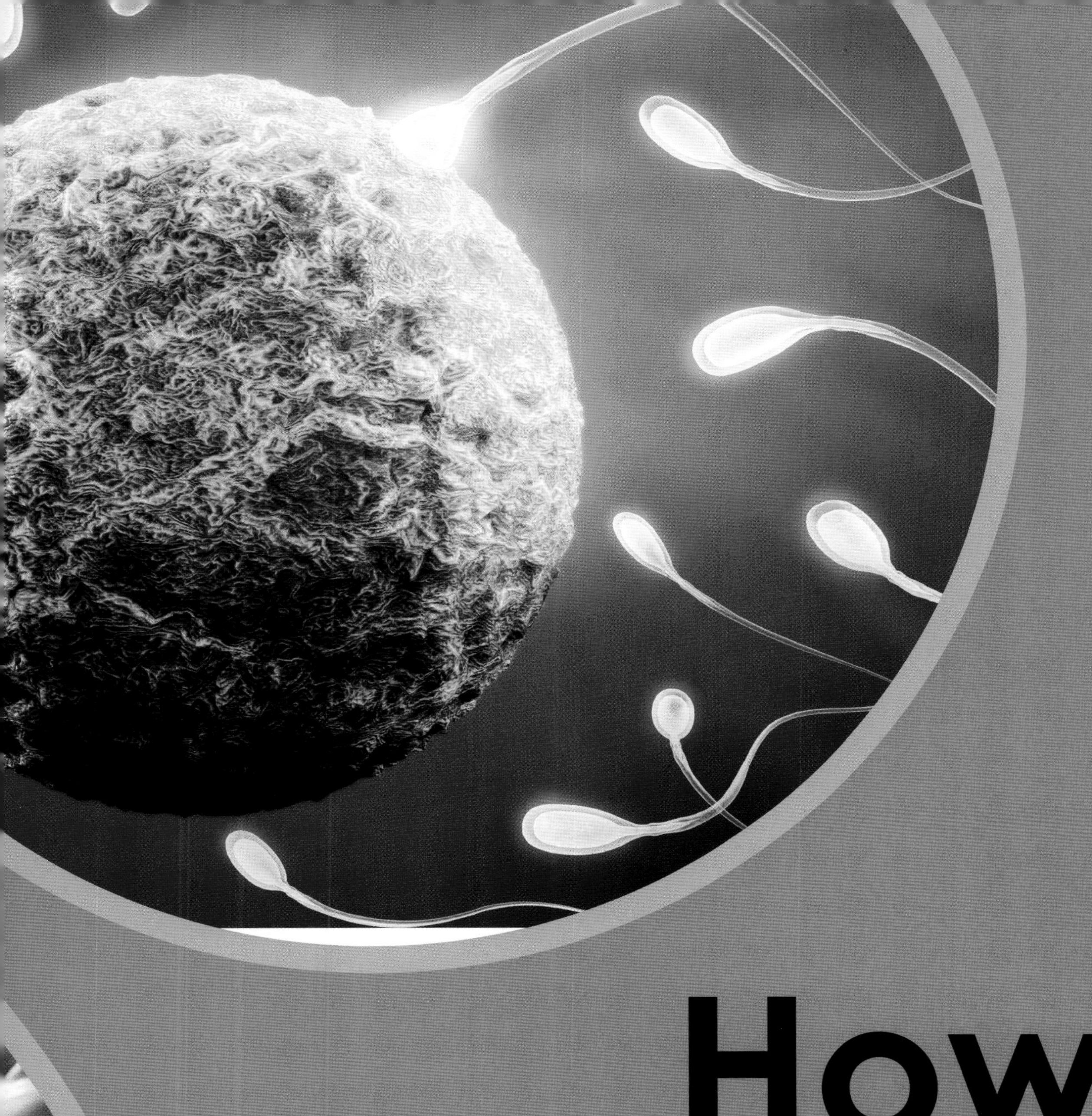

How it works

Your body is always working, even when you are asleep! Your brain receives information from your surroundings and your body reacts. When it gets dark, your pupils get bigger. When gases build up in your stomach, you burp. When you experience something new, your brain stores a memory.

How can I feel light things?

Your skin is a sensory organ. This means it has sensors that feel pressure, pain, temperature, movement, and even the lightest of touches. Areas with lots of sensors are called receptors. Fingers and hands have many touch receptors in them.

Light touch

Different touch receptors allow you to feel different things. Meissner's corpuscle and Merkel's disc are receptors that detect light touch and faint pressure.

Hair follicles can feel things because they have nerves attached to them.

How can I read using my fingers?

Braille is an alphabet that allows blind people to read. Each letter has a different pattern of raised dots. As the fingertips are highly sensitive, they can feel the raised dots and work out what the letters are.

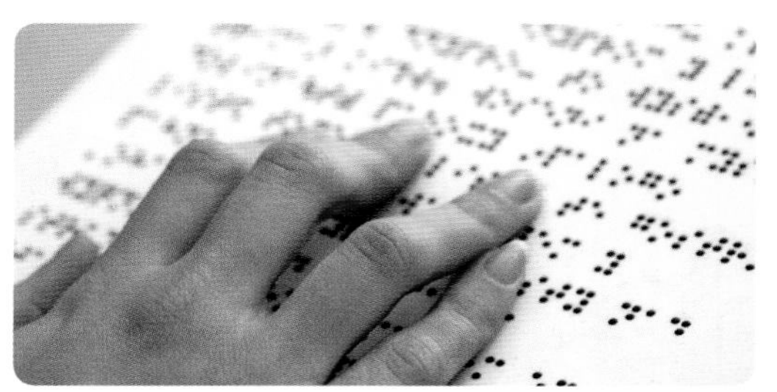

Sending signals

Receptors are different types of nerve cells or cells connected to nerves. They send electrical signals to the brain so it can tell you what you are touching.

Meissner's corpuscle

These are located just below the top layer of skin. They are found in hairless areas, such as the lips, fingertips, palms, eyelids, and soles, which are very sensitive to touch.

Merkel's disc

These disc-shaped cells are nerves that are connected to skin cells. They are found near the surface of the skin, in areas with body hair.

? Quick quiz

1. What are areas that have lots of sensors called?
2. Which alphabet allows blind people to read?

See pages 132–133 for the answers

How do I breathe?

When you breathe in, the muscles in your diaphragm and ribs contract. This makes the space in your lungs bigger, so air rushes in. The muscles relax as you breathe out, pushing air out of the lungs.

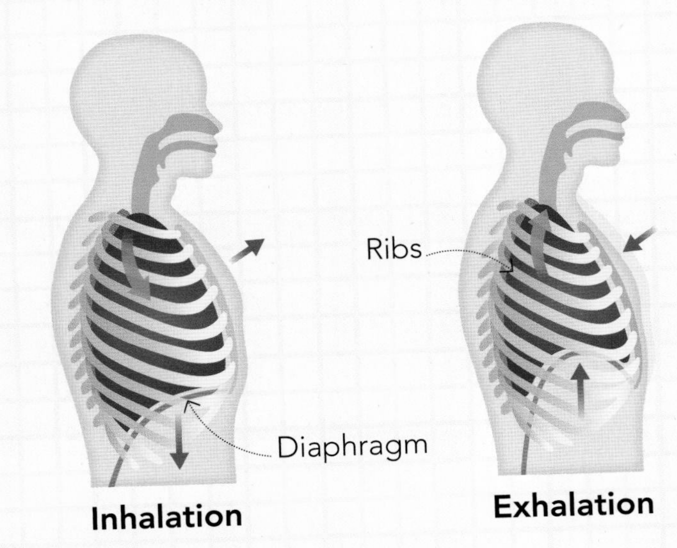

Brain stem

Breathing is controlled by the brain stem. It monitors the level of the waste gas carbon dioxide in the blood. When it is too high, the brain sends messages to the body telling you to breathe harder.

Nasal cavity

This space behind the nose cleans the air you breathe in before it passes down the windpipe.

Why don't I ever forget to breathe?

Breathing happens automatically, even when you're asleep. You don't need to think about it because your brain controls it. However, you can take over from your brain and choose to slow your breathing down, or blow at certain times and with varying force, such as to play an instrument.

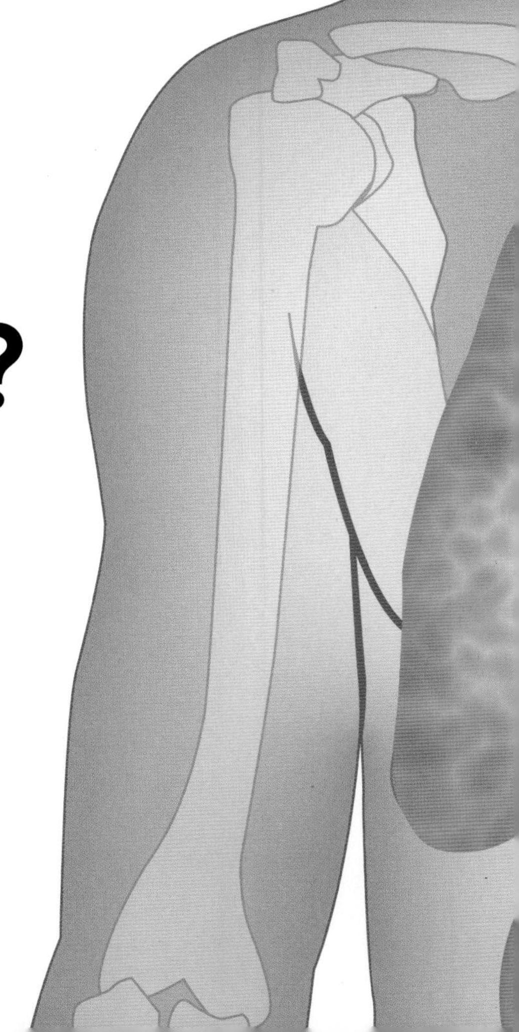

What else does my brain control automatically?

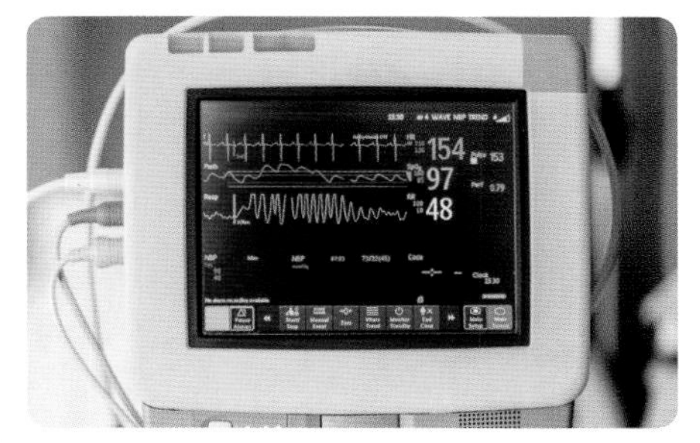

The brain controls the heart and keeps it beating to pump blood around the body, carrying oxygen from the lungs to all the other organs. Other muscles, such as those in the intestines, also work automatically.

Trachea

The windpipe, or trachea, carries air to your lungs. It splits into two tubes, one going to each lung.

Ribcage

The brain sends a message to the muscles in the ribcage to move faster when you need more oxygen in the body and less carbon dioxide.

Diaphragm

The diaphragm is a muscle that helps you breathe. When you inhale, the diaphragm becomes flat and when you exhale, it becomes a dome shape.

? Quick quiz

1. Why do you breathe out after holding your breath?
2. What happens to your diaphragm when you breathe out?
3. Can you choose when to make your heart beat?

See pages 132–133 for the answers

Why can I jump?

You can jump because you have both joints and muscles. Joints let the skeleton bend where bones meet. Muscles pull on leg bones, pushing the body up into the air.

Leg muscles

The leg muscles work as a team to lift and propel the body upwards and forwards to jump. These muscles also help to cushion your landing.

Knee joint

Muscles are attached to bones by tendons, which are a type of connective tissue.

Leg muscle

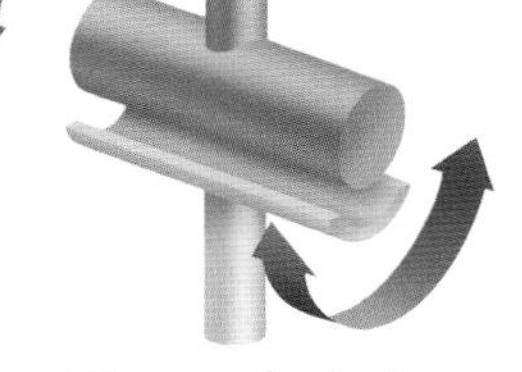

Knee joint

The hinge joint in the knees helps the lower legs move backwards and forwards. This joint has shock absorbers, which help your legs cope with the stress of jumping.

What's inside a joint?

At the end of each bone is a thin layer of cartilage, which helps joints to move and not be rigid. Synovial fluid is made in the synovial membrane. This fluid lubricates joints so they can move smoothly.

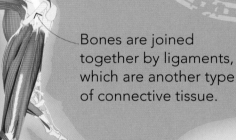

Bone
Ligament
Synovial membrane
Joint
Synovial fluid
Cartilage

Hip joint

The knee is the largest joint in the body.

Bones are joined together by ligaments, which are another type of connective tissue.

Hip joint

The ball-and-socket joint in the hips lets the upper leg move in many directions. This helps the body to move and adjust balance as you jump.

? Picture quiz

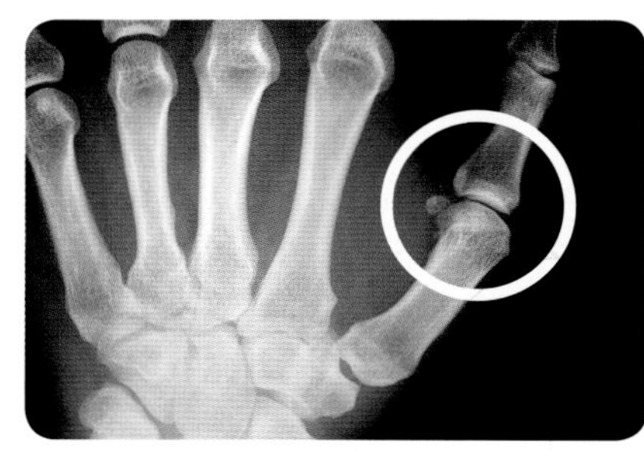

Where in the body is this joint?

See pages 132–133 for the answers

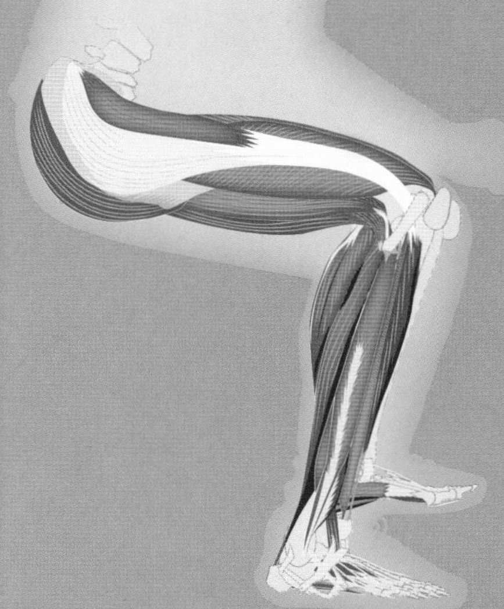

How do bones help me hear?

Sound waves hitting the outer ear travel to the eardrum, which sends vibrations through three tiny bones in the middle ear called the ossicles. These bones – the malleus, incus, and stapes – pass sound vibrations into a liquid in the inner ear. There, sensors collect the sound, sending it to the brain. The brain figures out what you're hearing.

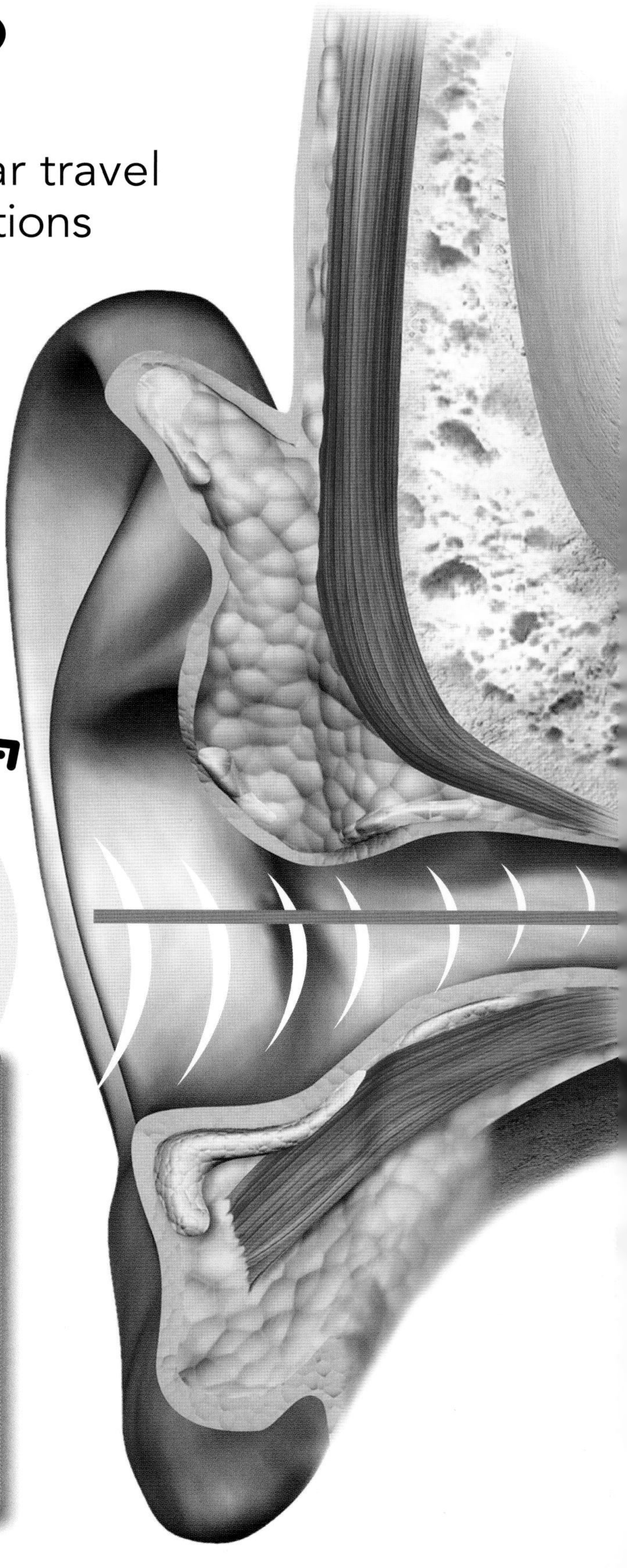

Outer ear

Your outer ear flap, or pinna, is shaped like a cup. It catches sound waves as they travel through the air as vibrations. The pinna is made from bendy cartilage.

What sounds can't you hear?

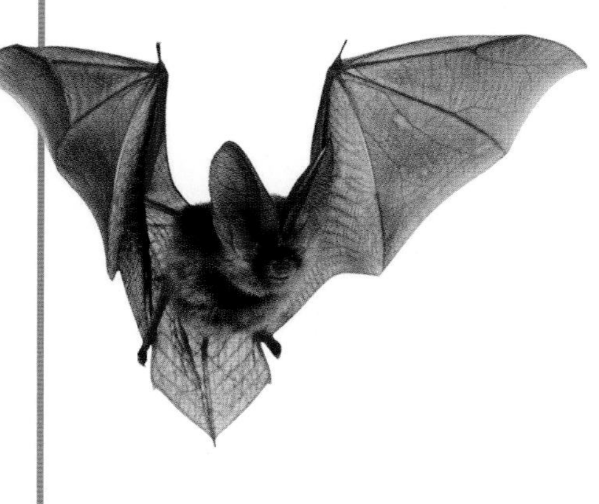

You can't hear sounds that vibrate too quickly or too slowly – your ears will not receive the vibrations. Dogs can hear high-pitched dog whistles. This high-pitched sound vibrates too quickly for humans to hear it. Children have better hearing than adults. Children can hear bats squeaking when adults cannot.

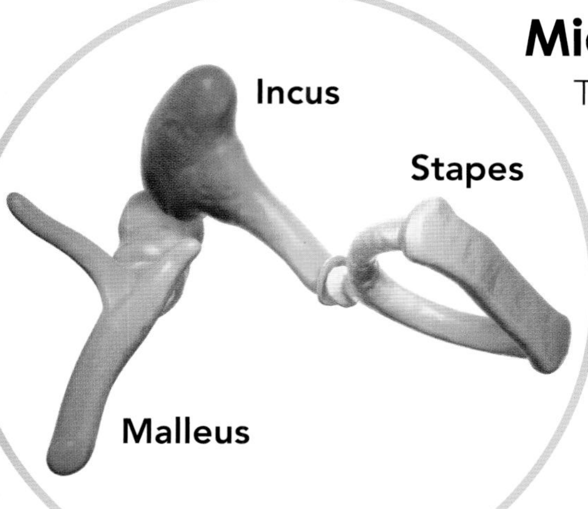

Middle ear

The ossicles are in your middle ear, behind your eardrum. When you hear sound, your eardrum pushes the malleus, which pushes the incus and the stapes. This domino effect is how sound travels through the smallest bones in your body.

? True or false?

1. Sound travels through gas in the outer ear.
2. Sound travels through fluid in the inner ear.

See pages 132–133 for the answers

Semi-circular canals

Inner ear

The semi-circular canals and cochlea in the inner ear are filled with fluid. Sound waves vibrate through this fluid to tiny hair-like sensors called receptors.

Receptors

The tiny hair-like receptors in the inner ear send electrical signals to the brain through a nerve called the vestibulocochlear nerve.

Inside the cochlea

Hair-like cells wiggle as the sound vibrations pass through them. They change the sound into electrical signals.

ardrum

his very tiny "drum" is nade from a disc with a nembrane stretched over t. The membrane vibrates vhen a sound hits it. It then iits the malleus, which makes he other ossicles move.

Small pupil

In bright light, the inner circles of muscles in the iris contract to pull the iris inwards. This shrinks the size of the pupil. This happens automatically to stop too much light getting into your eyes.

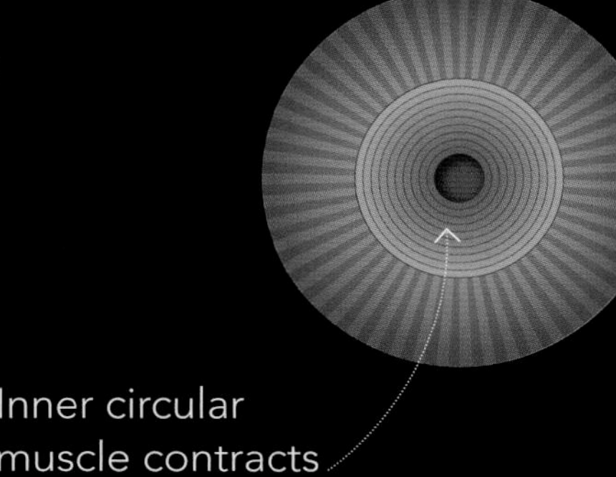

Large pupil

In dim light, the outer muscles in the iris contract, which pulls the iris outwards This dilates – or expands – th pupil, which allows more ligh in so you can see better.

Why do my pupils change size?

Pupils are holes that let light into your eyes so you can see. The colourful circle around each pupil is called the iris. It has two types of muscle in it that contract, or pull, in response to a change in light – the inner circular muscle and the outer radial muscle. These muscles change the size of your pupils.

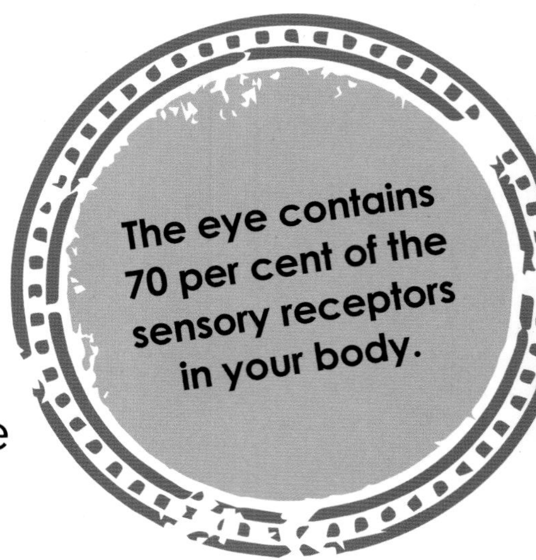

The eye contains 70 per cent of the sensory receptors in your body.

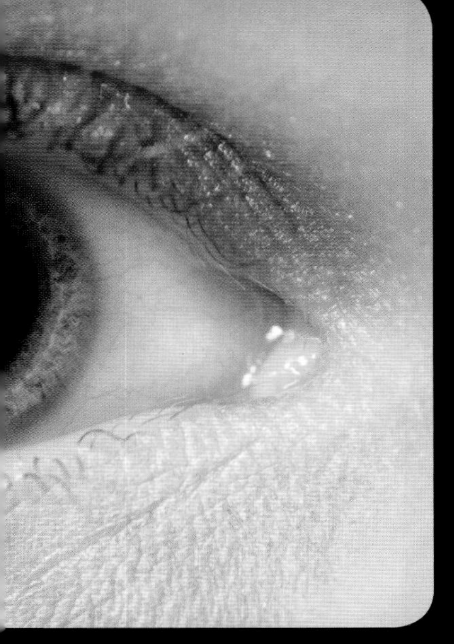

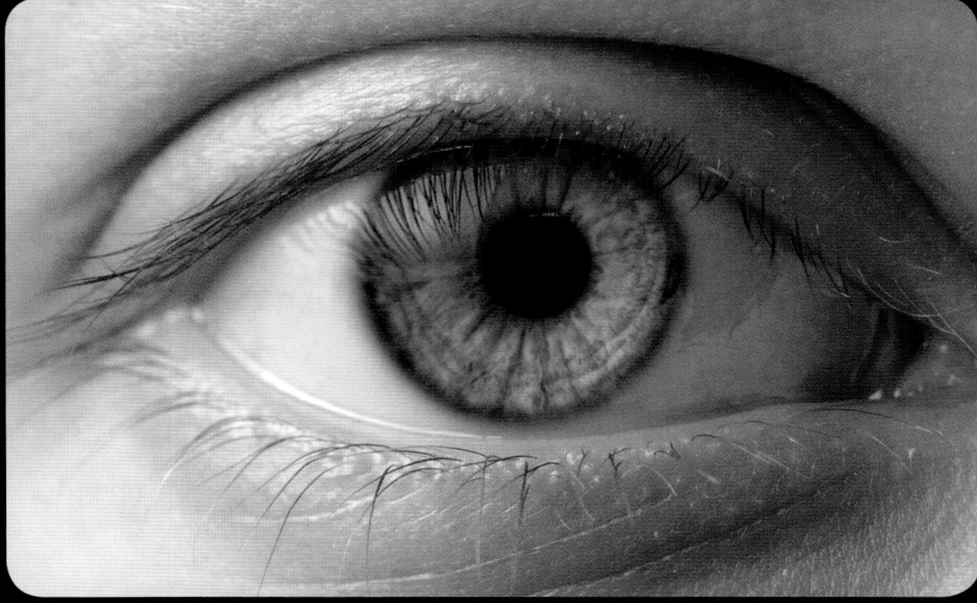

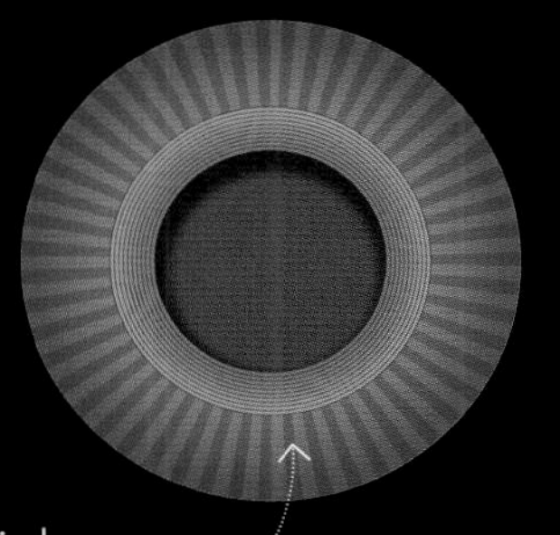

Normal pupil

In soft light, both rings of muscle in the iris contract a little bit at the same time. This balance keeps the iris and pupil in a normal shape.

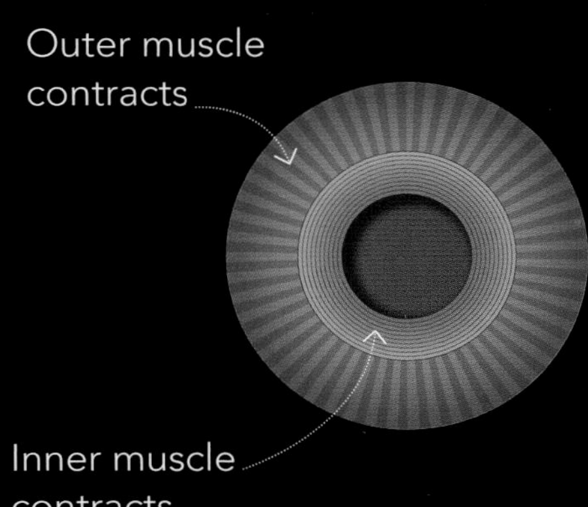

How do I see in 3D?

Light reflects from objects into your eyes. The light is detected by receptor cells at the back of each eye and they send signals to your brain. Each eye sends a slightly different signal to your brain. The electrical signals generated from both eyes combine together and your brain makes a 3D image.

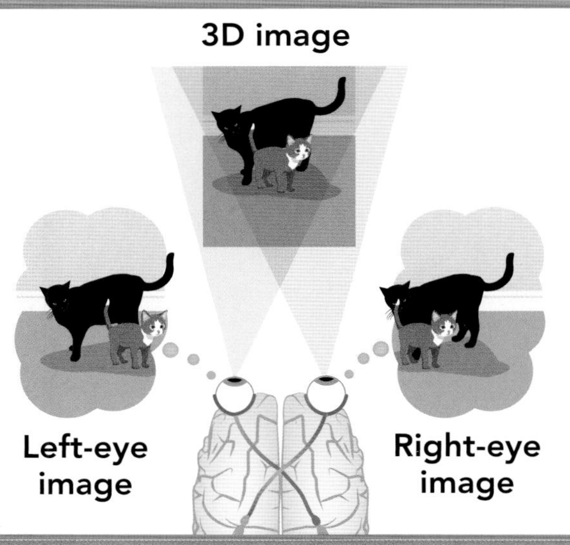

? Quick quiz

1. Why do your pupils get smaller when looking at bright light?
2. What is the colourful circle around each pupil called?
3. What happens to pupils when it is dark?

See pages 132–133 for the answers

How do I balance?

You learn to balance when your body receives information from different organs about where each part of your body is. Sensory organs and muscles help you to move and stay balanced, even as gravity pulls you downwards.

Inside the ear

In your ear are three small tubes called the semi-circular canals. These contain fluid, which moves around as you move your head.

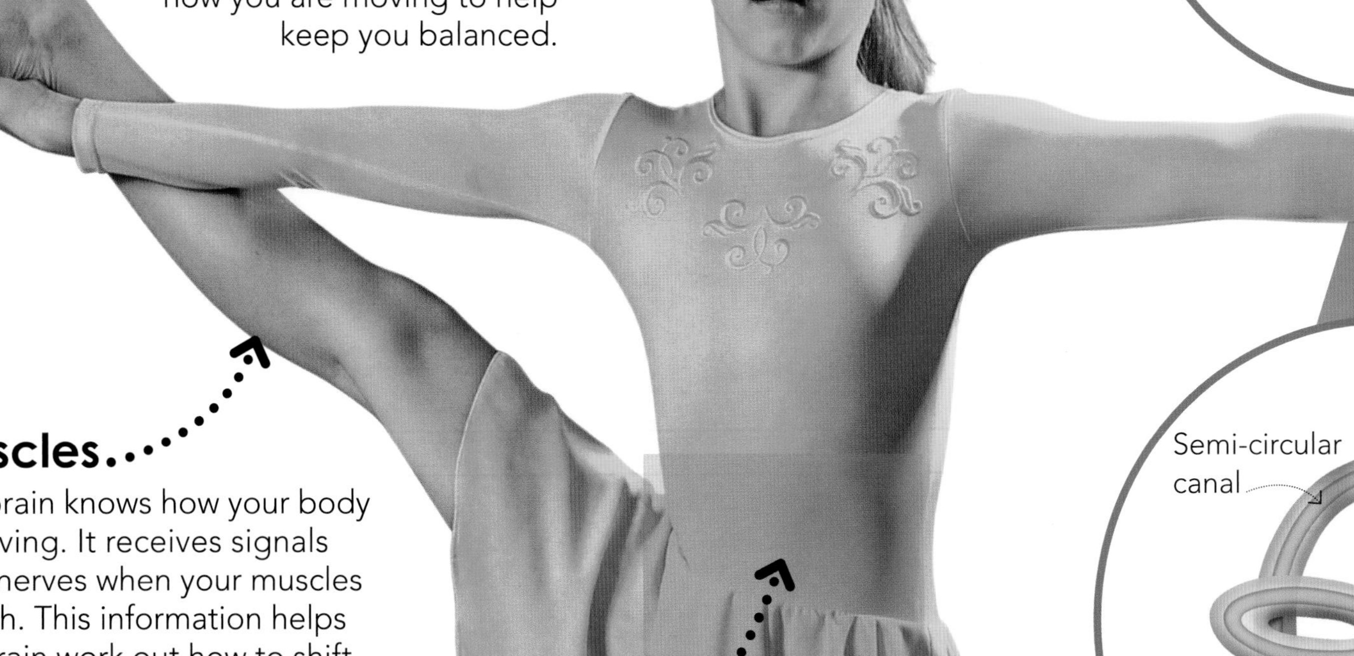

Eyes

Your eyes send information about what you can see to the brain. The brain uses this to work out where you are and how you are moving to help keep you balanced.

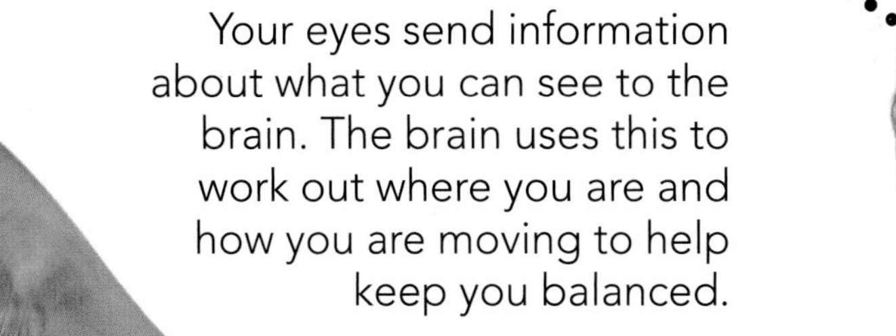

Muscles

The brain knows how your body is moving. It receives signals from nerves when your muscles stretch. This information helps the brain work out how to shift your weight to stay balanced.

entre of gravity

Your body has an invisible line going through it that helps you to balance. It is called the centre of gravity, and you automatically move your body around it so you do not fall over.

Pressure sensors

Your skin has sensors in it, which are called receptors. They can sense touch, temperature, and movement. This means you can feel the ground and balance your body weight.

Organs of balance

The movement of fluid in the semi-circular canals is detected by tiny hair-like sensors. The sensors send electrical signals through nerves to your brain. This helps your brain work out how you are moving and you adjust your body to stay balanced.

Gravity

This is an invisible pulling force that pulls everything – including you – towards the ground. It stops you from floating away.

? *True or false?*

1. The organs of balance are located in the brain.
2. If you close your eyes you cannot balance.
3. Your centre of gravity can move.

See pages 132–133 for the answers

Does my centre of gravity move?

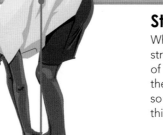

Bending

As you bend over, your centre of gravity moves forwards. You stick out your bottom to move your body weight backwards so you do not fall over.

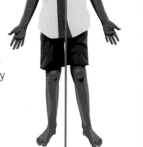

Standing

When you stand up straight, your centre of gravity goes through the middle of your body so you can balance in this position.

Why don't icy drinks make me cold all over?

Your brain monitors your body temperature inside and outside. If your temperature rises or falls, your brain reacts and sends signals to your organs to make changes. These changes help to move your body temperature back to a healthy temperature of 37°C (98.6°F).

Moving heat

Heat moves in one direction – from hot to cold. Only heat can move around, so something is cold because heat has left it.

Heat moves from your tongue to the ice lolly.

Heat moves from the hot drink to your hands.

Skin

When you touch something cold, the blood vessels in your skin get smaller. This means that less blood travels to your skin, helping your body to keep its heat. The hairs on your skin also stand up to trap warm air when your body temperature falls.

Internal heating

Your liver creates lots of heat when it helps to break down your food. Your blood carries this heat around the body. This keeps your body temperature normal when you drink something cold.

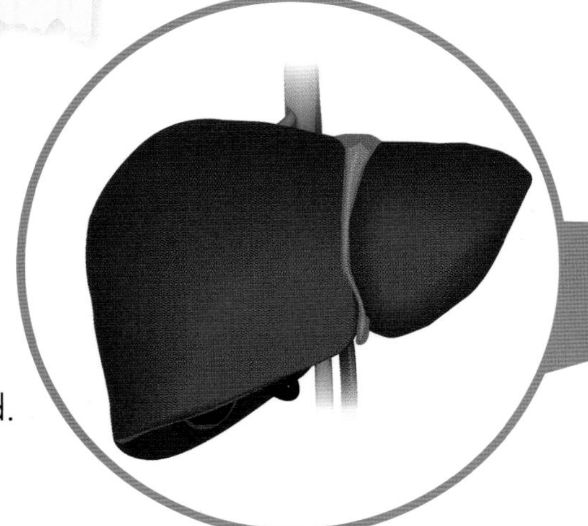

Controlling temperature

The hypothalamus in the brain monitors body temperature. It receives signals from receptors that detect cold, and tells your body to make changes to warm you up.

? Quick quiz

1. Which way does heat move?
2. What part of your body monitors temperature?

See pages 132–133 for the answers

Thyroid gland

Your thyroid gland produces a hormone called thyroxine. When you are cold, it releases more thyroxine. This hormone tells your cells to use more energy so they give off heat and you warm up.

Muscles

Your muscles send out heat when they change stored energy from food into movement energy. When you are really cold, you shiver. This is a reflex that causes your muscles to contract quickly, which creates more heat.

How does my body cool down when hot?

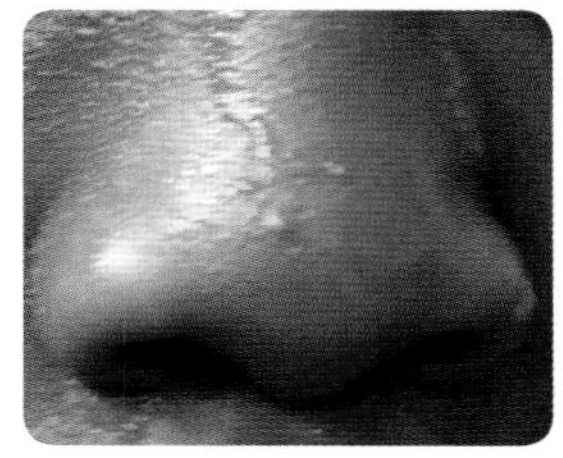

Sweating

When you are hot, you sweat. Sweat draws heat away from your skin. It takes heat with it as it evaporates (turns from a liquid to a gas). This cools you down.

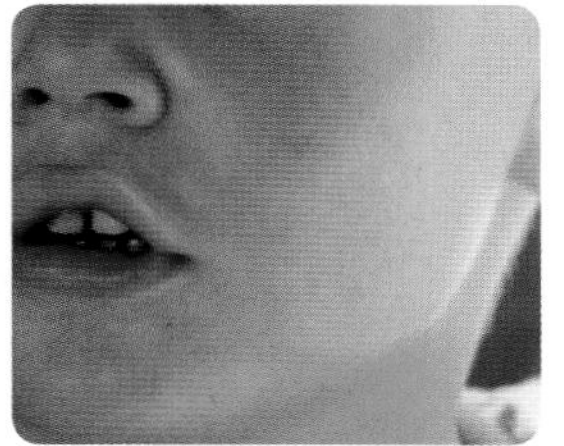

Flushing

Blood vessels in your skin get bigger when you are hot. This increases blood flow to the skin's surface so your blood can cool down. This often results in red patches on your face.

In the evening

During the day, gravity slowly pulls your body down from your head to your toes. This squashes your spine. By the end of the day, you are up to 2 cm (0.8 in) shorter than when you woke up!

Vertebrae in spine

When you stand up straight, the vertebrae in your spine are stacked vertically on top of each other. As gravity pulls on your body, the flexible cartilage in the discs between each vertebra gets squashed down. This makes you shrink throughout the day.

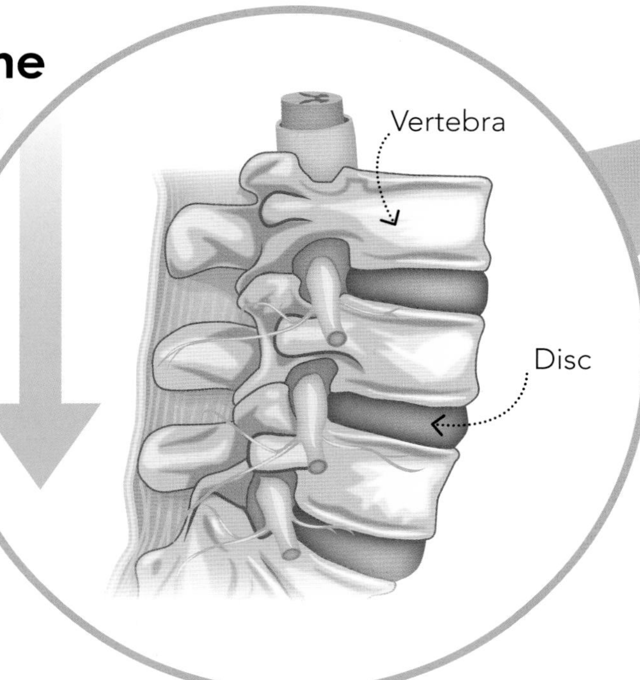

Am I taller in the morning?

Yes! Throughout the day, a force called gravity pulls your body downwards as you walk, sit, or stand. This makes you shorter as your spine gets squashed. When you go to sleep at night, your spine stretches out because you lie flat on your back. By the morning, you are a little bit taller again.

130 cm
120 cm
110 cm
100 cm
90 cm
80 cm
70 cm
60 cm
50 cm
40 cm
30 cm
20 cm
10 cm
0 cm

In the morning

You wake up taller after sleeping because your muscles relax and your spine extends out to its normal length. Gravity keeps you on the bed when sleeping, but it doesn't shorten your spine because you are lying flat.

True or false?

1. People get taller in space.
2. You shrink overnight.
3. Your spine bends when you get older.

See pages 132–133 for the answers

Why do we shrink as we age?

As you get older, the bones in your spine get smaller and the cartilage in your discs gets worn out. This means that the cartilage takes up less space and you shrink in size. When you shrink, your spine bends, which can make you look hunched over when you stand up.

What is gravity?

Gravity is a pulling force. When you use your muscles and joints to jump, gravity pulls you back down so you do not float away!

How do I remember things?

Memories are made when cells called neurons link together and store a pattern in your brain. When you remember something, electrical signals are sent between neurons in the same pattern as when you first made the memory.

What other types of memory do I have?

Working memory

This short-term memory type helps you remember things just after you learn them, such as the steps on your to-do-list.

Semantic memory

This helps you remember things that aren't related to you, such as when a specific castle was built.

Episodic memory

Episodic memory is when you remember how you felt at certain events, such as feeling happy at a party.

Implicit memory

This type of memory tells you if you believe something based on what else you have learnt about it.

Procedural memory

Learning

When you learn a new skill, such as kicking a football, you use a type of memory called your procedural memory. A new path is created between neurons in your brain, and electrical signals jump between these neurons.

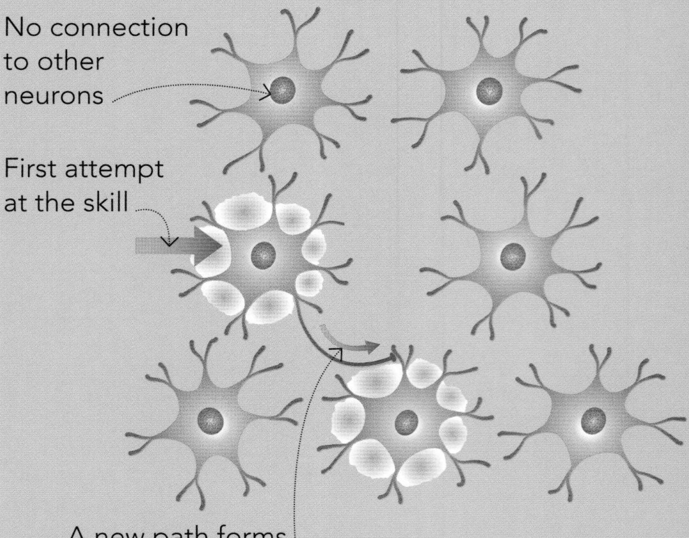

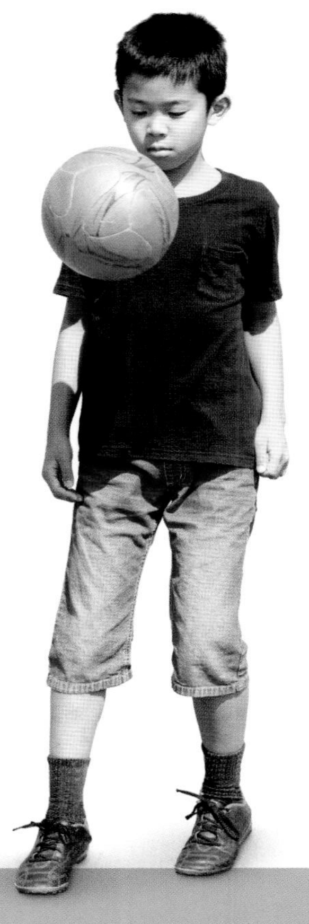

Quick quiz

1. How many types of memory are there?
2. Which cells store memory patterns?
3. What type of memory involves remembering emotions?

See pages 132–133 for the answers

Practising

When you practise a new skill, the pattern of neurons and electrical signals is repeated. You remember what makes it go right and wrong. You move your muscles based on those memories to get the skill right.

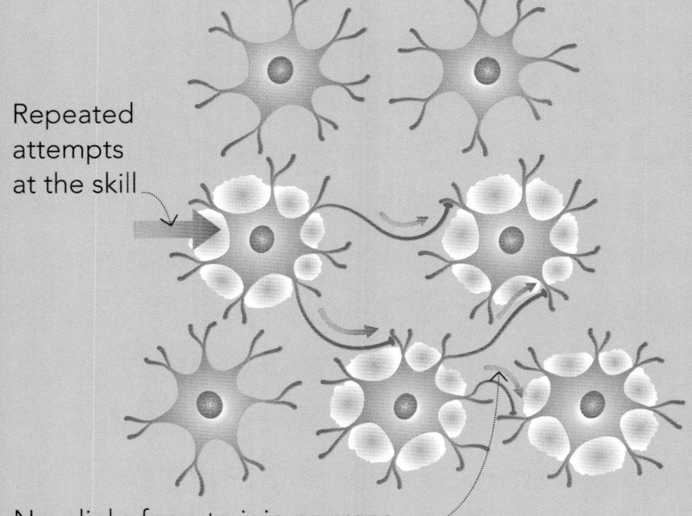
Repeated attempts at the skill
New links form to join neurons in a pattern as you practise.

Remembering

Every time you repeat a skill you have learnt, you improve. Your neurons also get better at repeating the correct pattern. This helps to reduce the amount of times you make a mistake, and you remember how to do it right.

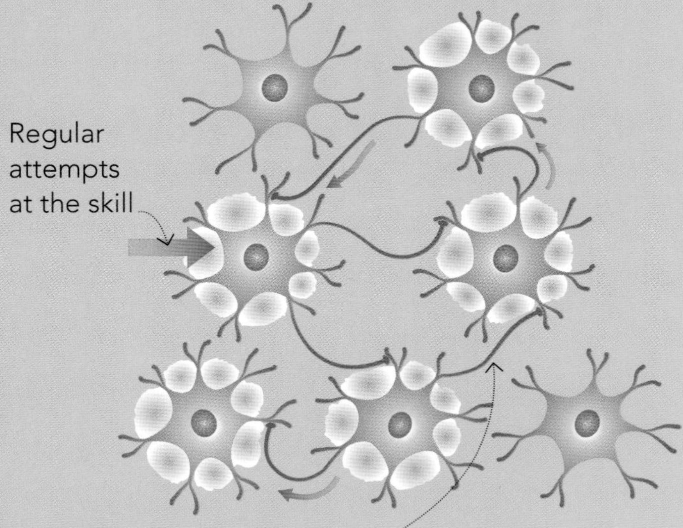
Regular attempts at the skill
The existing neuron pattern repeats when you remember the skill.

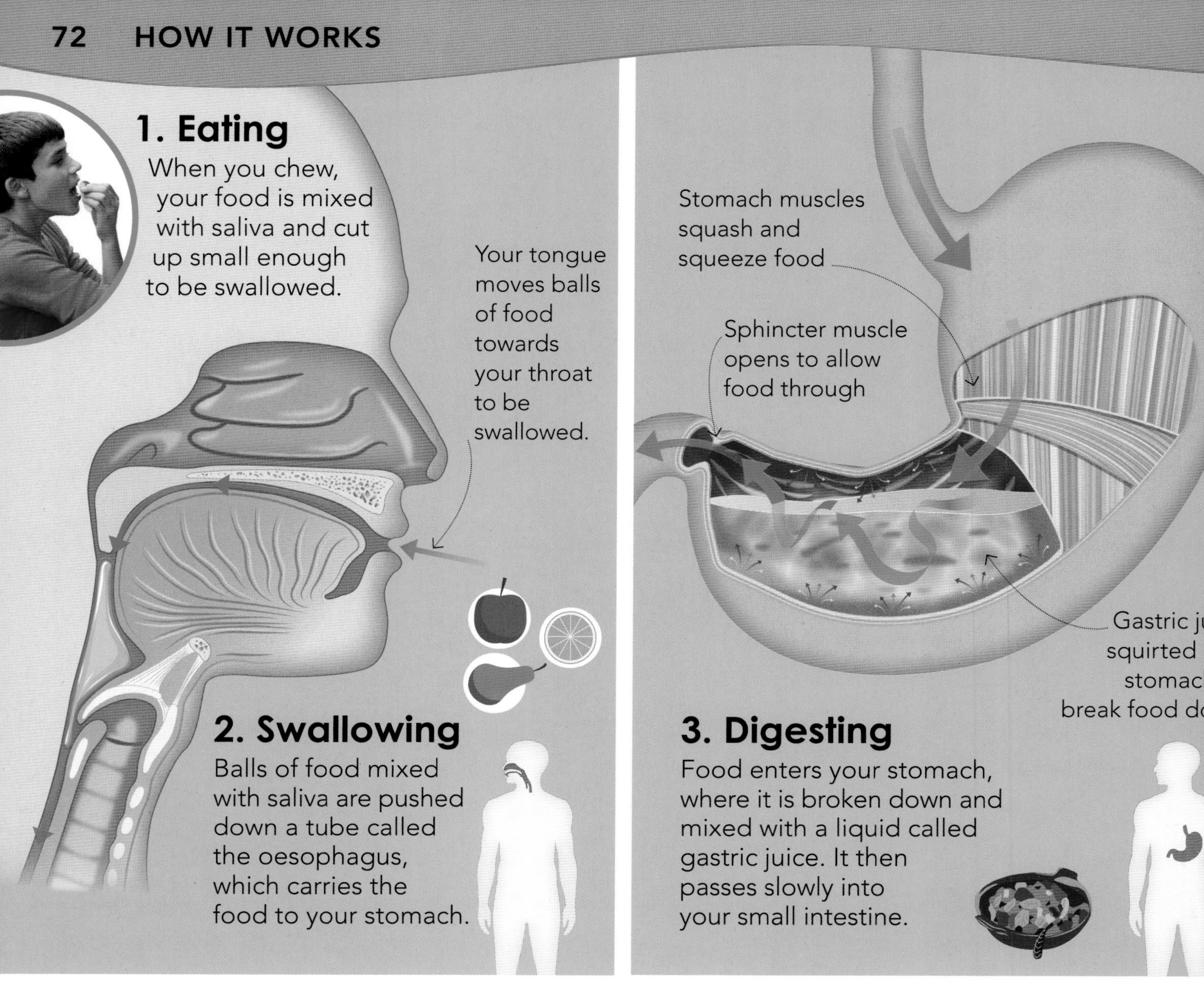

1. Eating
When you chew, your food is mixed with saliva and cut up small enough to be swallowed.
Your tongue moves balls of food towards your throat to be swallowed.
2. Swallowing
Balls of food mixed with saliva are pushed down a tube called the oesophagus, which carries the food to your stomach.
Stomach muscles squash and squeeze food
Sphincter muscle opens to allow food through
Gastric ju
squirted i
stomach
break food do
3. Digesting
Food enters your stomach, where it is broken down and mixed with a liquid called gastric juice. It then passes slowly into your small intestine.

What happens to the food I eat?

Your food goes on a two-day journey from your mouth to your bottom. This process is called digestion. Food is pushed along your digestive tract, where it is squashed and broken down with the help of chemicals, called enzymes. The nutrients and water from the food are absorbed into your blood and waste is pushed out of your body.

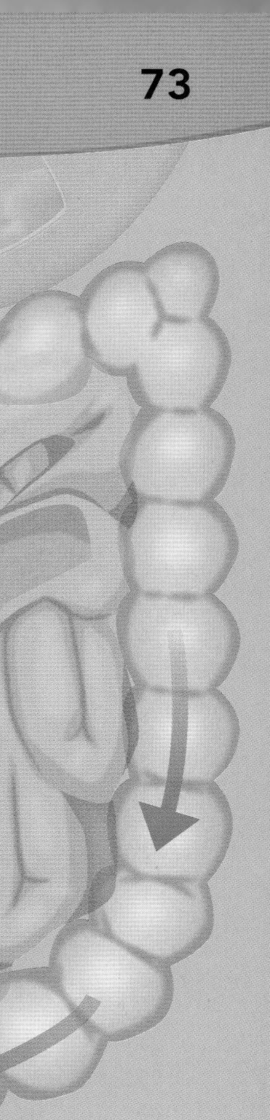

4. Absorbing

Partly digested food is squeezed along the small intestine and enzymes break it down into simple nutrients. These are absorbed into your blood.

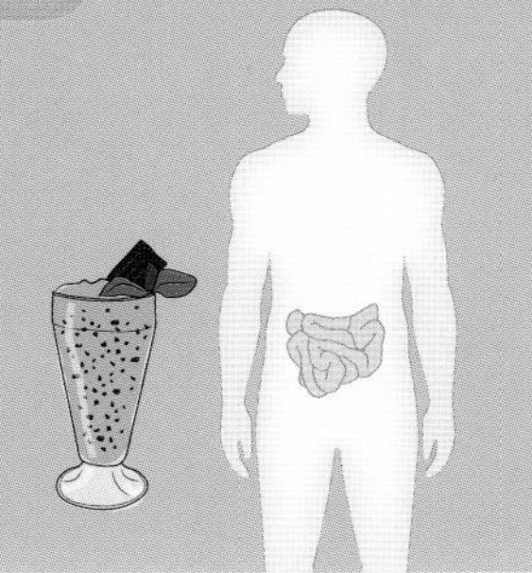

5. Leaving

The leftover waste food travels into the large intestine. Muscles squeeze the waste into segments, pushing it along until it leaves your body as poo.

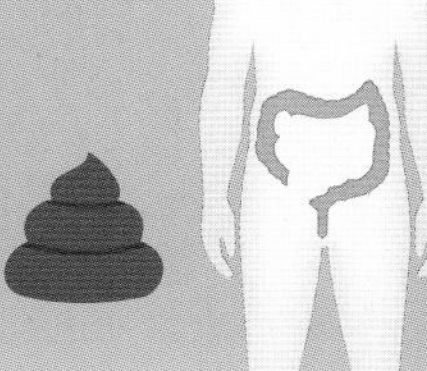

What do other parts of the digestive system do?

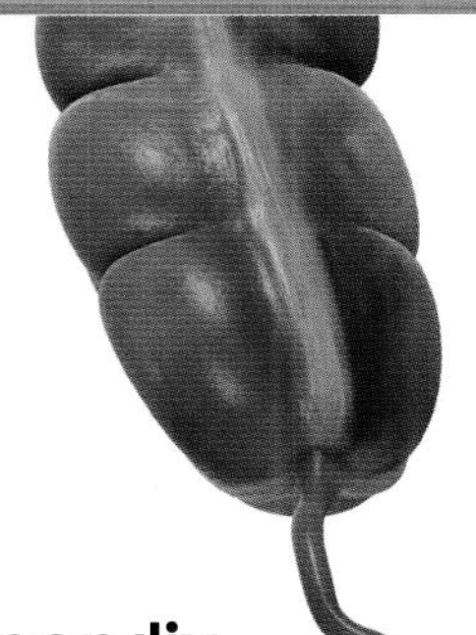

Appendix

The appendix can store good bacteria and contains cells that help fight against infection.

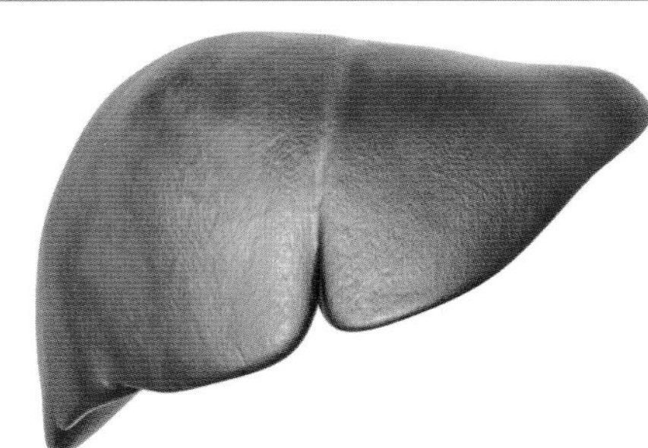

Liver

This makes chemicals and enzymes that speed up digestion. It uses bile from the gallbladder to break down fats. It also cleans blood.

? Quick quiz

1. What does bile help the body to do?
2. How long does it take for food to go through your body?

See pages 132–133 for the answers

Why can't I breathe underwater?

Living things need oxygen to survive. Animals get oxygen in different ways. Fish breathe underwater using organs called gills, which take oxygen directly from water. Humans have lungs that take oxygen in from the air. This means your lungs cannot work underwater.

Bubbles

When you're underwater, you can still breathe out, making bubbles. This helps you get rid of waste gases, such as carbon dioxide.

Using gills

A fish sucks water in through its mouth as it swims. As the water washes through the gills, they take oxygen from the water and release carbon dioxide from the body.

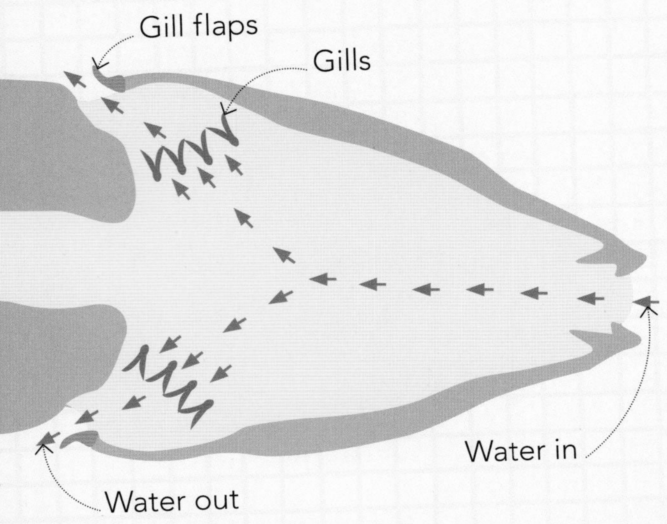

Top view of a fish

Picture quiz

What animal can breathe through its lungs and skin?

See pages 132–133 for the answers

Holding our breath

Even though you can't breathe underwater, you can hold your breath until you reach the water's surface. Most people can hold their breath for at least 30 seconds.

What other animals have gills?

Crabs

These creatures breathe underwater using gills. When crabs come out of the water, they still use gills to breathe – they just need to keep them moist to take oxygen in from the air.

Aquatic molluscs

Snails and clams use gills to take oxygen from the water into their blood. Most underwater snails have just one gill.

Why do I burp?

The main reason you burp is because you swallow air when you eat. The air gets trapped and comes back as a burp. Fizzy drinks have gas in them, so you burp more after drinking them, too.

The scientific term for burping is eructation.

Why do babies need to be burped?

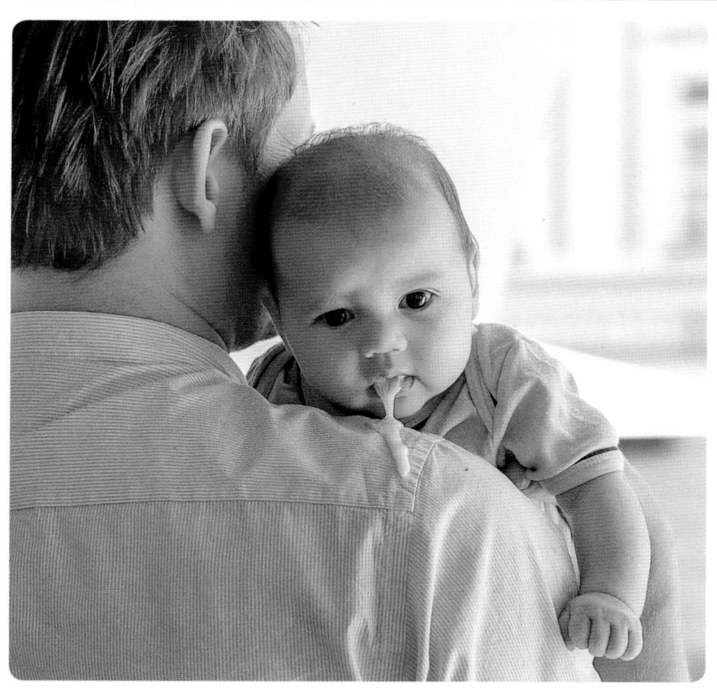

Babies swallow air when they drink milk. The air gets trapped in their stomach and can give them a tummy ache. So they need help to release the trapped air and burp it out. Sometimes they bring up a little milk, too!

Gas build up

As you eat, your stomach fills and stretches because there isn't enough space for the extra gas you swallow.

Sphincter muscle relaxes

As gas builds up it stretches the stomach. This causes the sphincter muscle at the bottom of the oesophagus to relax, opening the pipe so the gas can escape upwards.

Why does burping make a noise?

The gas that is released from the stomach creates vibrations at the top of the oesophagus and in the throat. The vibrations are what make the burp noise.

Oesophagus

Gas builds up in the oesophagus, trapped between the throat and the stomach. Eventually, you feel the need to release the gas as a burp.

Stomach acid

Food enters the stomach and mixes with an acid called hydrochloric acid. This turns the food into a thick, soupy liquid.

1. Can eating or drinking too fast make you burp?
2. What is the scientific name for burping?

See pages 132–133 for the answers

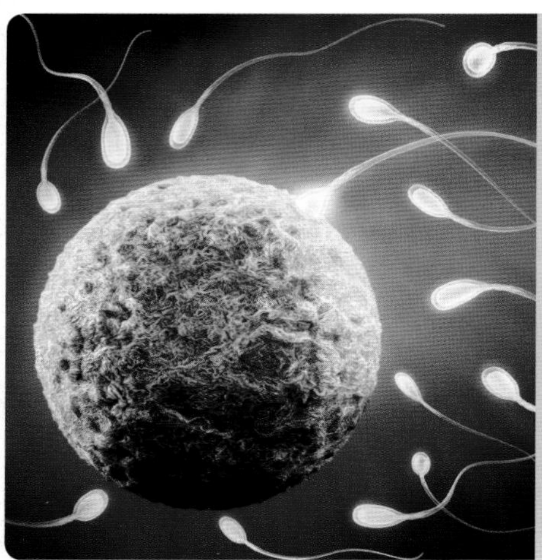

Egg and sperm

A sperm cell from the father fertilizes, or joins with, the egg cell from the mother. Each of these cells holds a set of instructions, or genes, that come together to make a new human.

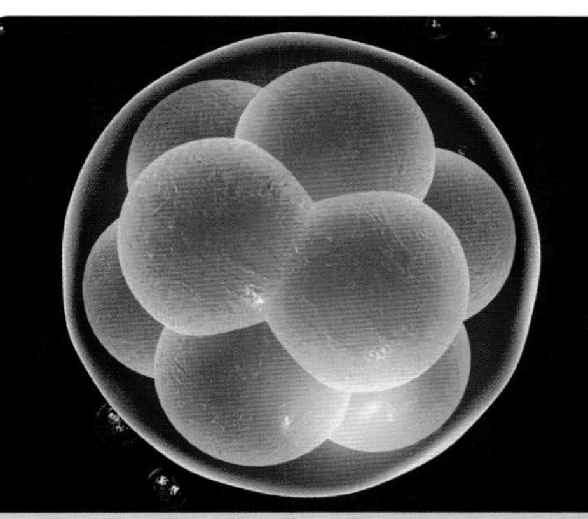

Early embryo

For the first two weeks after fertilization, the first cells make copies of themselves and are called an embryo. The cells in an embryo are stem cells, which means they have not become specific tissues yet.

How do babies grow?

Every baby begins as two cells, which are no bigger than a full stop. These cells divide and multiply, and after two weeks they start to become different tissues. At five weeks, the heart starts to pump blood, and eight weeks later the baby has a human shape!

Five weeks

At five weeks, the embryo is about the size of a pea. The head, eyes, arms, and legs begin to take shape and a tiny heart starts pumping blood around growing organs.

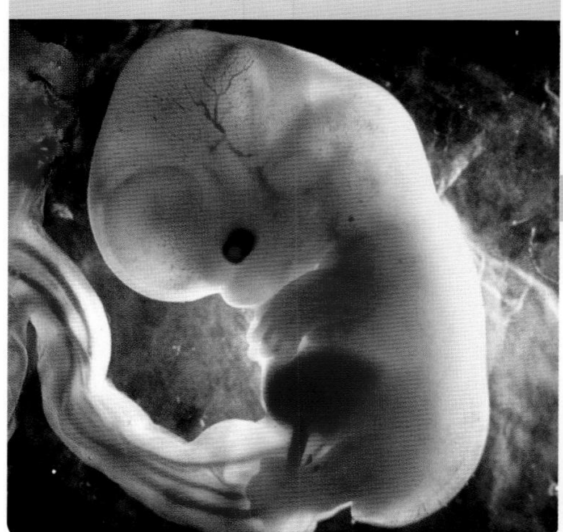

Where do babies grow?

Babies grow inside their mother in a chamber called the womb. The umbilical cord connects the baby to the walls of the womb. This cord provides the baby with food and oxygen, and it also removes waste.

? Quick quiz

1. What do we call a baby in the womb if it is more than eight weeks old?
2. What do we call a baby in the womb when it is under eight weeks old?
3. How does a growing baby get oxygen in the womb?

See pages 132–133 for the answers

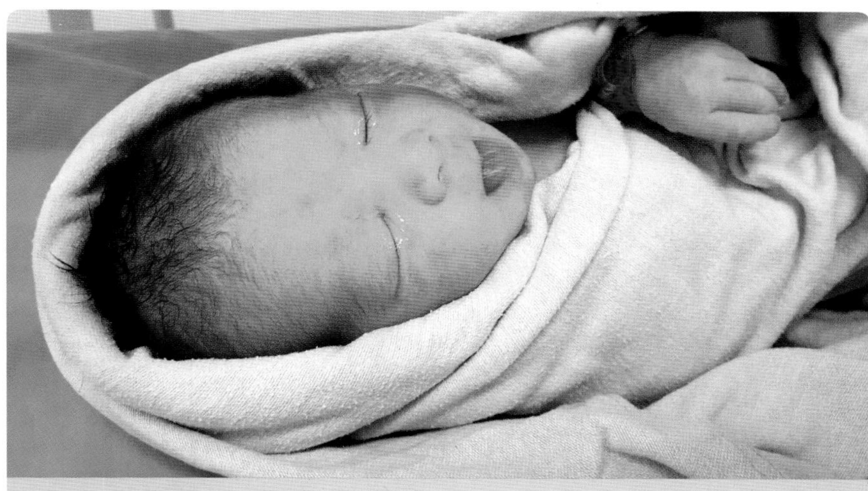

Newborn baby

The cushioning fluid leaves the womb just before the baby is born and the placenta comes away afterwards. The baby uses its lungs to breathe in oxygen, so no longer needs an umbilical cord – it is cut off and becomes the belly button!

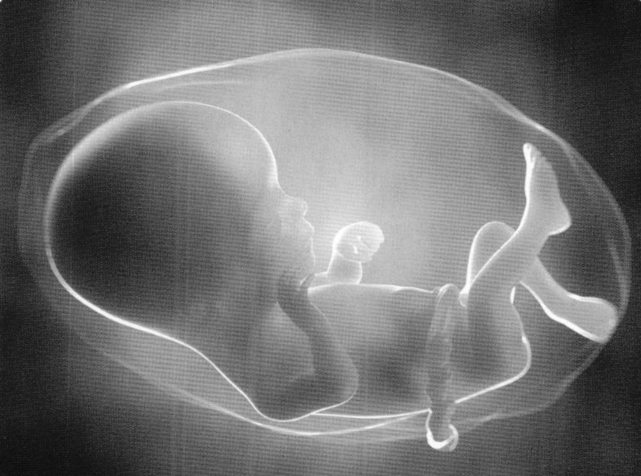

16 weeks

A baby is called a fetus from eight weeks onwards. At 16 weeks, the fetus is about 20 cm (8 in) long and can hear sounds. It responds to these sounds by kicking and turning around. At this stage, the main organs are mostly formed.

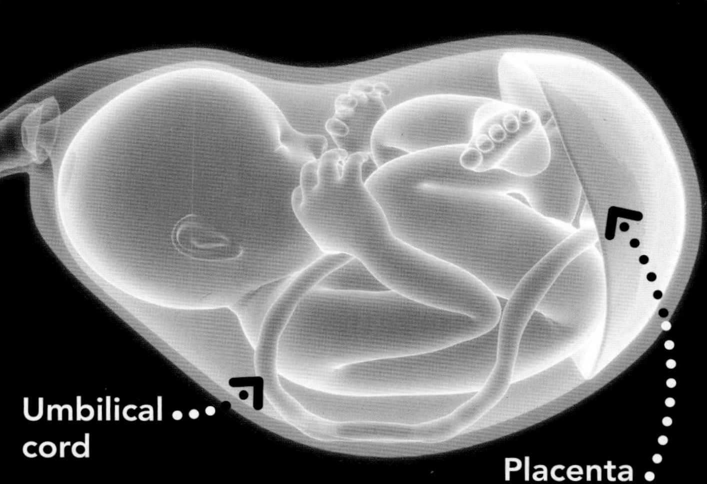

Nine months

The baby floats in cushioning fluid in the womb and is ready to be born. It gets oxygen from the mother's blood through the umbilical cord, which is attached to the placenta in the womb. The baby's lungs are full of fluid and cannot breathe in air.

Thick skin

The skin on the soles of your feet hardens as you use it all the time. These cells divide more frequently than other skin cells, so your skin here is thicker. The skin on your elbows stretches a lot when you move, so it is also thicker to allow for this repetitive movement.

Does my skin last forever?

No, your skin is constantly dying and remaking itself. The top layer of your skin is called the epidermis. About 35,000 dead skin cells flake off it every minute and are replaced by new ones. Skin cells are filled with keratin, which makes them strong.

Making new skin

Skin cells are created at the bottom of the epidermis layer. These cells are pushed upwards as new cells are made. It takes about three weeks for skin cells to reach the surface of the epidermis.

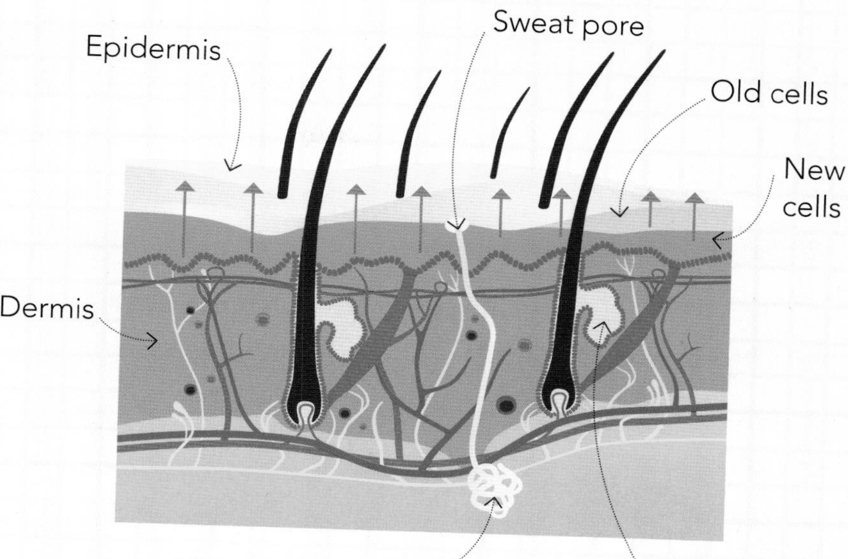

What does dead skin look like?

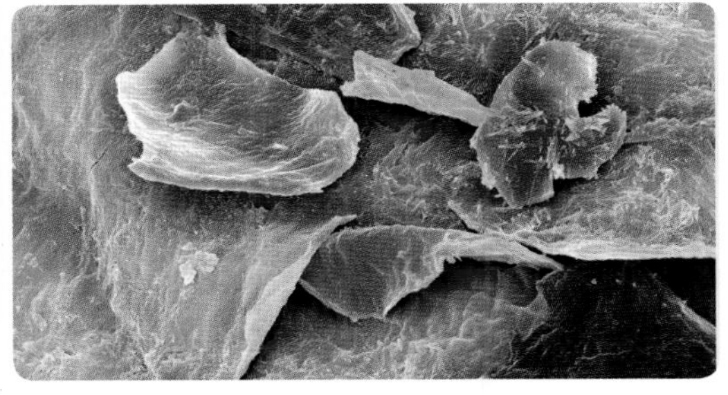

The skin you can see on your body is made from a protective barrier of dead cells, which are knitted together. These dead skin cells are arranged in a tessellated pattern, which means they fit together without gaps. This pattern makes the skin flexible.

? True or false?

1. Your skin is thickest around the belly.
2. New skin is made at the base of the dermis.

See pages 132–133 for the answers

How do I hold my pee?

You hold your pee using muscles in the bladder. The bladder is an organ that fills up with waste liquid that has been taken out of the blood by the kidneys. When your bladder is full, receptors send a signal to the brain and you feel the need to pee.

You produce about 1½ litres (3 pints) of urine a day.

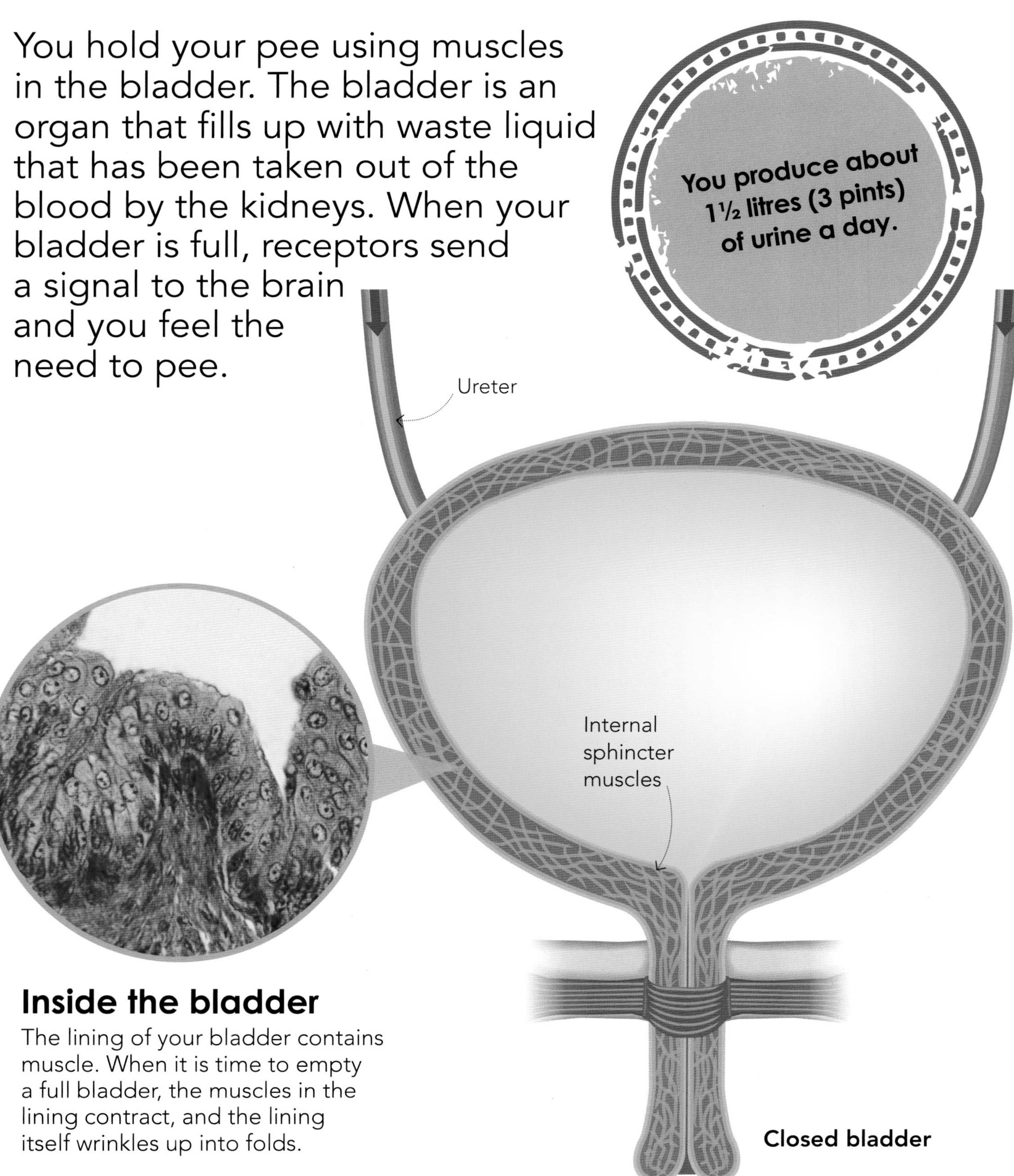

Inside the bladder

The lining of your bladder contains muscle. When it is time to empty a full bladder, the muscles in the lining contract, and the lining itself wrinkles up into folds.

Closed bladder

Why is my pee yellow?

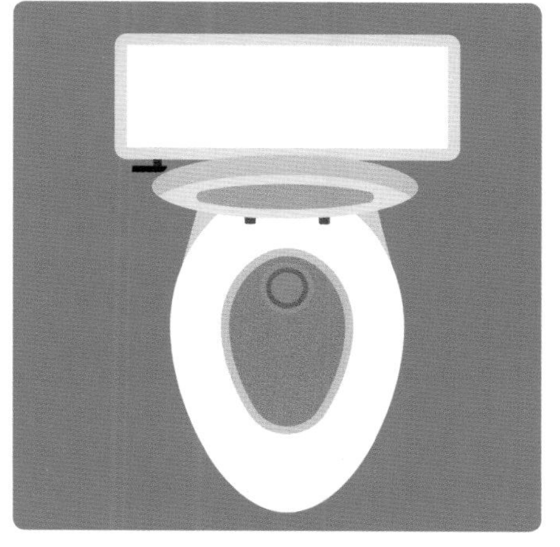

Kidneys add a chemical called urobilin to your pee. This chemical has a yellow colour. Urobilin breaks down in water, so if you drink a lot, your pee is pale yellow. If you don't drink enough water your pee is dark yellow. This means you are dehydrated.

? Quick quiz

1. How do you know when it's time to pee?
2. What happens to the bladder walls when you pee?
3. What keeps the bladder shut?

See pages 132–133 for the answers

Bladder control

Babies can't control their bladders, which is why they wear nappies. The sphincter muscles in their bladders always stay open, and pee automatically flows out when the bladder fills up. You learn to control your bladder from about two years old – this is often known as "potty training".

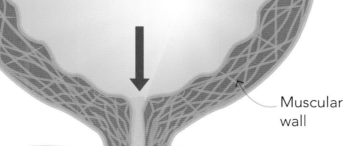

Muscular wall

External sphincter muscles

Urethra

Open bladder

Emptying the bladder

When you go to the toilet, the sphincter muscles in your bladder relax and the bladder empties. The stretchy muscular walls squeeze the pee out as they fold inwards and pee flows out along the urethra.

Adrenaline

Adrenaline is a hormone that is released into the blood. It controls tiny muscles, called arrector pili muscles, in your skin. They are attached to the top layer of your skin and the base of each hair follicle – a small hole where the hair grows from.

Feeling relaxed

When you feel relaxed, the arrector pili muscles are also relaxed. This means that the hair lies flat.

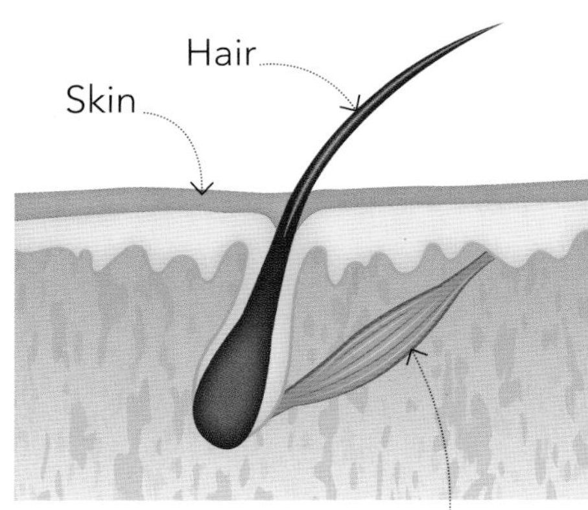

Feeling cold or scared

When you feel cold or scared, adrenaline makes the arrector pili muscles contract. This pulls the hair up straight and goosebumps form.

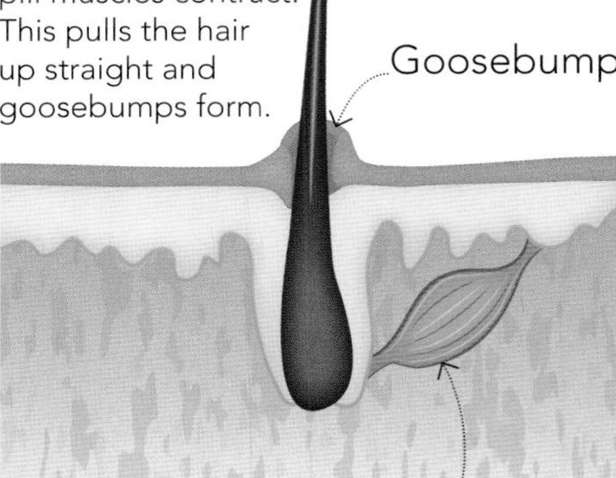

Why do I get goosebumps?

Small muscles in your skin pull up hairs and make bumps called goosebumps, when they detect a chemical signal called adrenaline. This hormone is released into the blood as a chemical signal when you're cold or scared.

Why do some furry animals make their hair stand on end?

To look big and scary

An animal looks bigger when all of its hair stands up. It makes the animal seem more dangerous, so it can scare off any threats.

To keep warm

When hair stands up, it traps air close to the skin. The trapped air heats up quickly and acts like a blanket, helping the animal to stay warm.

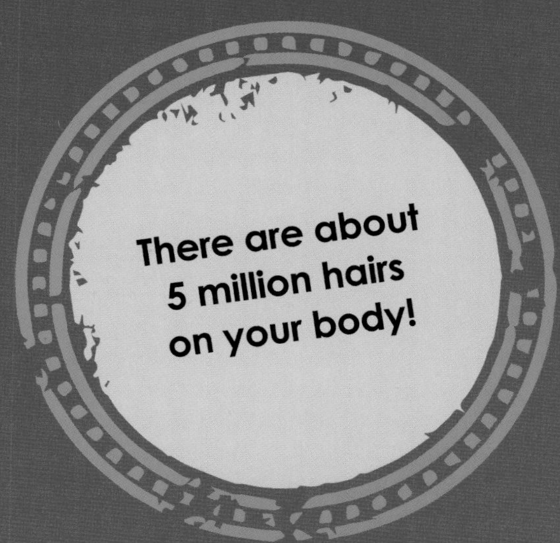

There are about 5 million hairs on your body!

? *True or false?*

1. The hormone adrenaline makes body hair fall out.
2. Your emotions can make you have goosebumps.
3. Tiny muscles relax to lift your hairs up.

See pages 132–133 for the answers

Why do I have eyebrows?

Eyebrows stop sweat from dripping into your eyes – this protects them so you can see! Your eyebrows also help you to show how you are feeling through your facial expressions. They can be used to display many different emotions.

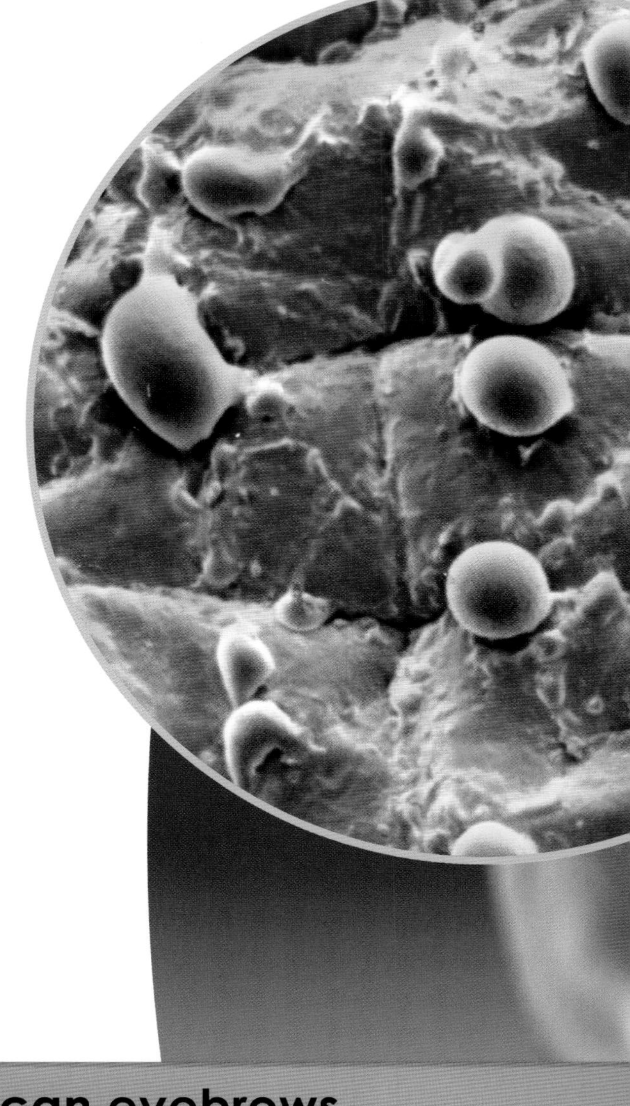

Sweat glands

Your sweat glands are in your skin. They are long and coiled, and produce sweat to cool you down. There are more than 4 million sweat glands in your body.

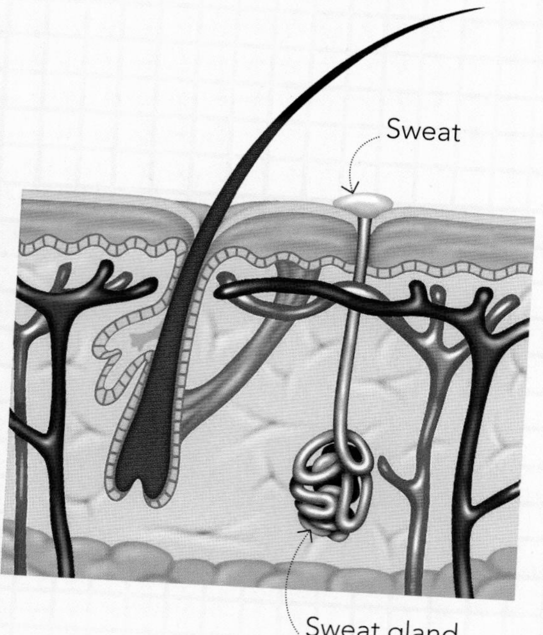

How can eyebrows show emotions?

Frowning

You might frown when you want to show that you do not like something. You do this by scrunching up your eyebrows.

Raised eyebrows

When you raise your eyebrows, you look like you are surprised about something. You may not realize you are doing this!

There are more than 1,000 hairs in your eyebrows!

Cooling down

Liquid sweat droplets evaporate, or turn from a liquid to a gas, on your skin as your body warms up. The heat from your body transfers to the sweat. As the droplets evaporate, your body cools down.

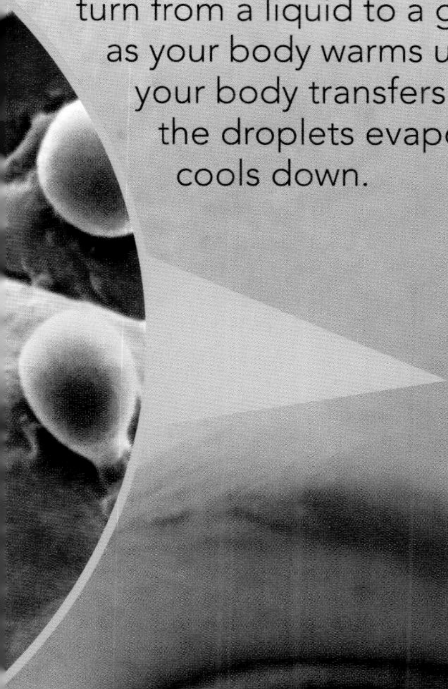

Sweating

You sweat when you are hot, when you exercise, and when you feel nervous. Sweat droplets react with bacteria on your skin to give you a sweaty smell.

? True or false?

1. Cows sweat through their noses.
2. There are more sweat glands in your armpits than on your arms.
3. You raise your eyebrows to show sadness.

See pages 132–133 for the answers

Why do my ears pop?

The pop you sometimes feel happens when the air pressure changes inside your ears, such as when you're in the sky in an airplane. Your middle ear, behind your eardrum, balances the air pressure inside your ear with the air pressure around you. This results in a pop!

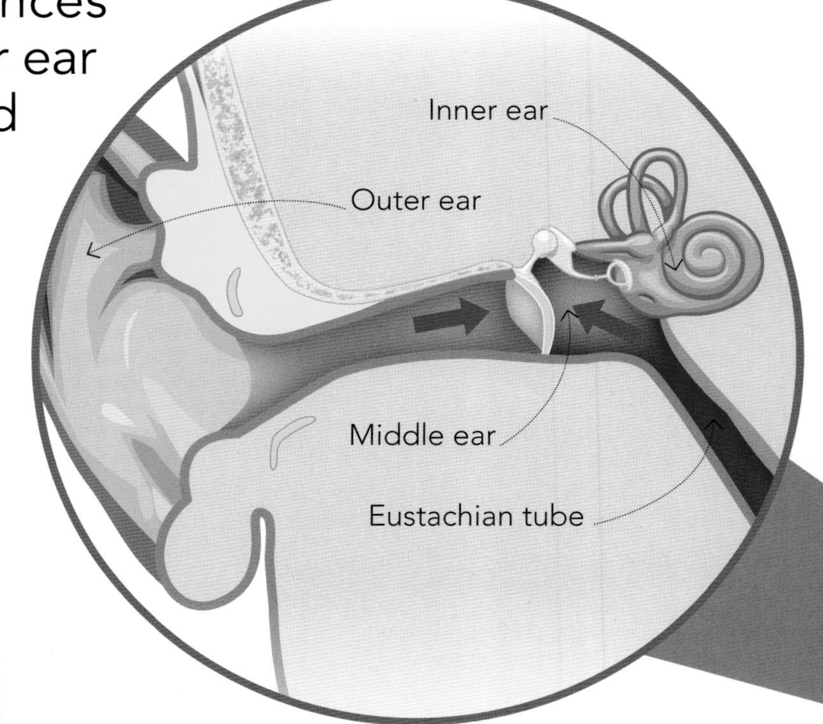

What is air pressure?

Air pressure is the weight of the air molecules around you. These are more spread out the higher up you go and so the air pressure is lower. High in the sky or on top of a mountain, the air pressure is very low.

Inside the ear

Your eustachian tube links the cavity, or space, behind your eardrum to your mouth and nose. When the tube opens, air flows into the middle ear from your throat. This flow of air helps to balance the air pressure in your ear.

How do you balance the air in your ears?

Yawning

When you yawn, air moves from your mouth into the middle ear, through the eustachian tube. This makes the air inside the ear the same pressure as the air outside.

Swallowing

When you swallow, the eustachian tube opens and air enters the middle ear. This balances the air pressure inside and outside the ear.

The eustachian tube also drains fluid away from the middle ear.

Popping ears

The air inside your ears is trapped in the middle ear. The pop happens when the air pressure inside your ear changes to match the air pressure outside. This pop can be quite painful for young children, but hurts less as you get older.

Picture quiz

What is the name of this bone in the middle ear?

See pages 132–133 for the answers

Healthy habits

Your body is powered by food, oxygen, and water. You can keep your body healthy by getting enough sleep, exercising regularly, and eating well. Your mental health is just as important as your physical health, and you can feel a range of emotions. It's important to remember that everyone thinks differently.

Why do I need food?

Food gives you energy, which you need to make all the parts of your body work. Your body breaks down food, and stores useful chemicals in your blood and cells. Your cells can convert stored energy into movement energy.

How does my body make energy?

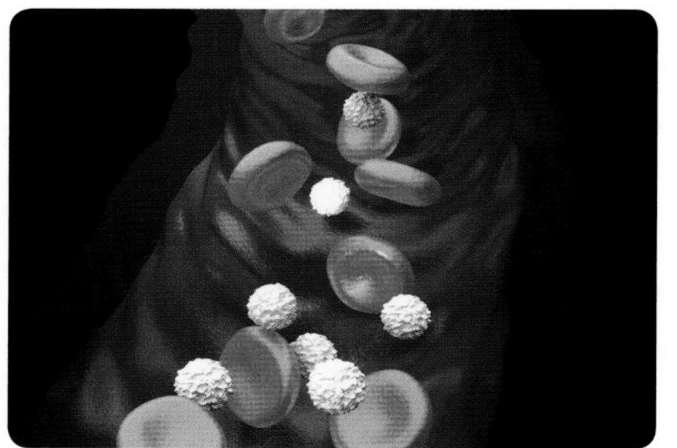

Stored energy
Sugar travels in the blood as glucose, which fuels cells. It is also stored in the liver and muscles. Extra glucose is stored as fat.

Movement energy
The body uses blood sugar to power your cells and make muscles move. Fat turns into sugar and enters the blood.

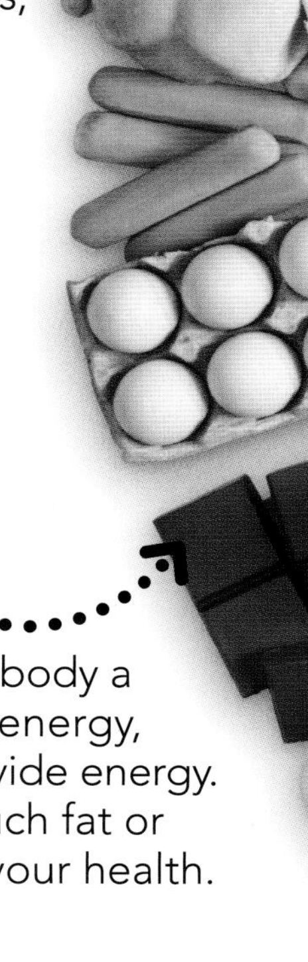

Proteins

We need proteins, such as those found in meat and eggs, to build cells and repair the body. These foods also contain fat for energy.

Fats and sugar

Sugar gives your body a quick release of energy, and fats also provide energy. However, too much fat or sugar is bad for your health.

Dairy

Dairy products, such as milk and cheese, have lots of calcium. This helps your teeth and bones grow.

Carbohydrates

Your body turns carbohydrates, such as those found in bread, pasta, and rice, into sugar (glucose). They are the main source of energy for the body.

? Picture quiz

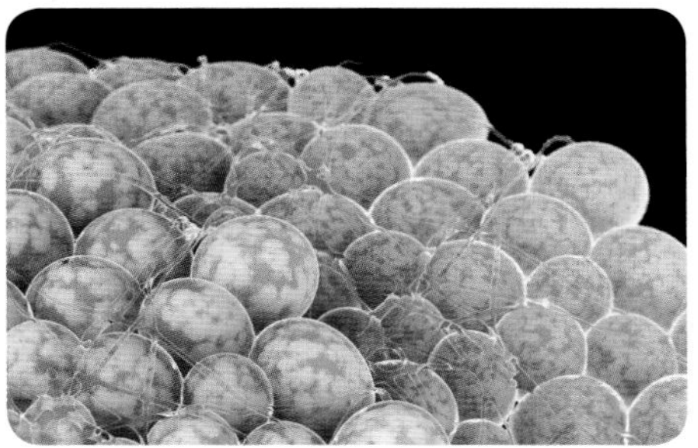

Where in the body is extra sugar stored?

See pages 132–133 for the answers

Vitamins, minerals, and fibre

These keep all the different parts of the body working properly. Fibre helps you break down food and get rid of waste in poo.

Respiration

Your cells convert oxygen gas (O_2) and sugar into movement energy. A waste gas called carbon dioxide (CO_2) is made, as well as water (H_2O). This process is called respiration.

Sugar + O_2 = CO_2 + H_2O + Energy

Feel good

When you exercise, your brain releases chemicals that make you feel happy, relaxed, and less worried. Exercise helps you to sleep better, too.

? True or false?

1. Climbing strengthens muscles and bones.
2. Muscles get bigger with exercise.
3. Exercising gives you extra calories.

See pages 132–133 for the answers

Burn calories

Energy in food is measured in calories. Extra calories are stored in the body as fat. Exercise uses up calories that the body doesn't need.

More energy

Regular exercise makes your heart and lungs work harder. This helps them grow stronger, so they are able to deliver extra oxygen and nutrients to your cells. This in turn makes you feel more energetic.

What happens when I exercise?

Exercise is good for your mind and body. It uses the energy you get from food and it makes you stronger. Regular exercise makes your heart and lungs work better, and gives you more energy. Exercise also reduces the chances of getting sick.

Stronger muscles

Exercising makes your muscles stronger. The more you use them, the stronger they get. You are also able to use your muscles for longer without getting tired. When muscles aren't used often, they become small and weak.

How often should I exercise?

You should get active every day, including exercise that makes you breathe faster, such as skipping, running, riding a bike, or playing sports. It is also important to do activities that keep your muscles and bones strong, such as climbing, swinging, and stretching.

Future health

Exercise greatly reduces the risk of serious health conditions later in life, such as strokes, high blood pressure, diabetes, anxiety, depression, cancer, and arthritis.

Signs that you are thriving

Enjoying life

When you're feeling good it's easy to have fun, and enjoy hobbies and activities. You feel positive about yourself, and it's easier to be friendly and spend time with other people.

Good relationships

You might start and keep good friendships when you're in good mental health. You ask for help when you need it. Your feelings are not easily changed and controlled by others.

Expressing feelings

You value your thoughts, opinions, and feelings, and are comfortable talking about and showing emotions. You know you can get through problems, even if it feels tough at times.

What is mental health?

Mental health describes a person's emotional health over time. This includes feelings, behaviour, thoughts, and interactions with other people. You can examine these things to understand if you are in good mental health.

How am I feeling?

You may have different behaviours based on how you feel mentally. The images on the left show some signs of good mental health, whilst on the right are some problems that may happen if you suffer from poor mental health.

·igns you might be struggling

·osing interest

·you're feeling sad or upset ·lot, you might stop caring ·oout doing your school work, · be less interested in your ·obbies. You might stop ·anting to meet your friends.

Sleeping problems

If you are feeling unhappy or stressed, you might have lots of trouble sleeping. You might feel more tired than usual during the day, or you can't fall asleep and feel worried about things at night.

Eating patterns

You may stop feeling hungry or don't enjoy food. On the other hand, you may overeat or crave only sweet things because they make you feel better for a little while.

What can help to improve my mental health?

Mindfulness

Noticing your feelings, taking time to reflect, and focusing on the here and now could help to make you feel good.

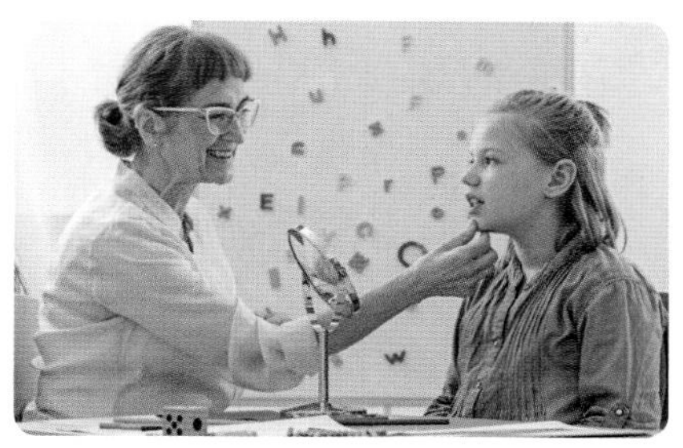

Counselling

Talking to a professional is an excellent way to start improving mental health if you need help.

? Quick quiz

1. What is one way to improve mental health?
2. What is one sign that you are thriving?
3. What is one sign that you might be struggling?

See pages 132–133 for the answers

Why do I feel happy and sad?

If you're feeling happy, it means that you are experiencing something you enjoy, which makes you feel good. Feeling sad is the opposite – you might feel sad when you are feeling hurt, scared, or disappointed.

Happiness

Your body releases happy chemicals when you do things you enjoy, when you feel loved, and when you think about things you like. Laughing helps you to feel happy. Give it a try!

Pyramid of needs

A scientist called Abraham Maslow came up with this pyramid to show what people need to feel happy. He said that needs are built upon one another from the bottom up, and the more levels of the pyramid you have, the happier you are able to be, with the top representing the best conditions for happiness.

What is empathy?

Understanding how others feel is called "empathy". Being able to communicate your feelings and show you understand how others feel is important because it makes them feel appreciated, loved, and accepted.

Quick quiz

1. What happens in your brain when you feel happy?
2. Why are your feelings useful?

See pages 132–133 for the answers

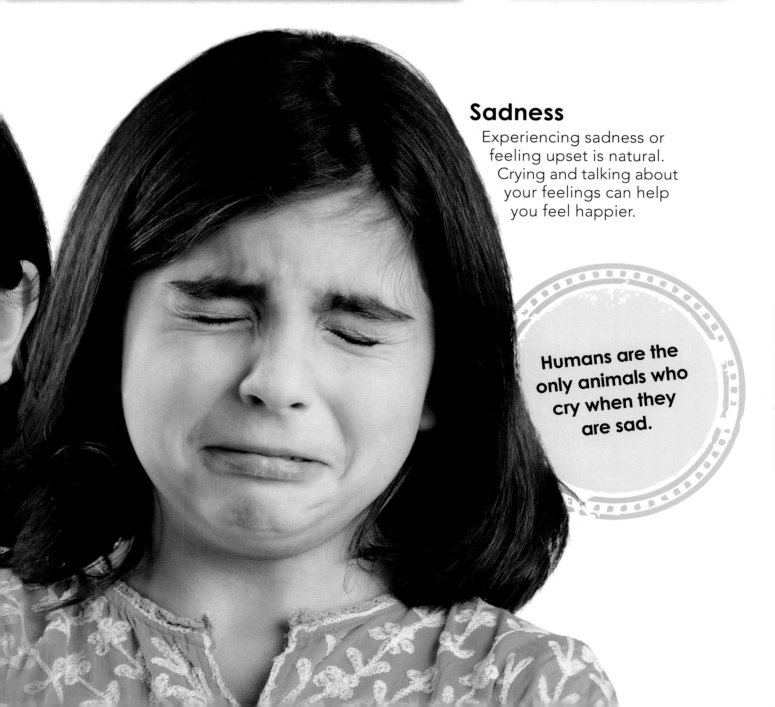

Sadness

Experiencing sadness or feeling upset is natural. Crying and talking about your feelings can help you feel happier.

Humans are the only animals who cry when they are sad.

How does soap kill germs?

When you wash with soap and water, the soap lifts germs off your skin. The soap breaks germs, such as viruses and bacteria, apart and surrounds them, so they can be washed away in water. Germs can make you sick if you do not wash them away.

Are germs there even if I can't see them?

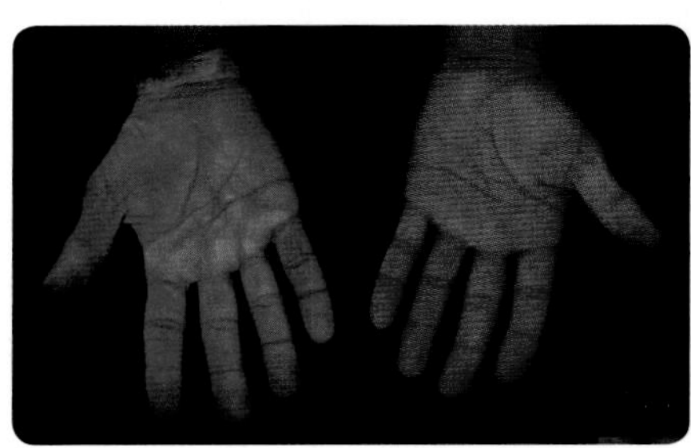

Germs show up in ultraviolet (UV) light. The blue hand is unwashed. It is covered in germs that are a blue colour in UV light. The pink hand has been washed with soap and water, and is germ-free.

Attracting

The tails of tiny particles of soap are attracted to germs. This means that the soap particles move towards germs and become attached to them.

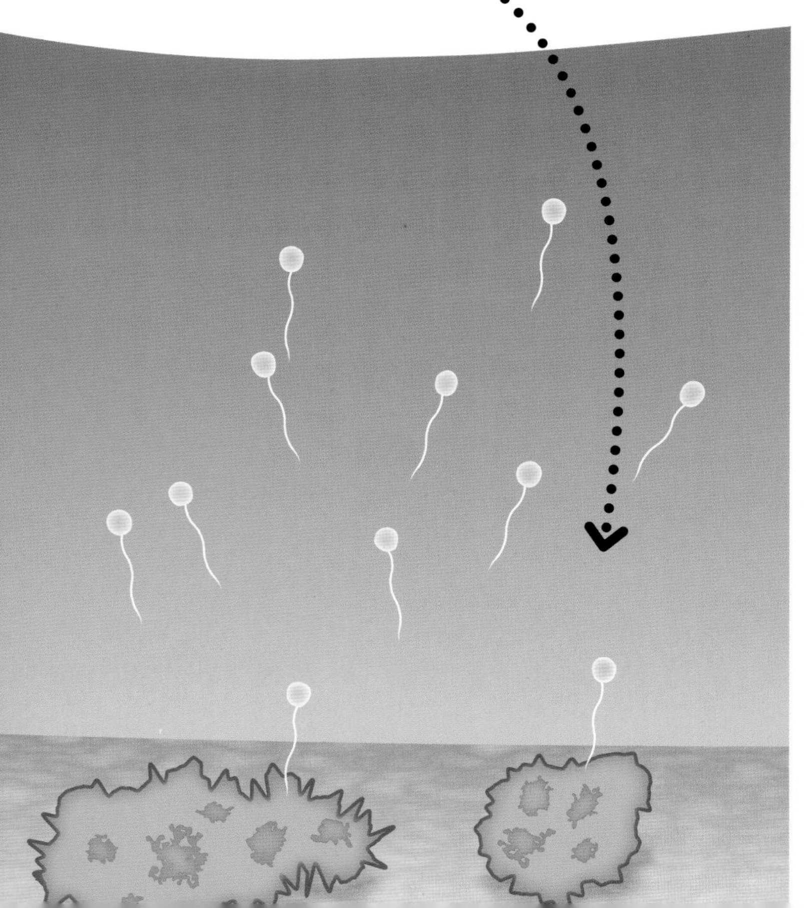

Lifting

When lots of soap particles are attached to germs, they lift them up and away from your skin. The tails of the soap particles poke into the germs, breaking them up.

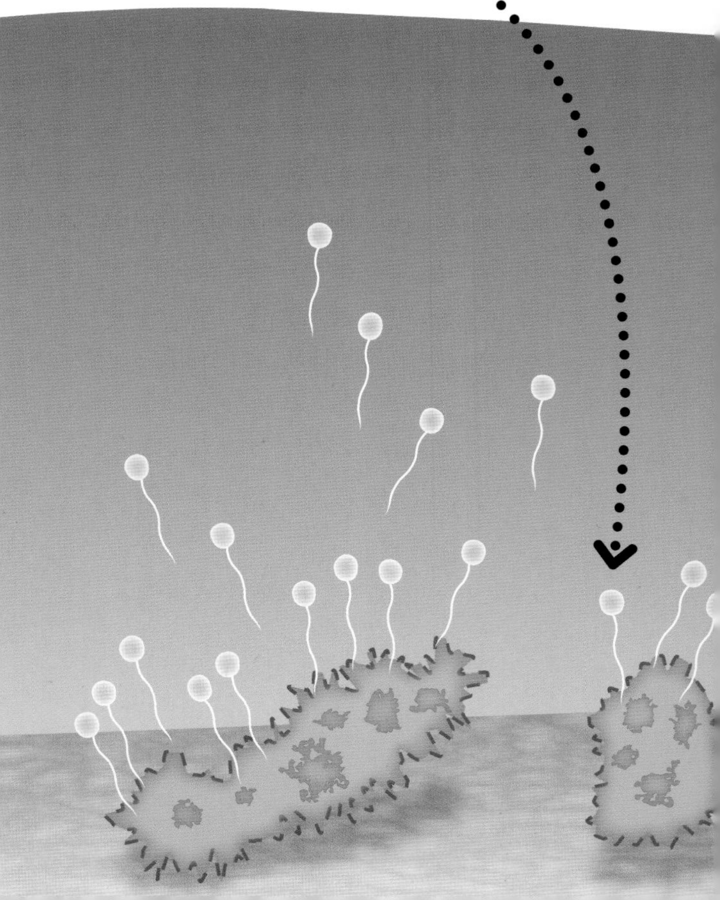

ow should I wash my hands?

ry to spend at least 20 seconds washing your ıands with soap and water. It's important to :lean every part of your hands thoroughly.

1. Wet your hands. Add soap and rub your hands to make a foam.

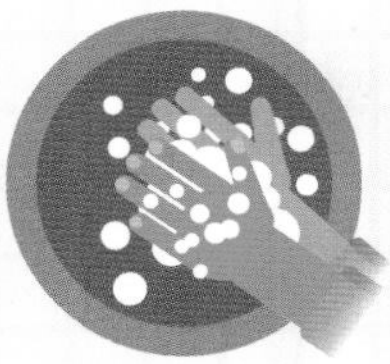

2. Make sure to clean your hands, palms, fingers, and wrists.

3. Rinse your hands with clean water to wash the soap off.

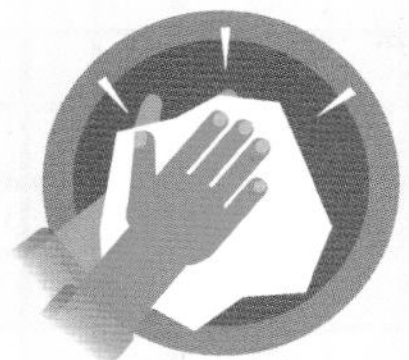

4. Dry your hands fully using a clean towel.

? Picture quiz

What type of germ is this?

See pages 132–133 for the answers

Surrounding

As soap particles surround and lift up each germ, the germs are pushed away from each other and they float in the water.

Removing

When you rinse your hands with clean water to remove the soap, the germs floating in the water are washed away. You are left with clean hands.

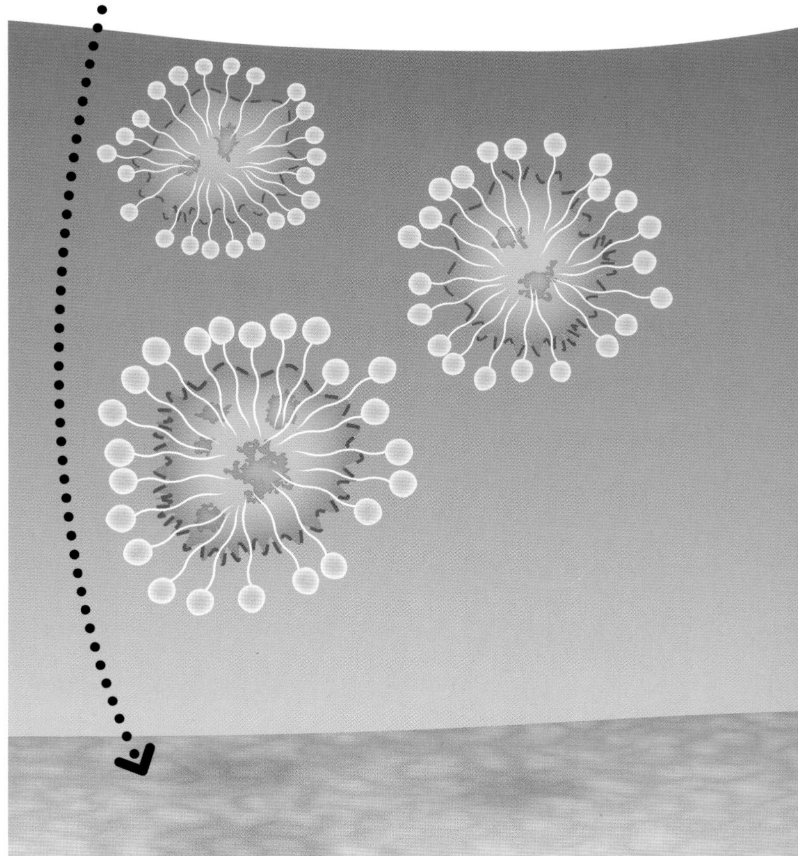

Why do people think differently?

We are all born with different personalities and we all think in a different way. How your brain works can affect how you learn, and how you relate to others.

Dyspraxia

This is a condition that causes poor coordination. Children with dyspraxia might find drawing, writing, and playing sports difficult. They often have good talking skills.

Down's syndrome

Children with Down's syndrome have a learning disability, which means they might take longer than other children to learn certain skills. They have their own personalities, and have likes and dislikes the same as everyone else.

Dyslexia

Dyslexic children find reading and writing more difficult than other children their age. Their strengths may include creativity, visual thinking, and working with their hands.

Autism

Autistic children may find sounds or bright lights uncomfortable. They find it hard to understand how others feel. They often have strong concentration and memory skills, and are good at seeing details.

ADHD

Children with ADHD may have lots of energy. They might be easily distracted, find it hard to focus on certain things, and could do things without thinking. They are often very creative.

How can my family affect the way I think?

Family rules

Family behaviours can affect the way you think and react to others. People learn different ways of doing things or sharing feelings from their family.

Core beliefs

Children who are shown love and respect often grow up feeling loved and valued. Those who are treated poorly may grow up thinking badly of themselves.

? Quick quiz

1. How does dyslexia affect children's reading ability?
2. What is one outside factor that can affect the way you think?

See pages 132–133 for the answers

What happens when I age?

Your body changes as it ages. Over time, the cells in the body get weaker, and lose the ability to repair and replace themselves. Ageing is a natural part of being human.

How can we repair joints that can't repair themselves?

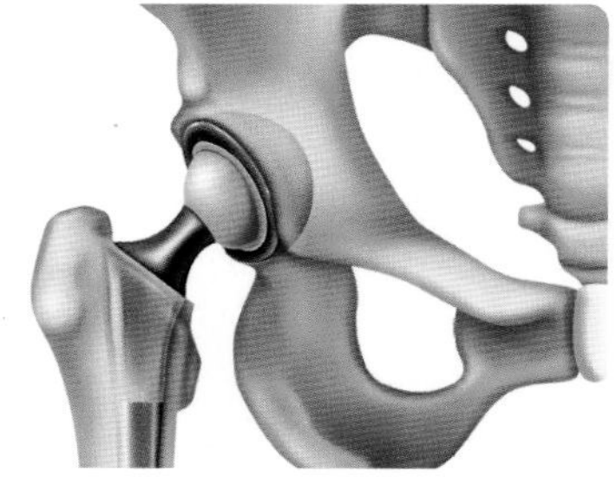

Hip replacement
The top part of the thigh bone is taken out and a metal replacement bone is put in. A metal cup is put into the hip.

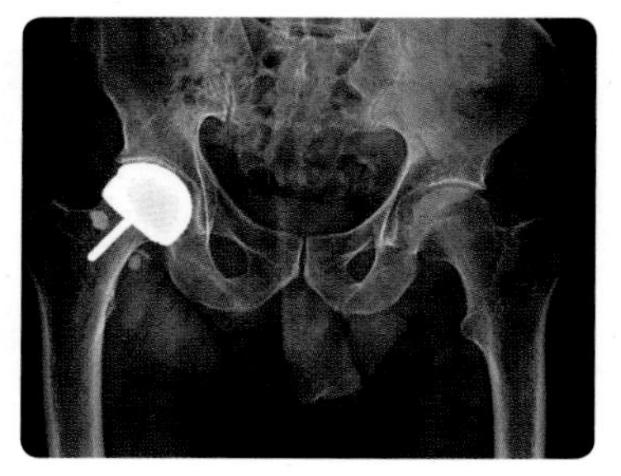

Hip resurfacing
The damaged bone is removed from the hip joint and metal plates are put in. Bone can then grow around the plates.

? True or false?

1. Your bones break more easily as you age.
2. Your skin becomes more oily as you age.

See pages 132–133 for the answers

Why does hair go grey?

The cells that give your hair its colour are called stem cells. These cells decrease and disappear around the root of the hair as you age, so the new hairs grow without colour and look grey.

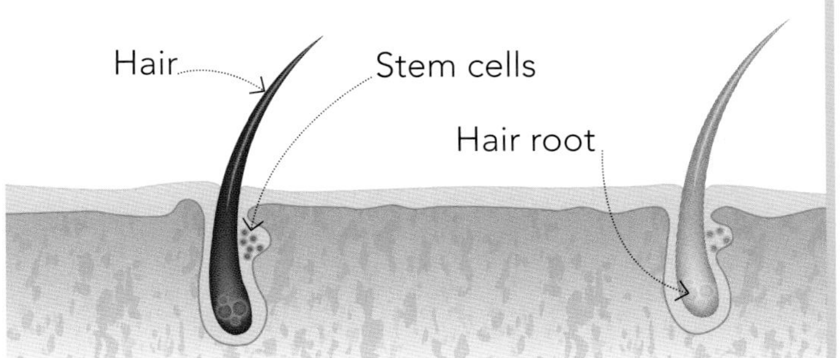

Loss of vision and hearing

Wear and tear of muscles and tissue in the eyes and ears makes them gradually get worse. Ear and eye diseases are also more common in older people.

Wrinkles

The skin gets thinner and produces less collagen, the protein that makes it elastic. Less oil is made by skin, so it dries out. Lines appear in places where the skin is stretched, such as around the eyes and mouth.

Lower energy

Muscles start to lose strength and flexibility so they can't work for as long as they used to. Your body clock also changes as you get older, which means you sleep less and get tired more quickly.

Stiff joints

The cartilage and fluid between joints that keeps them moving smoothly decreases. This means bones can start to rub together, and become stiff and sometimes painful.

Fragile bones

Bones lose calcium and minerals as they age, so they become weaker. Older people often break bones if they fall.

Why do I need water?

Your body needs a regular supply of water to work. Every part of your body is made of cells, and every cell contains water. The important jobs carried out by cells take place in water. Blood is mostly water, so it flows easily through the body. Water is also found in other fluids, such as saliva, sweat, and pee.

Why do I feel thirsty?

The brain monitors the water levels in the body and makes sure you always have the right balance. If you need more water, it signals you to feel thirsty so you drink. It also tells the kidneys to pee less so you lose less water.

Water in

Most of the water in the body comes from the fluids you drink. The food you eat also contains some water. Your body also makes water when it turns food and oxygen into energy.

Water out

Extra water in the body is removed when you pee and poo. When you sweat, water is lost through the skin. Water also leaves the body in the air you breathe out.

Water in

Water out

How much of me is water?

The amount of water in a person's body depends on their age. A newborn baby is almost three-quarters water. An elderly person, however, is less than half water.

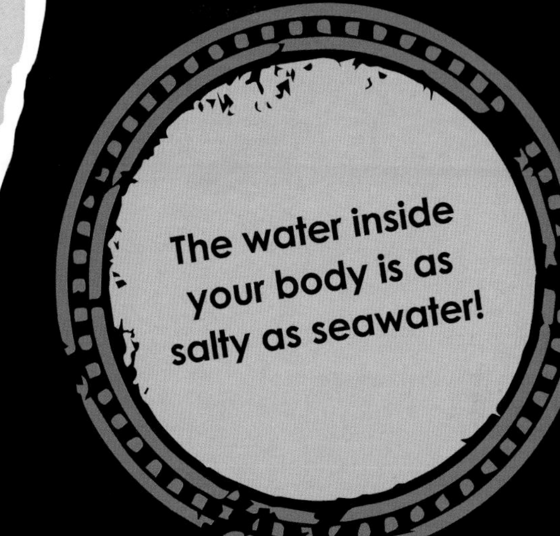

The water inside your body is as salty as seawater!

How much water is in cells?

Different cells have different amounts of water in them, based on the jobs they do. Muscle cells are three quarters water, whereas fat cells are only one quarter water.

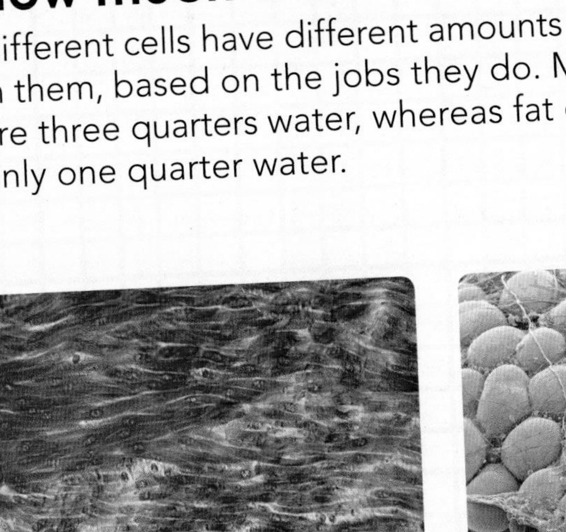
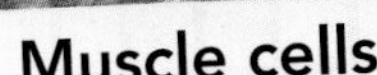
Muscle cells

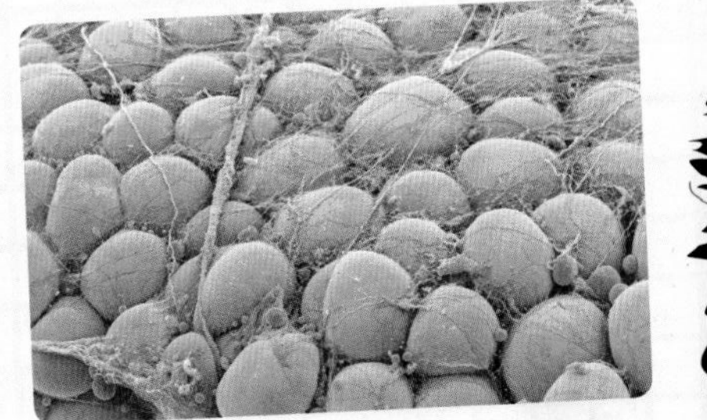
Fat cells

? Quick quiz

1. Where is the water in your body stored?
2. How does excess water leave the body?
3. What happens to your pee when you are thirsty?

See pages 132–133 for the answers

What is my body clock?

Your body clock is your natural alarm clock and calendar. Your organs slow down and speed up at different times of the day, and things also change during the year. For example, your body speeds up in the morning to keep you alert, and your hair grows faster in the summer.

High alertness

At about 9 am your brain is really good at thinking and solving problems. It's good to do school work at this time of the day.

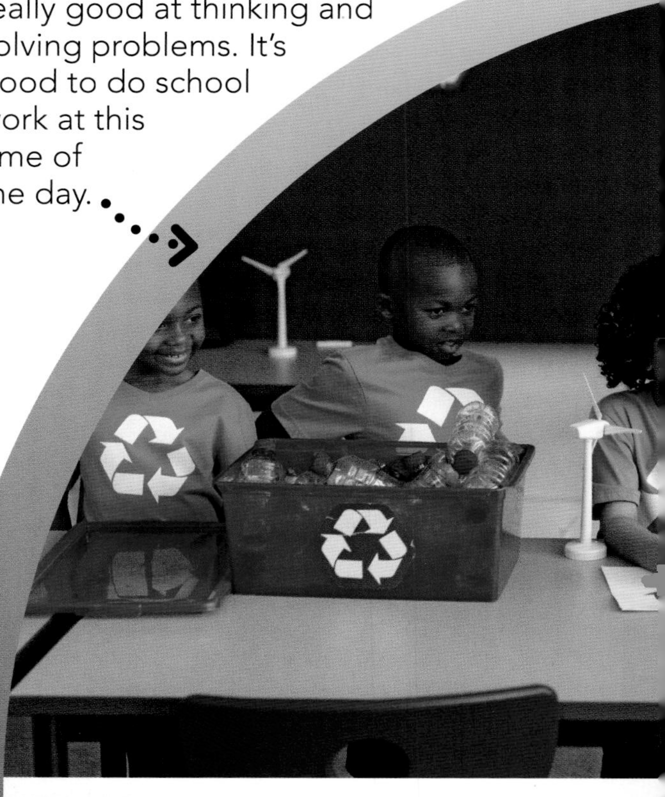

6 AM

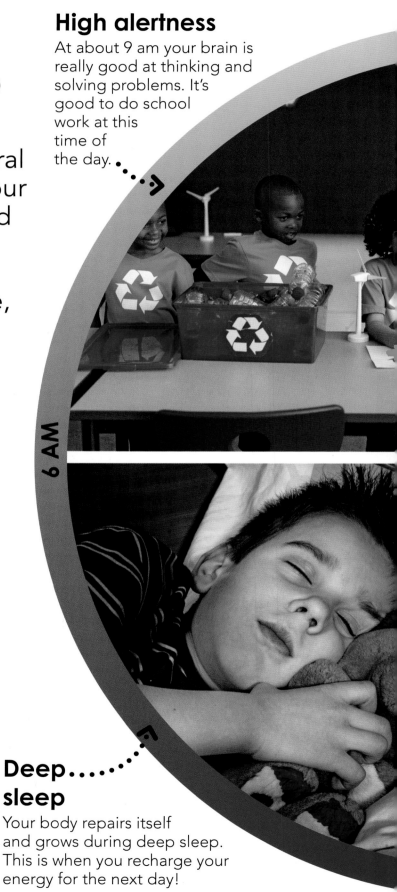

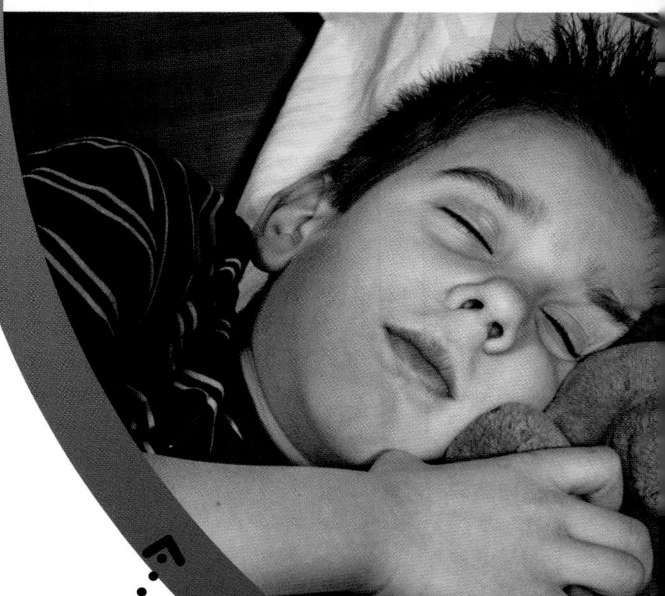

Deep sleep

Your body repairs itself and grows during deep sleep. This is when you recharge your energy for the next day!

What is a sleep cycle?

After you fall asleep, you go through a cycle of different types of sleep. First, you fall straight into a shallow sleep, then a deep sleep, then a light sleep, and finally start dreaming. This cycle repeats about four or five times each night.

- **Awake**
- **Dreaming**
- **Light sleep**
- **Shallow sleep**
- **Deep sleep**

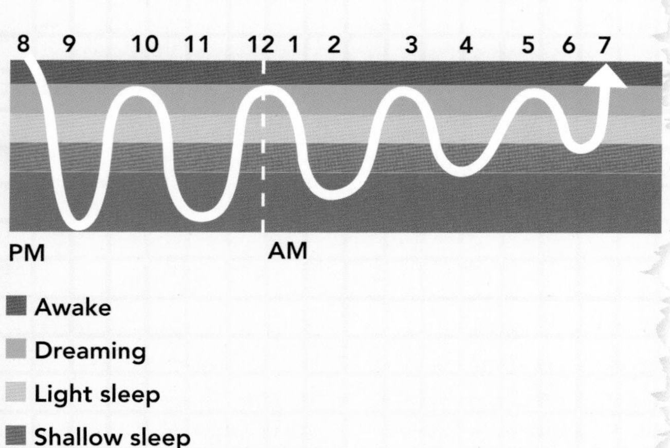

Best coordination

In the afternoon you have good coordination, which means you can use different parts of your body together well. This is a good time to play ball games, or do arts and crafts with your hands.

Physical peak

Just after 6 pm your blood pressure and body temperature are at their highest. This means your body is really active, so it's a good time to do physical activites, such as running.

Feeling sleepy

Your eyes sense light and dark, and send signals to your brain. This helps to measure day length, which means you should feel sleepy at the same time each day.

When it's dark, the hormone melatonin is released to help you fall asleep.

What does my brain do when I sleep?

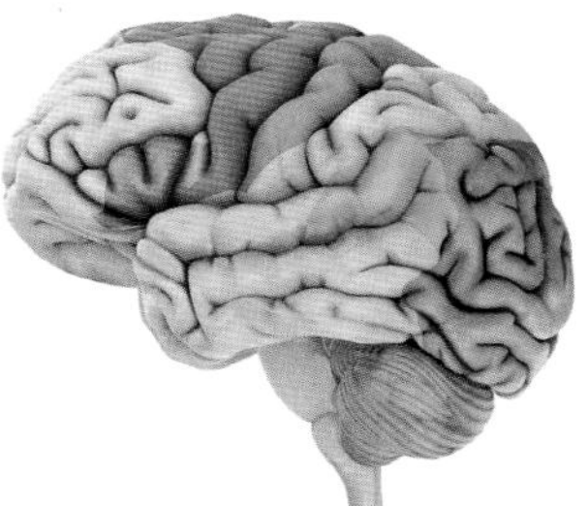

When you're asleep, your brain sorts out the information sent to it by your senses throughout the day. Some of the information is deleted, but some is stored as memories.

? True or false?

1. Your hair grows faster in the winter.
2. Newborn babies sleep for up to 19 hours a day.

See pages 132–133 for the answers

What happens when I'm scared?

When you feel frightened, your body gets ready to fight off the danger or run away from it. This is called the "fight or flight" response. The brain sends electrical signals to the body, telling it to release chemicals and prepare the body for action.

Pupils dilate

The dark spot in the centre of each eye gets bigger, and lets in more light. This is so you can see better to face the danger and plan an escape.

Sweaty palms

The body heats up, so you make more sweat to cool down. Hands, feet, and armpits have a lot of sweat glands.

Heart races

The heart beats faster and you breathe quicker to send oxygen and blood to the leg and arm muscles. This prepares you to fight or run away.

Digestion slows down

Activity in the stomach stops and digested food moving through the body slows down. Blood is sent to other areas of the body needed for fighting or running away.

How does my body know I'm in danger?

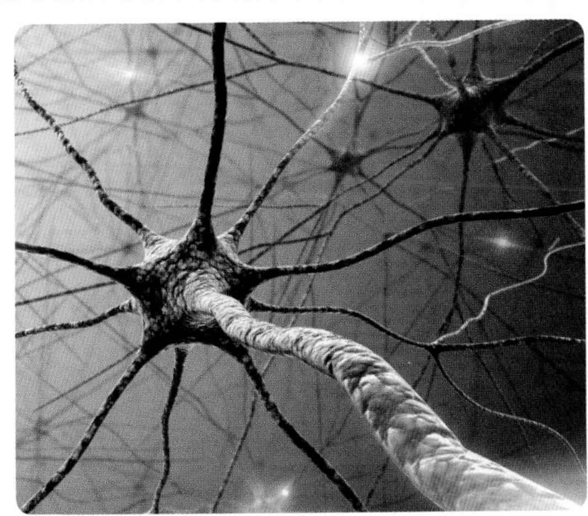

Electrical signals

The brain receives information from the senses as electrical signals through nerve cells. It then sends out other electrical signals. These cause chemicals to be released as hormones.

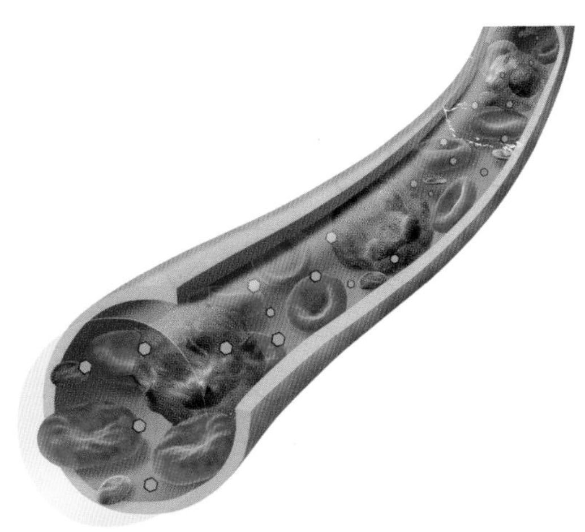

Chemical signals

These are hormones that change the way our body works. The adrenal glands release a hormone called adrenaline into the blood to prepare the body to fight or run away.

Bladder empties

The sphincter muscle, which controls the bladder, relaxes. This is why people sometimes pee themselves when they are scared.

Bigger blood vessels

Blood vessels get bigger in the muscles needed to fight or run so that more blood and oxygen can flow into them. Blood vessels in the brain expand so that the nutrients in the blood can help it to work faster.

? Quick quiz

1. Where are most of the sweat glands in the body?
2. What does the hormone adrenaline prepare the body to do?
3. What happens to digestion when you are scared?

See pages 132–133 for the answers

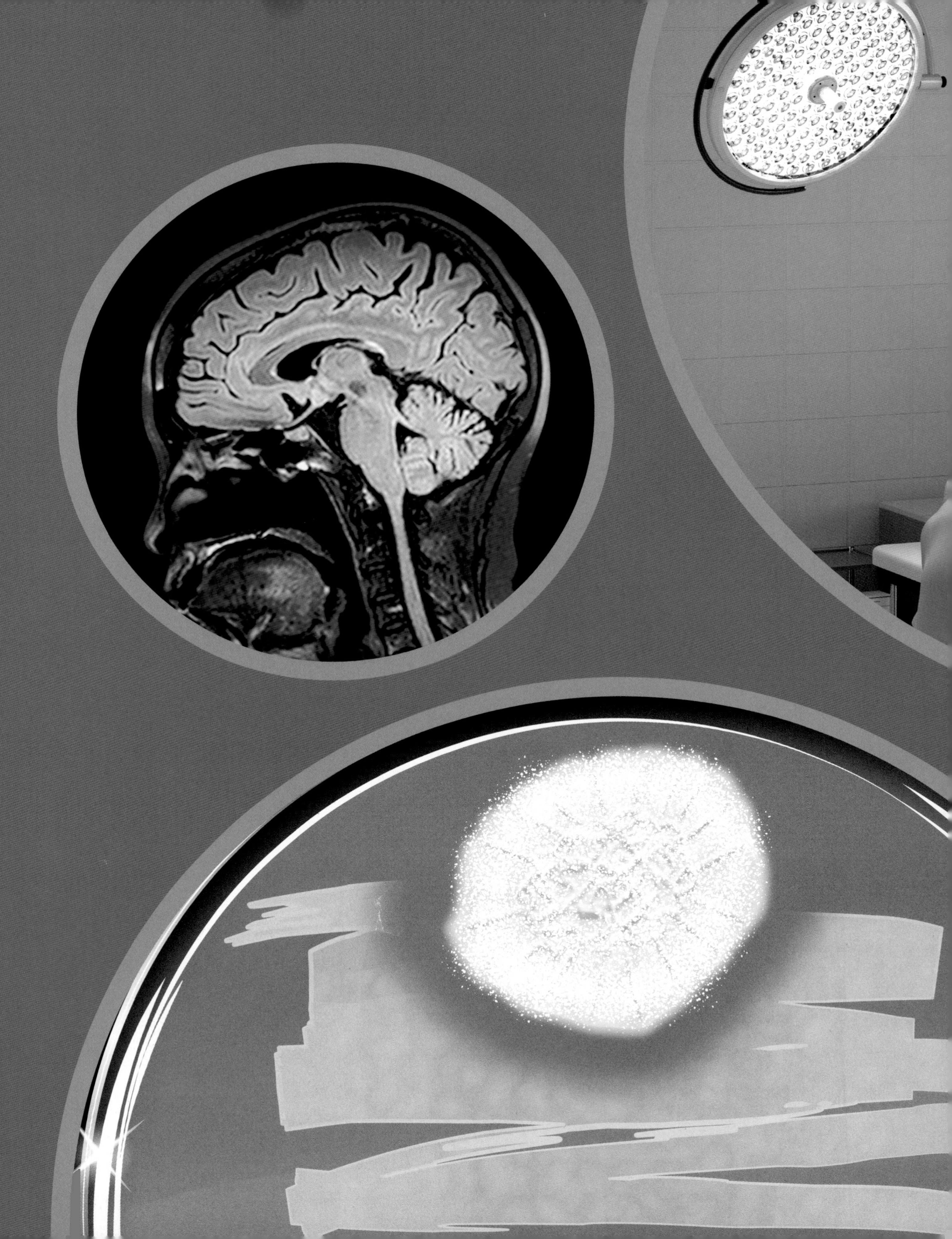

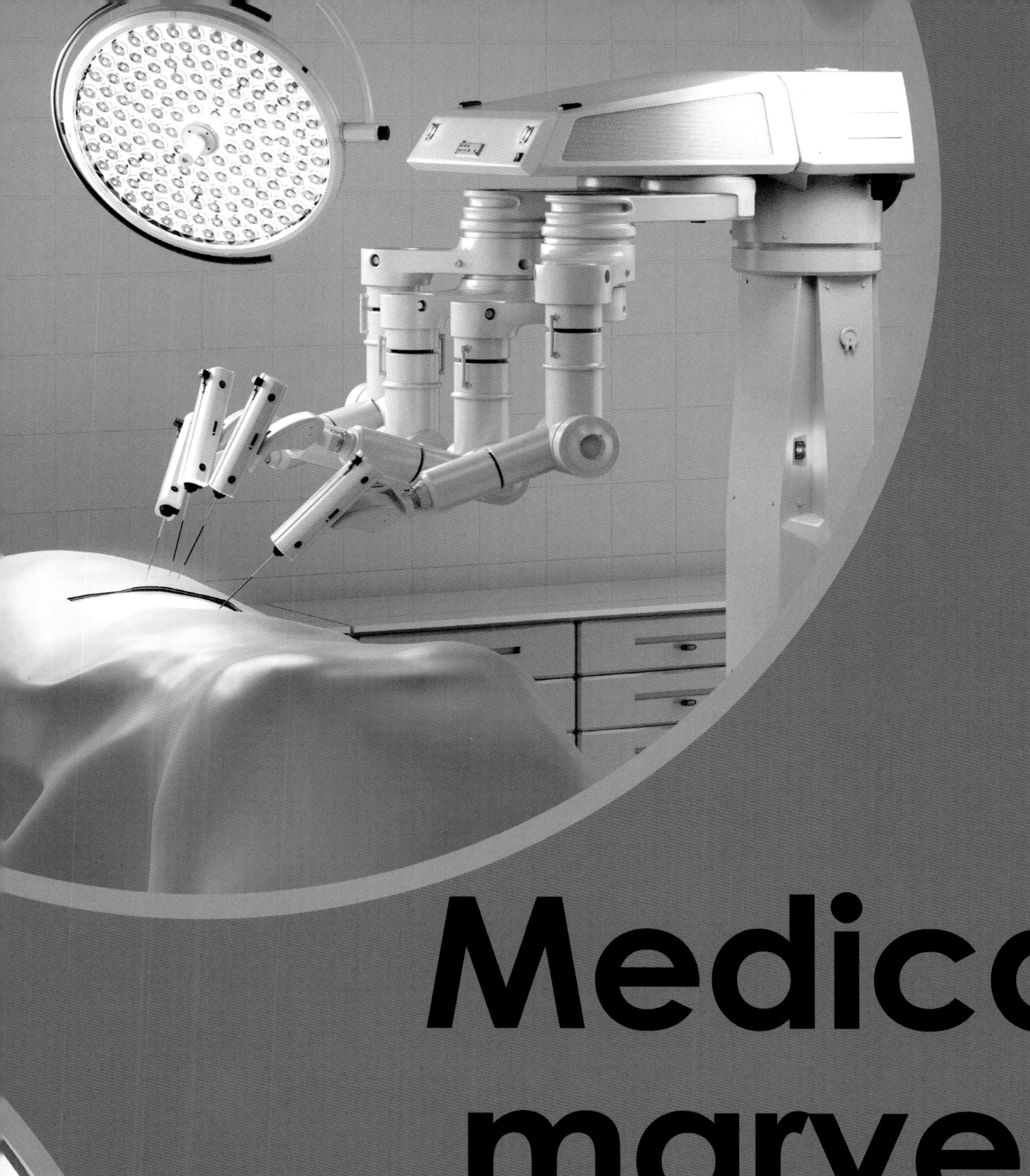

Medical marvels

From bionic hands to organ transplants, medical discoveries have completely changed the way we examine and repair the human body. Now, doctors can use magnets to see inside your body, antibiotics can kill bacteria, and robots can perform operations!

How do X-rays work?

X-rays are invisible beams of light that pass through soft tissue, and are absorbed, or soaked up, by thicker tissue, such as bone. This means that on an X-ray image, soft tissue and air are darker shades, but bones show up in white. This is useful because doctors can see if any of your bones are broken.

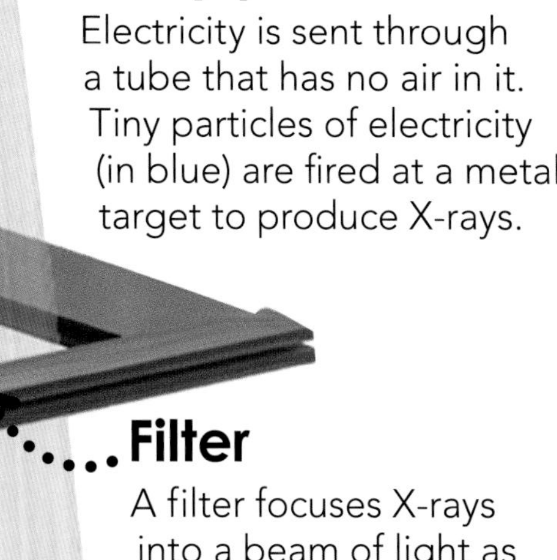

X-ray production

Electricity is sent through a tube that has no air in it. Tiny particles of electricity (in blue) are fired at a metal target to produce X-rays.

What did the first X-ray look like?

German physicist Wilhelm Röntgen took the first ever X-ray image in 1895. It was of his wife's hand, and showed her bones and a metal ring. Wilhelm discovered X-rays by accident when experimenting with another type of ray, cathode rays.

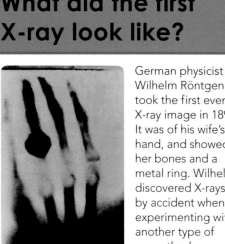

Rays

You can't see or feel an X-ray as it hits your body. However, X-rays are a form of radiation, which means they can damage your body if they are used too often.

Filter

A filter focuses X-rays into a beam of light as they pass through it. This means the X-rays can be sent to a specific

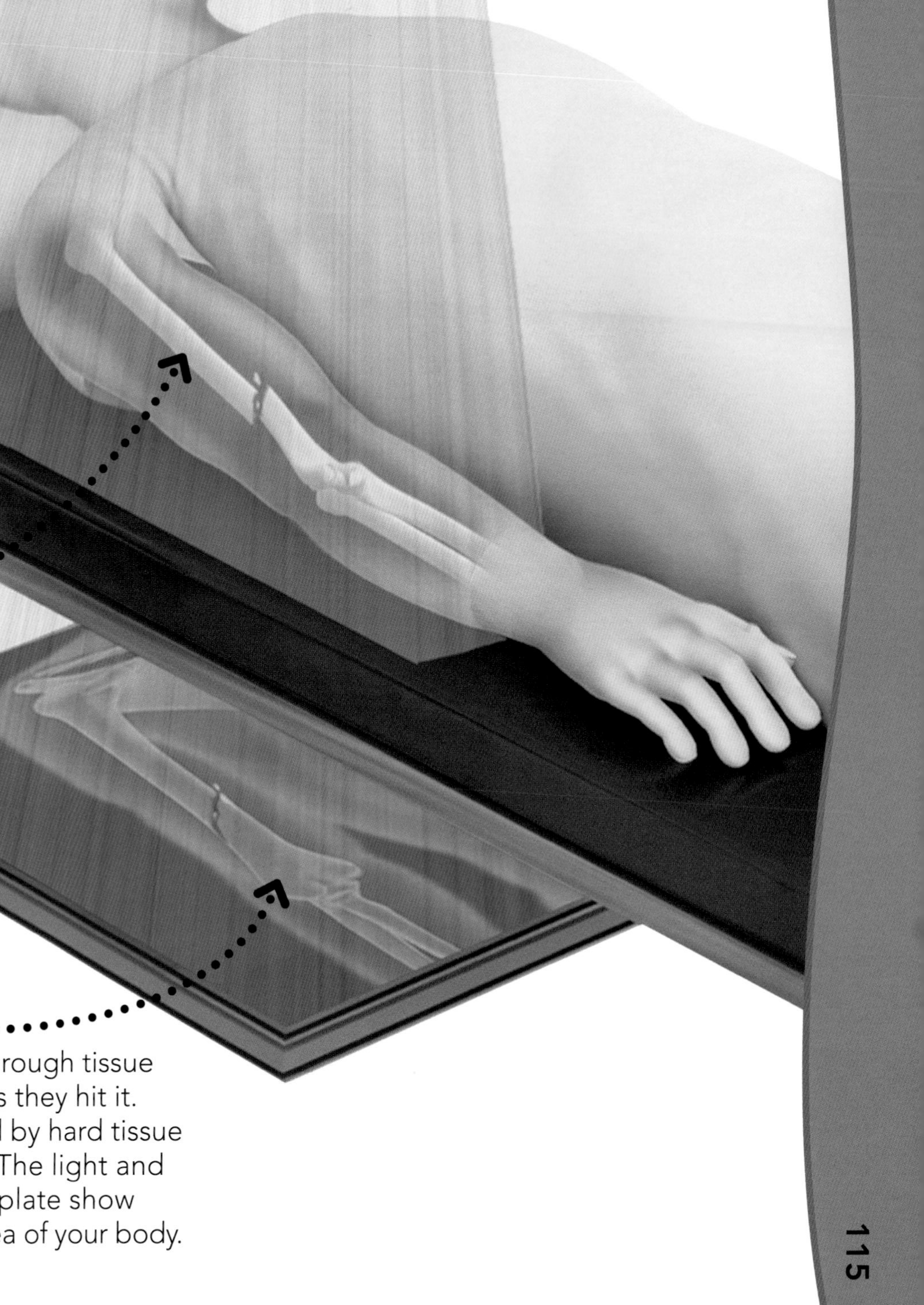

X-rays are used in airport security to see what's inside your luggage.

Body tissue

X-rays easily pass through soft tissue, such as skin and muscles. However, they are absorbed as they pass through harder tissue, such as bone or metal.

X-ray plate

X-rays that easily pass through tissue darken the X-ray plate as they hit it. X-rays that are absorbed by hard tissue lighten the X-ray plate. The light and dark areas on the X-ray plate show you a 2D image of an area of your body.

? Picture quiz

Which one of these can be seen on an X-ray image?

a) What you're thinking about.

b) Holes inside your teeth.

See pages 132–133 for the answers

Why do I need vaccinations?

Vaccinations protect you from viruses, which can cause diseases. A weak form of the virus is put into your body so your white blood cells can make virus-fighting proteins, called antibodies.

You can also be injected with antibodies from another person to kill a virus.

Vaccination

A weak form of the virus is injected into your blood or given to you to swallow. Your body recognizes that this virus is bad for you and starts to make antibodies to fight it.

Making antibodies

Your white blood cells create antibodies that attach to and destroy the invading virus. Your body then remembers the virus and can easily make antibodies if the virus tries to infect you again.

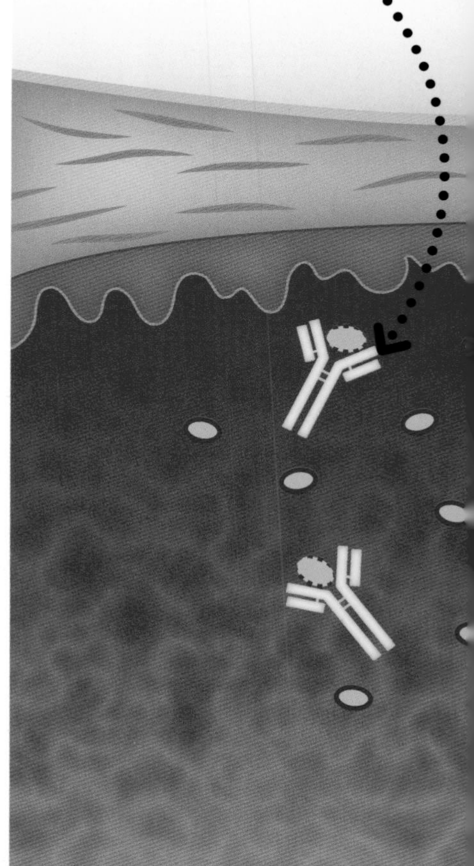

What is COVID-19?

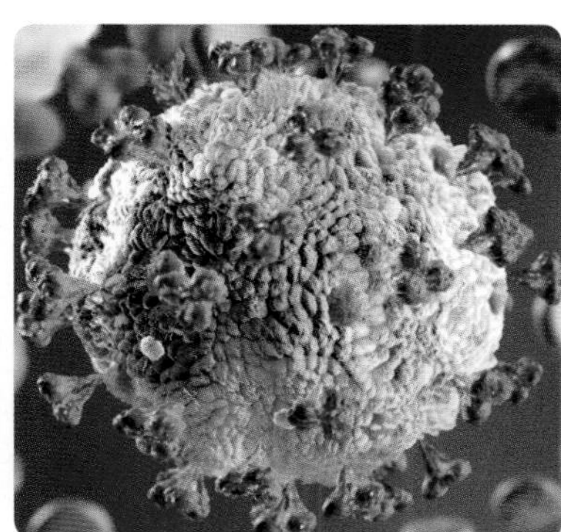

COVID-19 is a disease caused by a type of virus called a coronavirus. COVID-19 was discovered in 2019, and spreads very easily through droplets in the air or on surfaces when people cough. Most people who get COVID-19 recover quickly, but around one in five people need hospital treatment.

First vaccination

The very first vaccination was developed by a doctor called Edward Jenner in the 18th century. This vaccination was created to fight off a deadly virus called smallpox.

Edward Jenner

Quick quiz

1. What do antibodies do?
2. Which blood cells fight a virus?
3. How can you be given a vaccination?

See pages 132–133 for the answers

Immunity

If the virus comes back, antibodies are made quickly and can easily defeat the virus. This is called being immune. When you have immunity, it means you cannot get sick from that virus again.

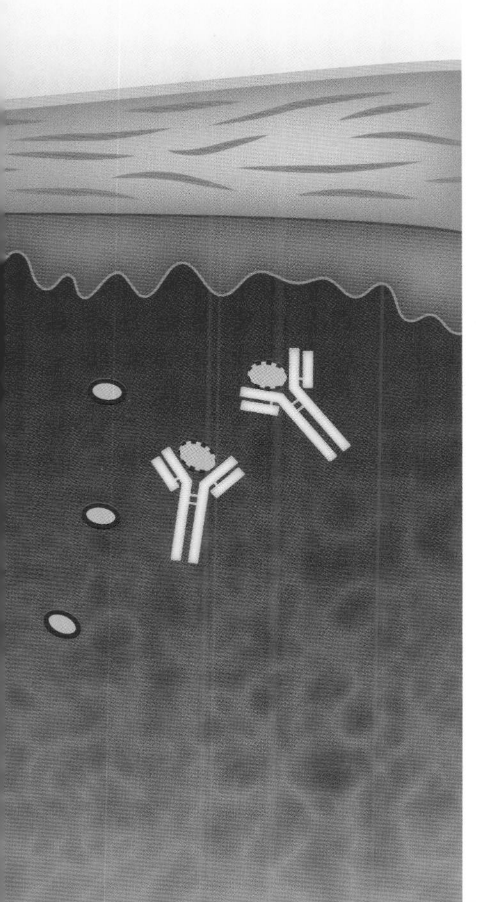

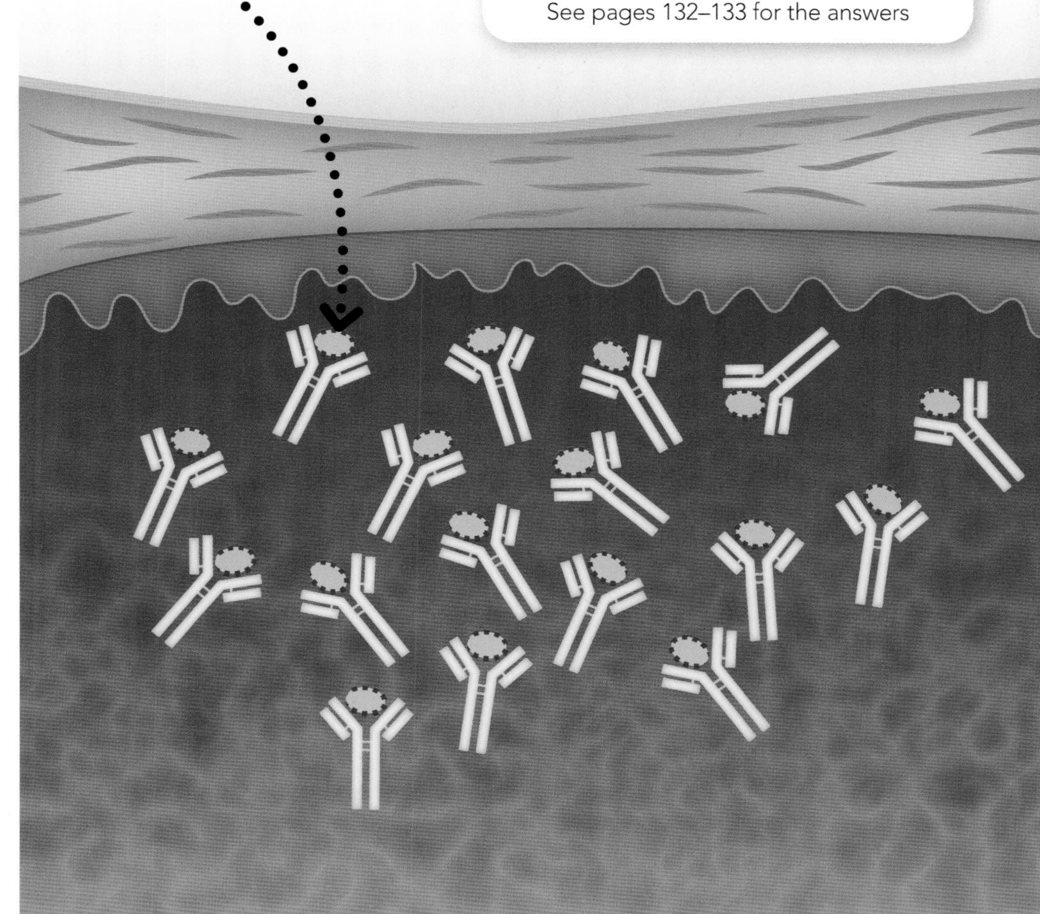

Can magnets show what's inside my body?

Yes! Doctors can use magnetic resonance imaging (MRI) to see inside your body. In an MRI scan, magnets make atoms in your body line up in a certain way and give off a signal in radio waves. A computer turns the signal into pictures of the inside of your body.

Slices

Each image taken by the MRI scanner is a slice of your body at a certain angle. A computer then puts these images together to make a 3D model.

What's it like to have an MRI scan?

An MRI scanner is a long tunnel that you lie inside. When you're being scanned, you must remain still. The scanner moves up and down as it takes images of your body. The machine vibrates and clicks loudly, but it doesn't hurt.

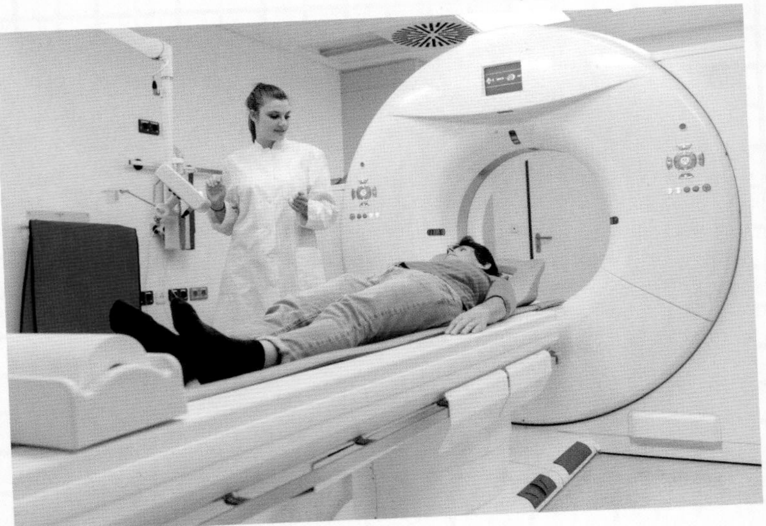

You can't wear anything magnetic, such as metal earrings, when you have an MRI scan.

3D organs

Specific organs can be scanned by an MRI. This means doctors can see the whole organ, such as the brain.

Different colours

Different tissues in your body give off slightly different radio waves when they are scanned. A computer gives these different colours, so doctors can see the different parts of your body at a glance.

Clear picture

MRI scans give a clear picture of the inside of your body. This means that doctors can find out if something is wrong without having to operate on you.

How else can we see inside the body?

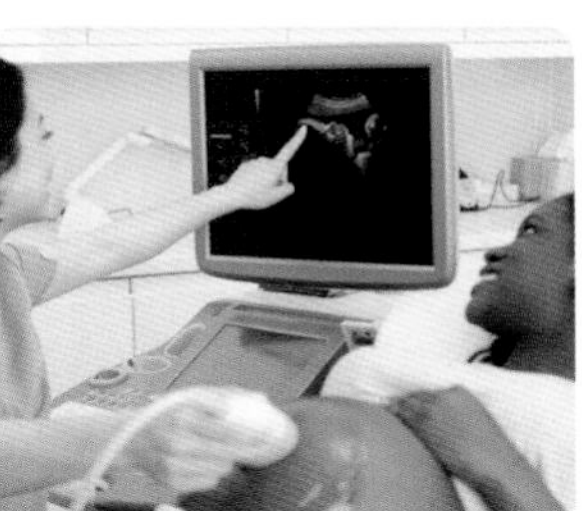

Ultrasound

Sound waves are sent into the body by a scanner. These waves bounce off solid objects inside your body and produce an image, such as a baby.

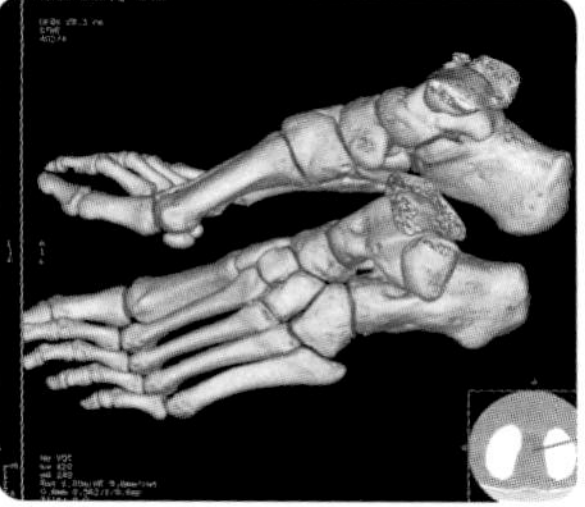

CT scan

Computer tomography (CT) scans send X-ray beams into the body at different angles. A computer puts the X-ray images together to make a 3D picture.

? Quick quiz

1. What does MRI stand for?
2. Why do we take pictures of the inside of the body?
3. What type of wave does your body give off during an MRI scan?

See pages 132–133 for the answers

How do antibiotics kill bacteria?

There are many different antibiotics. They are produced by fungi and bacteria. Antibiotics fight types of bacteria that can make you ill. They work by killing, or slowing down bad bacteria so the body can fight them off. Antibiotics cannot be used to kill viruses.

Kill zone

This area is bacteria-free as the penicillin has killed them. Any bacteria that grow and get near the penicillin will be killed here.

What are superbugs?

Bacteria can change over time to try and survive when their environment changes. Occasionally, super-strong bacteria cannot be killed by antibiotics. Instead, they survive and multiply, and become superbugs, which are hard to kill.

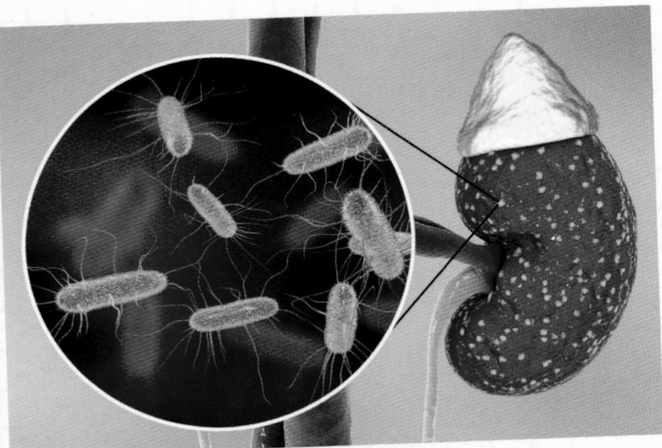

Superbugs can attack your organs, such as your kidneys, and cause infections.

Accidental discovery

Penicillin was discovered by accident in 1928. A scientist called Alexander Fleming left some bacteria uncovered when he went out for the day and a fungus grew on them, killing the bacteria!

Penicillin

This antibiotic is called penicillin. It works by weakening the bacterial cell walls so they burst open. Doctors give you penicillin as either a pill or a liquid, or inject you with it.

Bacteria

This is the area where bacteria has been added to the Petri dish (a flat dish with a lid used in laboratories). The white streak of bacteria here grows bigger as the bacteria multiply.

How can bacteria make me ill?

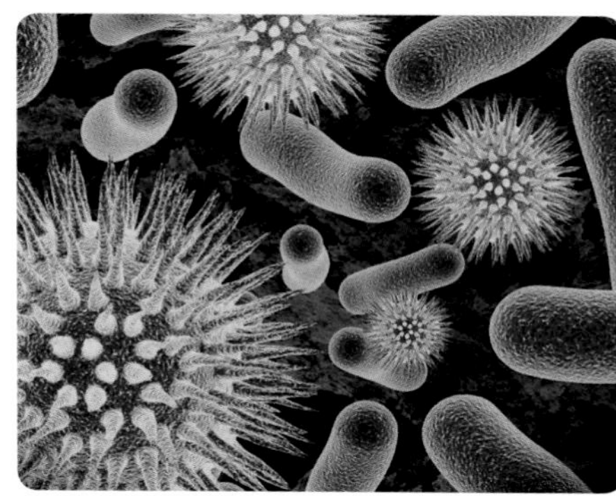

Multiplying

Bacterial cells copy themselves and split into two. New bacteria do the same. When bacteria multiply quickly the body can't fight them off properly. This means that you get ill.

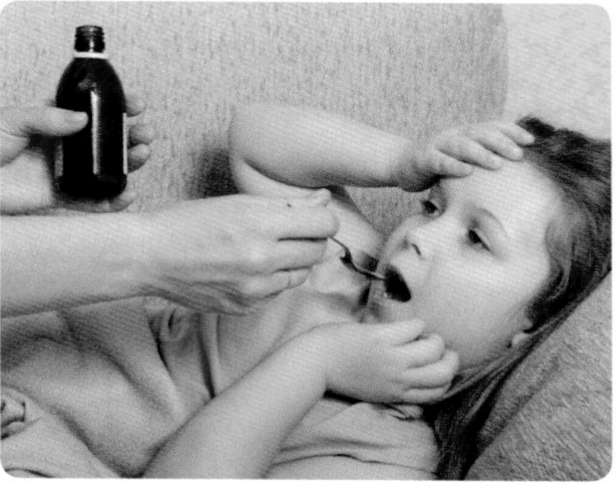

Chemicals

Bacteria can release poisonous substances that damage cells and make you feel unwell. Your body raises its temperature to fight bacteria because they do not like heat.

? *True or false?*

1. Bacteria are living things.
2. Soap can kill bacteria as well as antibiotics.

See pages 132–133 for the answers

How do doctors know what's wrong?

When you're feeling ill, a doctor will ask you questions to understand your symptoms, or signs of your illness. They do tests to work out what is wrong, and may give you medicine to see if it makes you feel better.

Temperature

The average human body temperature is 37°C (98.6°F). When your body is fighting off sickness, your temperature increases. A thermometer measures temperature, and is often placed in your mouth or ear.

What fluids can be tested?

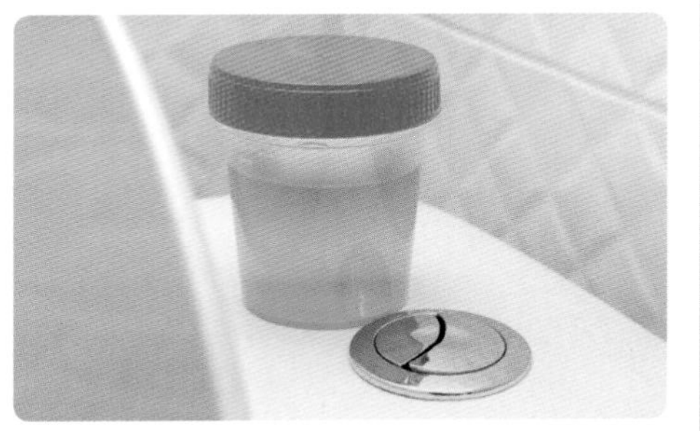

Doctors test blood, urine, and poo. The results show us many things, including if there is inflammation, bacteria, bleeding, disease, or hormone imbalances.

Swab

A stick is put on your tongue or in your throat to take out saliva. The stick is then put into a machine to test for bacteria and viruses.

Blood test

Sometimes doctors need to test your blood. To do this, they put a needle into a vein in your arm and draw blood into a syringe. This blood is tested for different illnesses in a laboratory.

Diagnosis

Doctors use questions and tests to give you medicine for what they think is making you sick. This is called making a diagnosis.

Blood pressure

Doctors use a blood-pressure machine to see how well your heart is pushing blood around your body. They put a band around your arm, which pushes on your arm to squeeze your blood vessels.

Listening

To listen to how you are breathing, a doctor will use a stethoscope. It is put on your chest and back. Doctors can then hear if your lungs are blocked with anything.

? Quick quiz

1. What is the average human body temperature?
2. What is the name for when a doctor thinks they know what is wrong with you?
3. What do doctors use to listen to your lungs?

See pages 132–133 for the answers

Can my cells change jobs?

Stem cells are cells that can permanently change to become another type of cell. Adult stem cells are made in bones. Stem cells in an embryo can develop into any type of cell, but in an adult they only change into certain types of cell, such as blood cells.

Bone marrow
Adult stem cells are made inside bone marrow. They can multiply and divide to create copies of themselves, and then they can change into different types of cell.

How do cells divide?

When a cell divides to make another cell, it first copies its DNA, then splits the DNA in two by a process called mitosis. The cell then divides in two by a process called cytokinesis, which produces two cells, each with a copy of the original DNA.

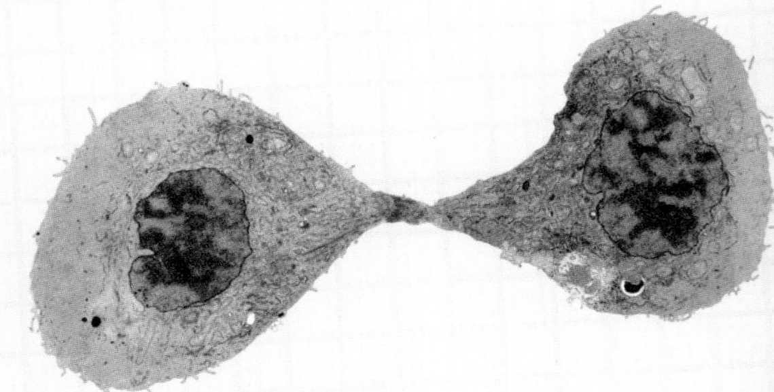

Picture quiz

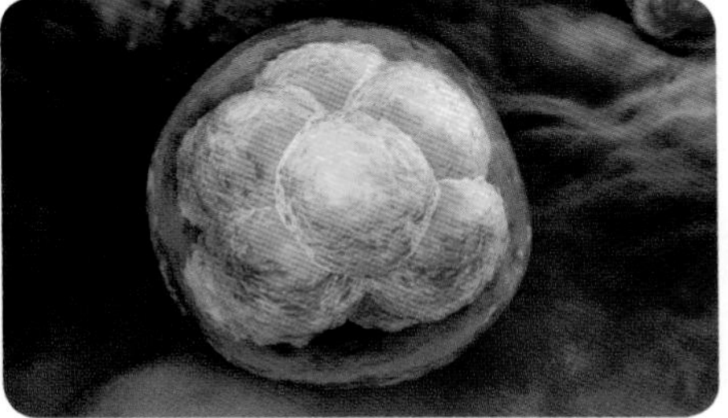

Where would you find this ball of stem cells?

See pages 132–133 for the answers

Stem cells

Becoming specialized
When stem cells change into another type of cell, they become specialized. For example, stem cells can change into different types of blood cell, such as red blood cells, white blood cells, or platelets. Once the cell has changed, it stays that way.

How could we use stem cells in the future?

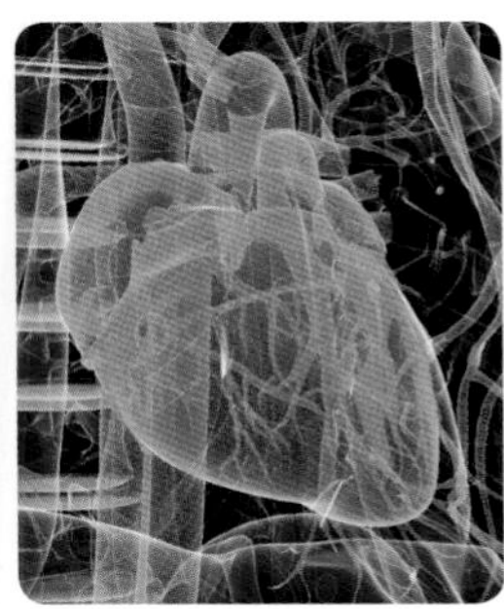

To grow organs
Stem cells in embryos can change into any cell in the body. This means we could use them to repair diseased or damaged tissues. We might even be able to grow new organs!

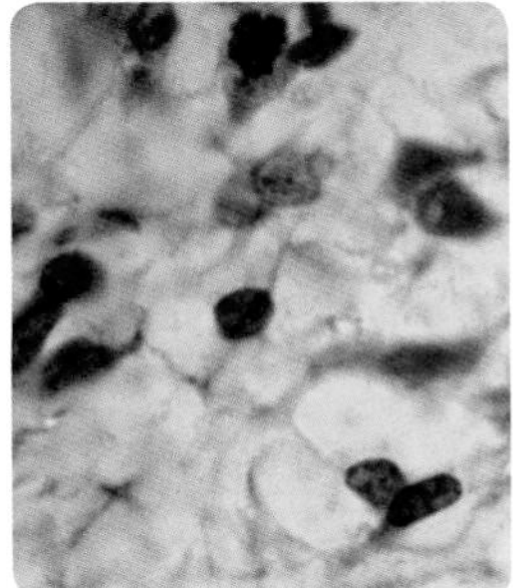

To repair genes
The umbilical cord attached to a newborn baby contains many stem cells. These could be used to repair or replace faulty genes in a sibling, in a process called gene editing.

How does sun cream work?

There are two types of sun cream – physical and chemical. Physical sun cream, or sun block, creates a barrier between the sun and your skin. This blocks harmful rays and reflects them away from you. Chemical sun cream absorbs these rays so they don't reach your skin and it also reflects some rays away.

Vitamin D

Some sunshine is good for you. Your skin can absorb ultraviolet (UV) light to make vitamin D. This vitamin helps your body grow and take in nutrients from the food you eat.

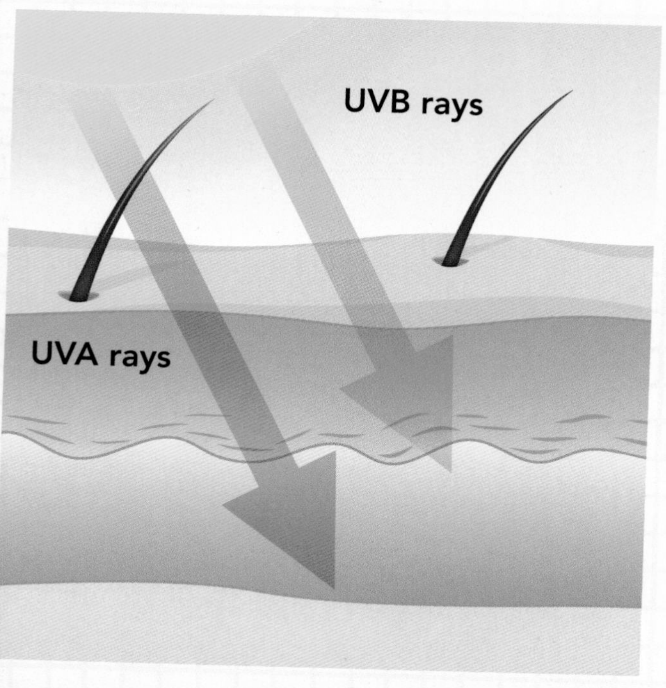

Sunglasses

Sunglasses reflect UV rays so they don't damage your eyes. They also make it easier to see when it is bright. Never look directly at the sun, even when wearing sunglasses.

Physical sun cream

Sun block forms a physical barrier on your skin, which means that harmful UV rays bounce off of it. Your skin is protected beneath the sun block.

UV rays

UV, or ultraviolet, light is an invisible light from the sun that can damage your skin. There are two types of UV light – UVA and UVB. UVA rays enter the skin and cause wrinkles. UVB rays affect the top layer of your skin, causing sunburn and sometimes a disease called skin cancer.

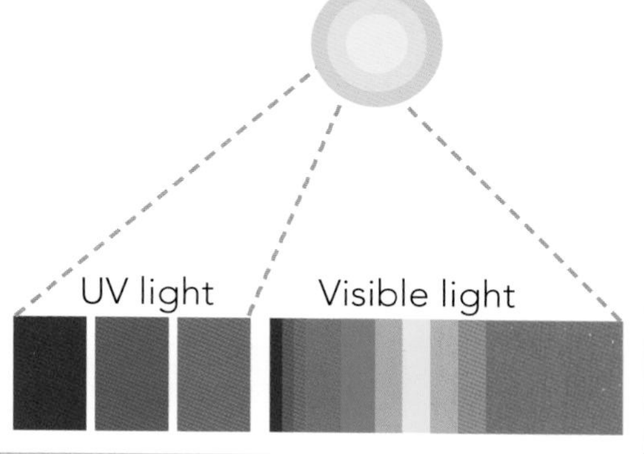

White hat

Hats keep your face in the shade. White clothing reflects sunlight, which keeps you cool, too.

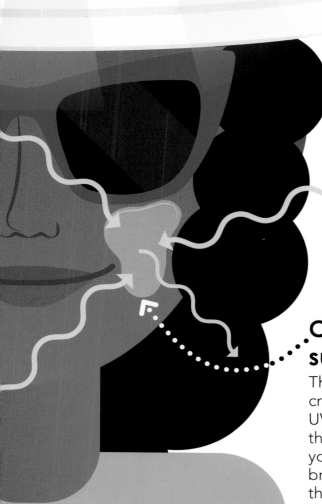

What happens when I get sunburn?

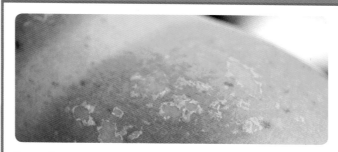

If you don't use enough sun block or sun cream, you can burn in the sun. This is called sunburn. Some people get a painful, red patch of sunburn, while others have skin that starts to peel. People with different skin tones experience different effects from the sun, but you should always wear sun cream when you're exposed to it.

Chemical sun cream

The chemicals in sun cream absorb harmful UV rays, which stops them from damaging your skin. Sun cream breaks down during the day, so you need to reapply it regularly.

? *True or false?*

1. You can see UV light.
2. Some sunshine is good for you.

See pages 132–133 for the answers

Can robots perform surgery?

Yes – robot operations are happening in hospitals all around the world right now! Robot arms can make smaller, more careful cuts than humans can, and they can also speed up operating times. These machines can be remotely controlled by a surgeon during an operation, or programmed beforehand.

Remote-controlled

This is the da Vinci Surgical System. It uses remote-controlled robotic arms to perform operations. The surgeon makes all the decisions and they control the robotic arms.

What is keyhole surgery?

In keyhole surgery, a small hole is made in the body and surgical tools are inserted. A camera and light tube are also placed inside to help the surgeon see as they perform the operation.

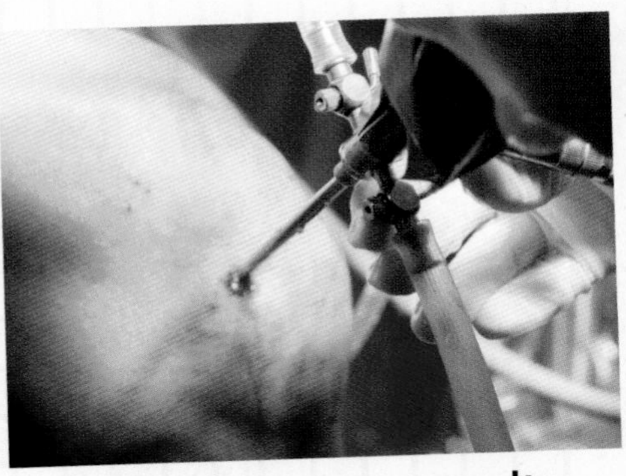

Keyhole surgery results in less pain and bleeding.

What else do robots do to help us?

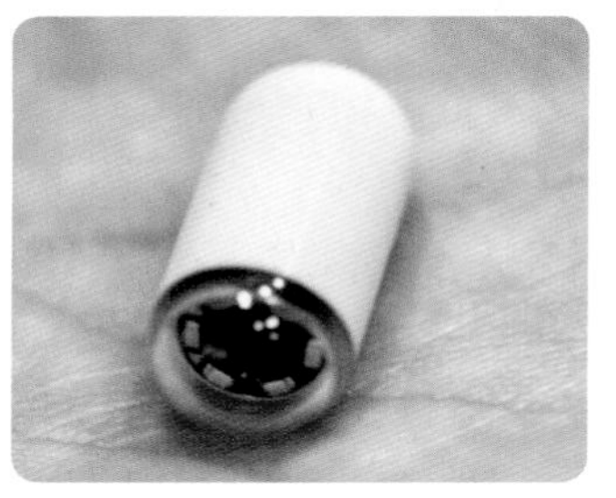

Capsule endoscope

A tablet-sized robotic pill, called a capsule endoscope, can travel all the way through your digestive system. It shines a light as it moves, and takes pictures that are sent to a computer for a doctor to see.

Robot exoskeleton

Robot exoskeletons can be strapped onto people who have nerve and muscle damage. They help people stand, turn, and walk. These exoskeletons are also used to help people lift heavy things without using a machine.

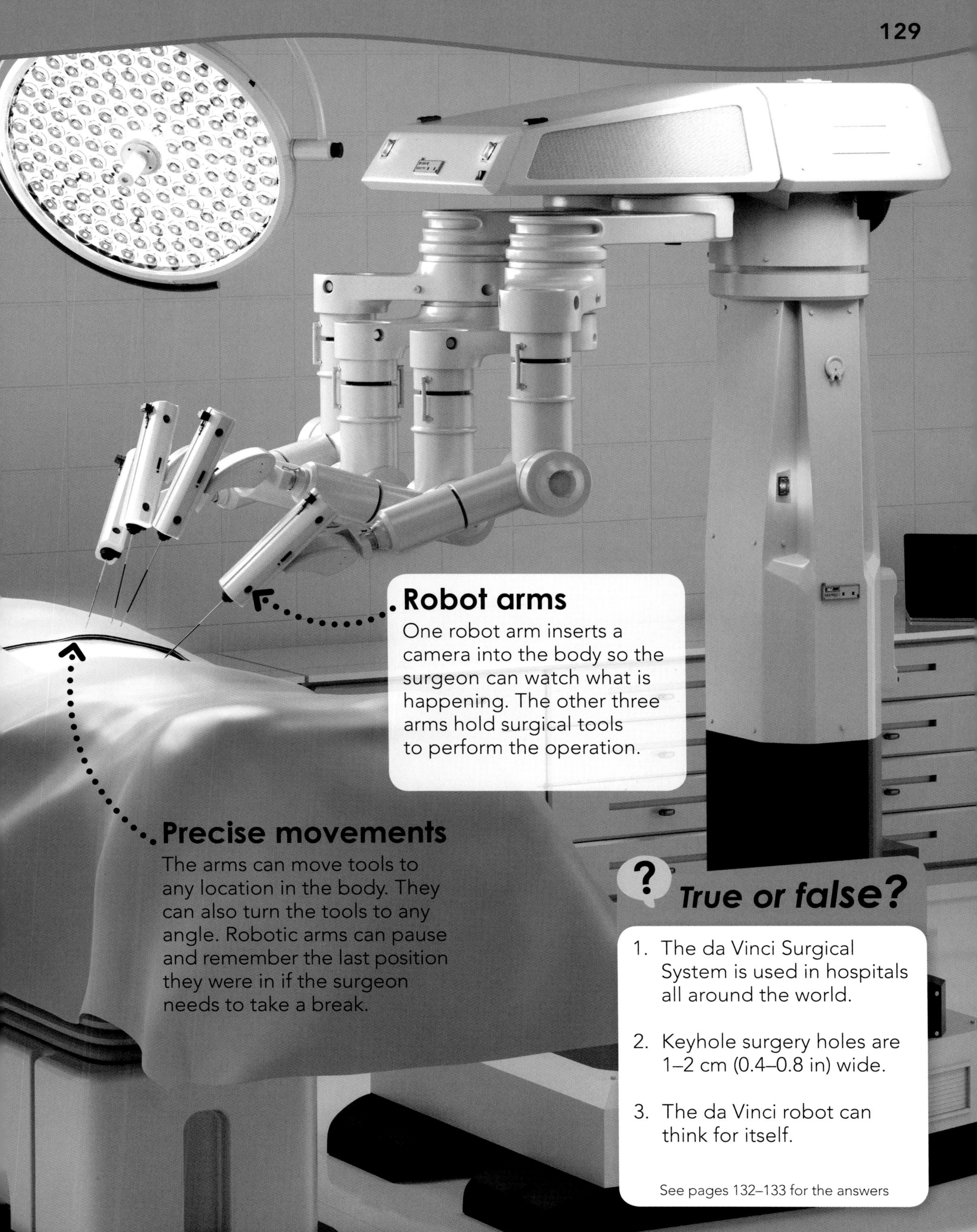

Robot arms

One robot arm inserts a camera into the body so the surgeon can watch what is happening. The other three arms hold surgical tools to perform the operation.

Precise movements

The arms can move tools to any location in the body. They can also turn the tools to any angle. Robotic arms can pause and remember the last position they were in if the surgeon needs to take a break.

True or false?

1. The da Vinci Surgical System is used in hospitals all around the world.
2. Keyhole surgery holes are 1–2 cm (0.4–0.8 in) wide.
3. The da Vinci robot can think for itself.

See pages 132–133 for the answers

How can doctors create body parts?

Some people are born without certain body parts, and others lose them due to sickness or an accident. Some of these people find it helpful to have a doctor create a body part for them. Doctors can also perform a transplant operation. This is when an organ from one body replaces an affected organ in another body.

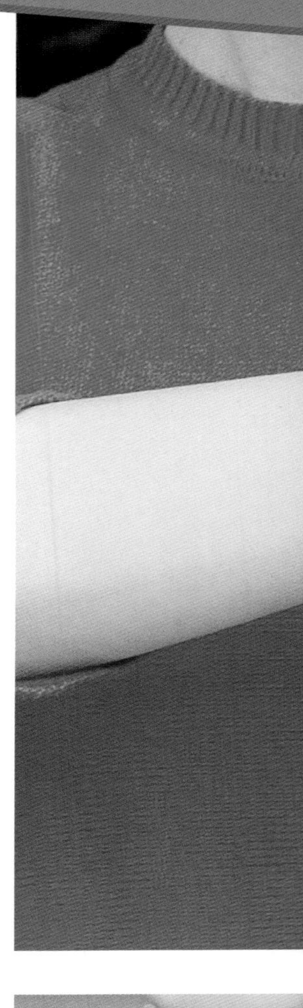

What is a transplant?

When an organ is not working properly, doctors can remove the same organ from another body to replace the affected organ. Many body parts, such as the liver, can be transplanted. After a transplant, the body needs medicine to make sure it doesn't reject the new organ.

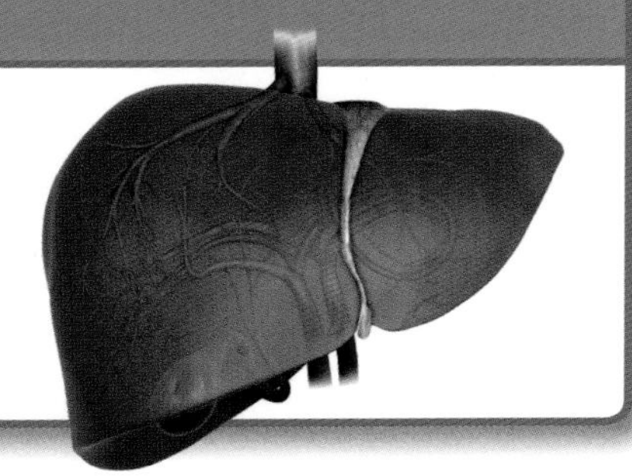

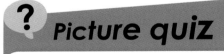

? Picture quiz

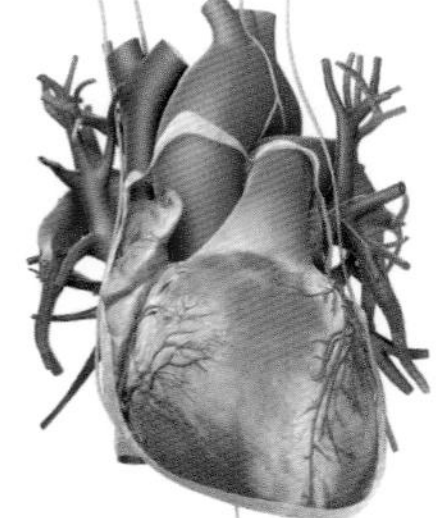

This organ can be transplanted into the body. What is it?

See pages 132–133 for the answers

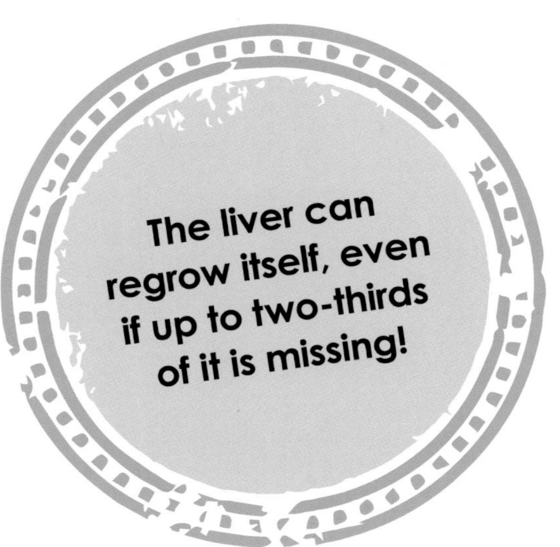

The liver can regrow itself, even if up to two-thirds of it is missing!

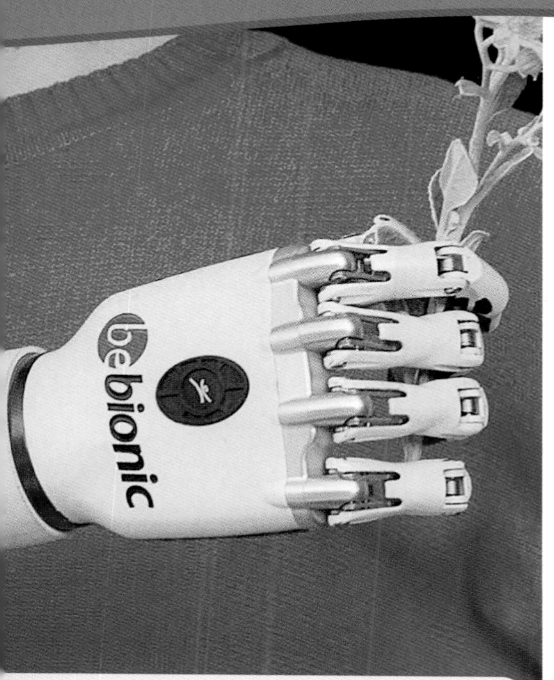

Bionic hand

This electrical hand is wired into the arm muscles. The brain sends signals to the muscles in the arm, which in turn move the hand.

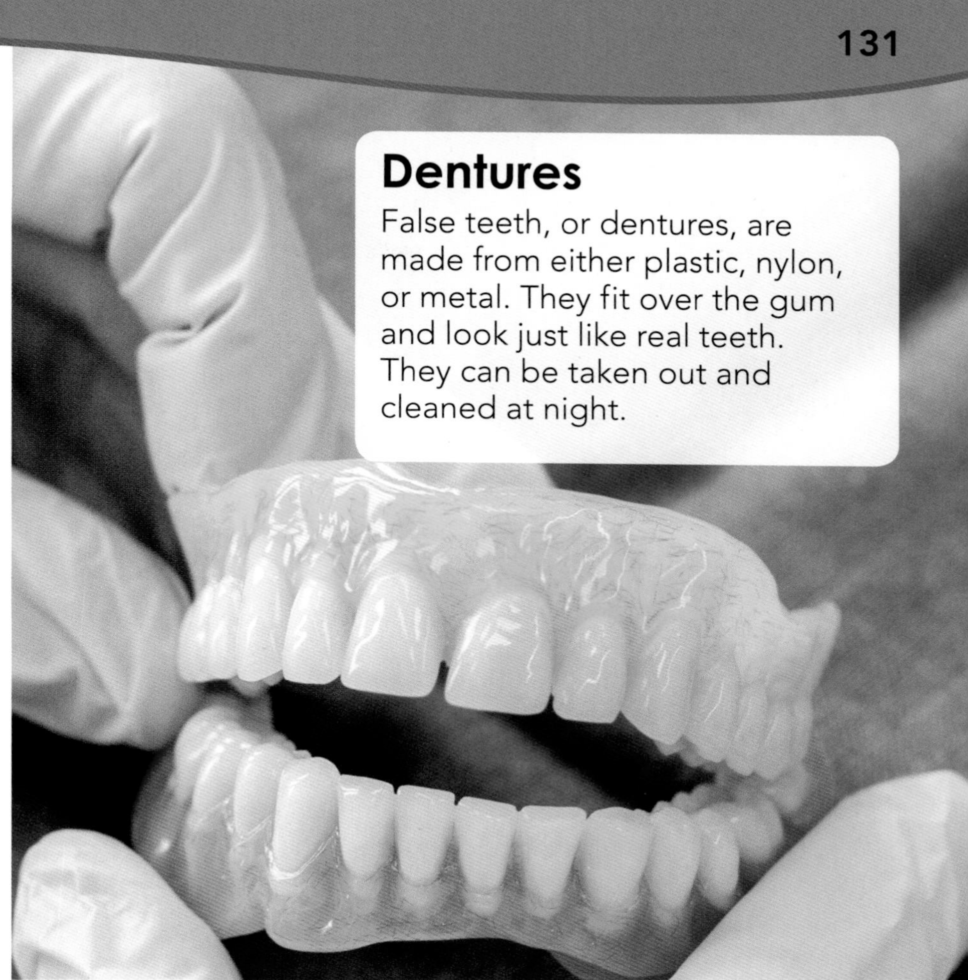

Dentures

False teeth, or dentures, are made from either plastic, nylon, or metal. They fit over the gum and look just like real teeth. They can be taken out and cleaned at night.

Prosthetic leg

This prosthetic leg is made from a lightweight material called carbon fibre. It can bend without breaking, which makes it useful for runners. Prosthetic legs can also be made of foam padding and plastic.

Pacemaker

A metal pacemaker is fitted when a heart needs help to pump. A tiny computer in the pacemaker sends out an electrical signal, which makes the heart pump at the right time.

Answers

Page 9 1) Cells. 2) The nucleus. 3) Organs.

Page 11 1) True. They are also part of the respiratory system. 2) False. The largest organ is the skin. 3) False. You can survive with one kidney.

Page 13 A red blood cell.

Page 15 1) False. Veins carry blood to the heart. 2) True. 3) False. White blood cells fight off germs.

Page 16 1) In the nucleus. 2) Genes switch on and off to tell the cell what to do. 3) A double helix.

Page 19 1) It's very thin and tightly coiled up. 2) Nothing! Only about 2 per cent of DNA does something. 3) Half of your DNA comes from each of your parents.

Page 21 1) One set comes from each of your parents. 2) Inheritance.

Page 23 1) True. 2) True.

Page 25 1) True. 2) False. They are chemical signals. 3) False. Nerves are the fastest signals in the body.

Page 29 1) Fat. 2) They are arranged with spaces in between layered tubes, which make the bones really strong when pushed from above. 3) Cartilage.

Page 30 1) Skeletal muscles. 2) Biceps.

Page 33 1) Three. 2) Supplies nutrients and acts as a shock absorber. 3) Your spinal cord.

Page 34 1) The valves snapping shut. 2) Oxygen. 3) Arteries.

Page 37 1) False. 2) False.

Page 39 1) Discs of cartilage. 2) By fluid and membranes.

Page 41 1) False. They do this during respiration. 2) False. They are located in the lungs. 3) True.

Page 43 1) Hippocampus. 2) Four.

Page 45 1) Old, dead skin cells. 2) The nail matrix. 3) In summer.

Page 46 1) True. 2) True. It also protects them. 3) False. Most babies are born with no teeth.

Page 48 1) False. Too much sugar is bad for your health. 2) False. Taste detectors are only in the taste buds. 3) True.

Page 50 A nerve cell.

Page 55 1) Receptors. 2) Braille.

Page 57 1) To release carbon dioxide. 2) It relaxes. 3) No. The brain controls it.

Page 59 In the thumb.

Page 61 1) True. 2) True.

Page 63 1) To stop too much light getting in. 2) The iris. 3) They get bigger.

Page 65 1) False. They are located in the ear. 2) False. You eyes help you to balance but you use other information, too 3) True.

Page 67 1) From hot to cold. 2) The hypothalamus.

Page 69 1) True. There is no gravity in space to squash you down. 2) False. You stretch out overnight. 3) True.

Page 71 1) Five. 2) Neurons. 3) Episodic memory.

Page 73 1) Break down fat. 2) Usually around two days.

Page 75 A frog.

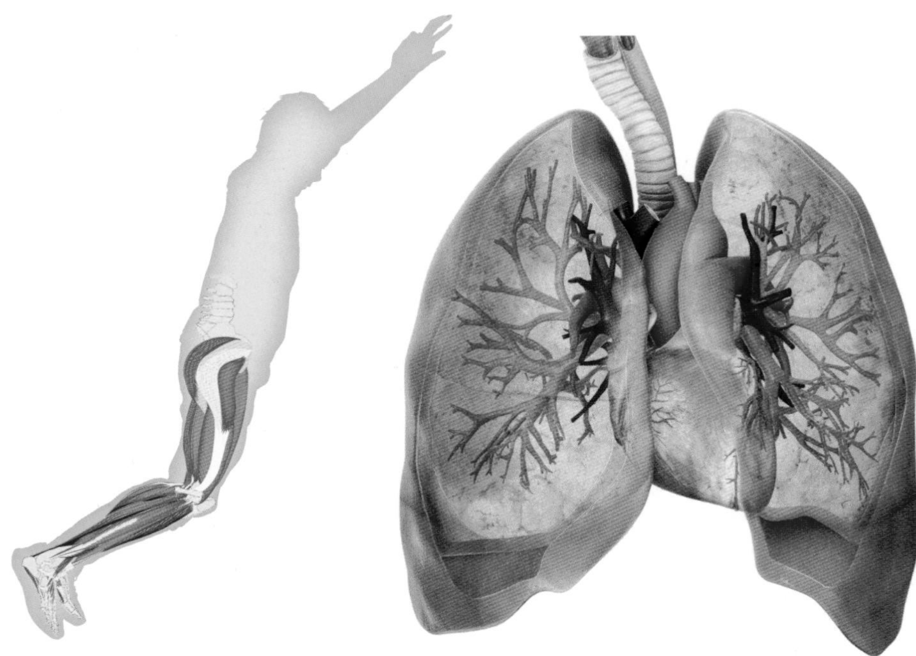

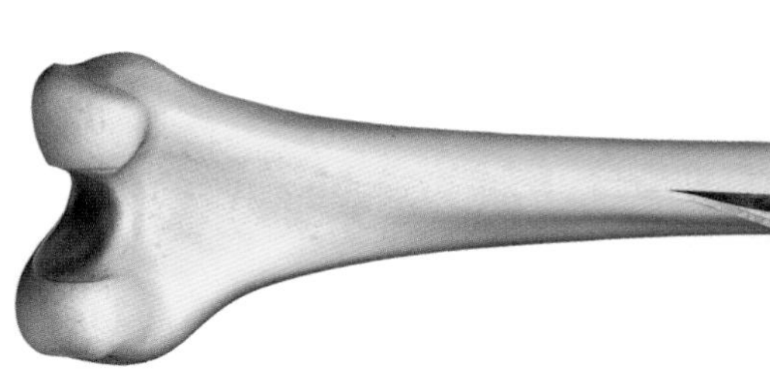

Page 77 1) Yes. When you eat or drink very fast you swallow more air than if you eat slowly. 2) Eructation.

Page 79 1) A fetus. 2) An embryo. 3) From the placenta and through the umbilical cord.

Page 81 1) False. It's thickest on your elbows and feet. 2) False. It's made at the base of the epidermis.

Page 83 1) Receptors send a signal to the brain. 2) They fold. 3) Sphincter muscles.

Page 85 1) False. It makes it stand up. 2) True. 3) False. They contract, or pull.

Page 87 1) True. 2) True. 3) False. You raise your eyebrows to show surprise.

Page 89 The stapes.

Page 93 In fat.

Page 94 1) True. 2) True. 3) False. You use up calories when you exercise.

Page 97 1) Practising mindfulness or talking to a counsellor. 2) Having good relationships, enjoying life, or expressing your feelings. 3) Losing interest in things, having problems sleeping, or a change in your eating pattern.

Page 99 1) Chemicals are released. 2) They connect us to others and they signal how we are.

Page 101 A virus.

Page 103 1) Children with dyslexia find it more difficult to read than other children their age. 2) Your family's behaviour can affect the way you think.

Page 104 1) True. 2) False. Your skin produces less oil as you get older, so it dries out.

Page 107 1) In cells. 2) Through your pee and poo, through sweat, and through your breath. 3) You pee less and in smaller amounts.

Page 109 1) False. It grows faster in the summer. 2) True.

Page 111 1) In the hands, feet, and under the arms. 2) It prepares the body to fight or run away. 3) It slows down.

Page 115 b) Holes inside your teeth.

Page 117 1) Attack and destroy viruses. 2) White blood cells. 3) It can be injected into your blood or given to you to swallow.

Page 119 1) Magnetic resonance imaging. 2) To see if there is a problem without having to operate. 3) Radio waves.

Page 121 1) True. 2) True. Washing your hands is a great way to kill bacteria.

Page 123 1) 37°C (98.6°F). 2) Diagnosis. 3) A stethoscope.

Page 125 In the uterus as it's an early embryo.

Page 127 1) False. It is outside the visible spectrum of light, so it is invisible. 2) True.

Page 129 1) True. 2) True. 3) False. They are remote-controlled and can't make their own decisions.

Page 130 A heart.

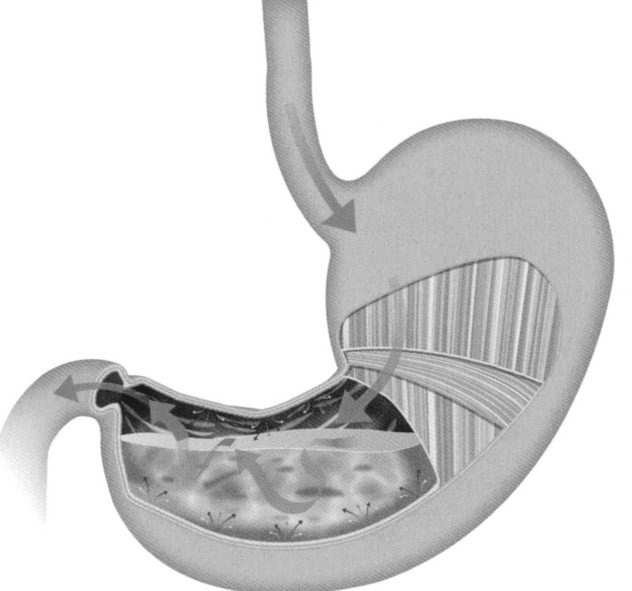

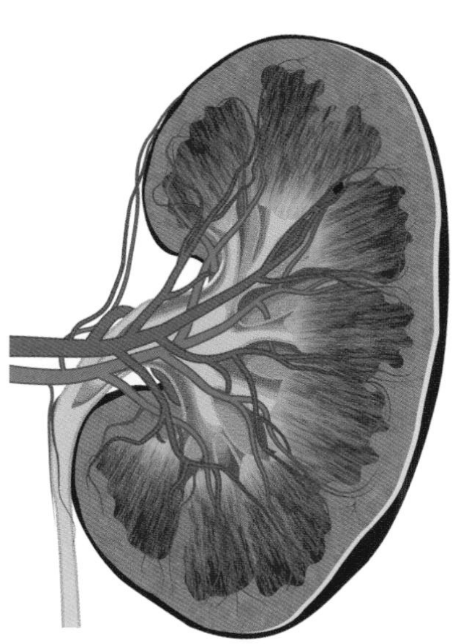

Quiz your friends!

Who knows the most about the human body? Test your friends and family with these tricky questions. See pages 136–137 for the answers.

Questions

1. What is the smallest organ in the body?

5. What is the **top part** of the **tooth** called?

8. What are the **three bones** in your **middle ear** called?

12. What type of **scan** uses **magnets** to show what's **inside your body?**

2. What are **rod-shaped bacteria** known as?

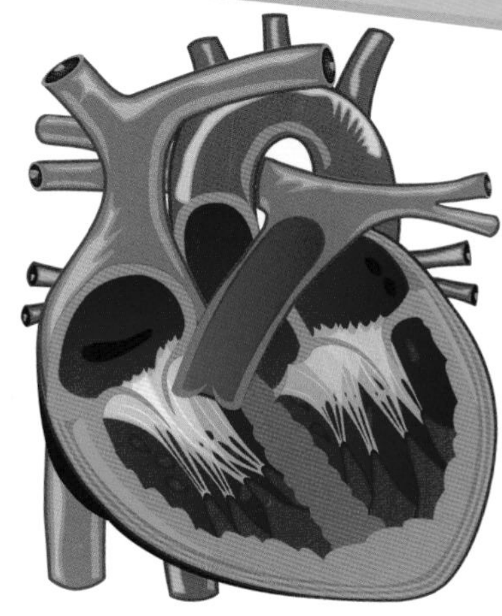

3. How many **chambers** are **inside** your **heart**?

4. Where in the body is **keratin** found?

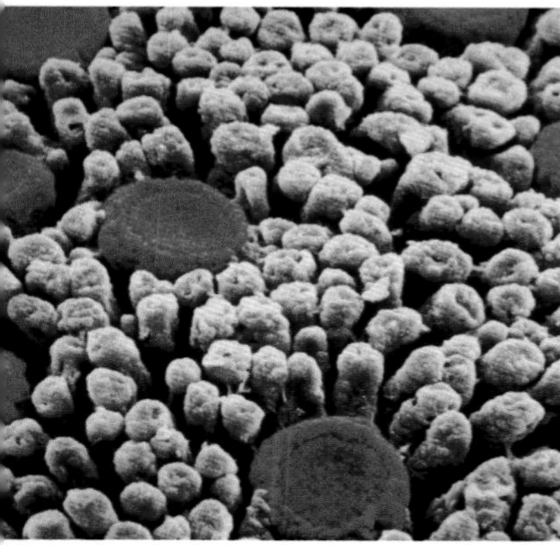

6. What are the **tiny bumps** that **cover your tongue** called?

7. What pattern are dead skin cells arranged in?

9. **Who** invented the **first vaccine?**

10. What device can be used to **measure your temperature**?

11. Which **organ can regrow** itself if some of it is missing?

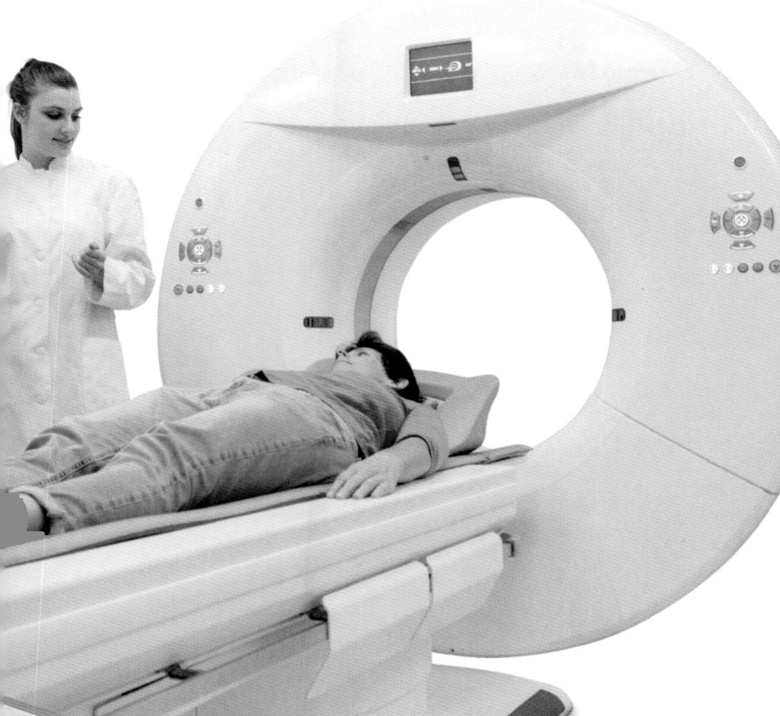

13. Where are **adult stem cells** made?

14. For how long should you wash your hands?

Answers

1. The smallest organ in the body is the **pineal gland**.

7. Dead skin cells are arranged in a **tessellated patter**

11. The liver.

13. **Adult stem ce** are made in th bone marrow

2. Bacillus bacteria.

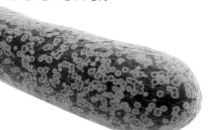

3. Your heart contains **four chambers**.

4. Nails, hair, and skin.

5. The crown.

6. The tiny bumps that cover your tongue are called **papillae**.

9. Edward Jenner.

8. The three bones in your middle ear are called the **malleus, incus, and stapes**.

10. A thermometer.

12. Magnetic resonance imaging (MRI) scan.

14. You should **wash your hands** for at least **20 seconds**.

Glossary

absorb
Take in something. Your blood absorbs oxygen from your lungs

allele
Particular variant of a gene. We get alleles from each parent for the same thing, such as nose shape

bacteria
Tiny, one-celled living things that live almost everywhere. Some cause disease, and others help your body

blood vessels
Tubes that carry blood through your body

body clock
Natural clock in the body that controls daily functions, such as sleeping

carbon dioxide
One of the gases in the air. You release carbon dioxide when you breathe out

cartilage
Tough, flexible tissue in the body

cells
Smallest living part of your body

cerebrospinal fluid
Fluid that surrounds and protects the brain, also known as CSF

characteristics
Features of your body that are controlled by genes, such as nose shape

chromosomes
Tiny bundles of wound-up DNA

diagnosis
Process of identifying someone's illness by looking at their symptoms and doing tests

diaphragm
Muscle under your lungs that helps you to breathe

DNA
Long molecule made from chains of four different types of chemical (represented by the letters ACGT) that can be used to create a code to build each part of the body. Stands for deoxyribonucleic acid

dominant
Used to describe an allele of a gene that shows up in your characteristics over a recessive allele

emotions
Inner feelings that affect the brain and body. These include happiness and fear

empathy
Ability to share in and understand another's feelings

enzyme
Substance that speeds up chemical reactions in the body. For example, digestive enzymes speed up digestion

epidermis
Thin, outer layer of your skin

follicle
Hole from which a hair grows

genes
Coded sections of DNA. Genes control the way your body works and develops

glands
Group of cells with the job of making and releasing specific hormones and other substances

haemoglobin
Red-brown coloured protein found in red blood cells

hormones
Chemical messengers that are created in glands and organs. They travel through your blood to tell another body part what to do

joint
Connection between two bones

keratin
Tough, waterproof protein found inside dead cells that make up the epidermis, hair, and nails

ligament
Slightly stretchy, connective tissue that holds bones together

meninges
Three flat layers of tissue that are located between your brain and skull

molecule
Chemical unit that is made up of atoms

MRI
Type of body scan that uses magnets. MRI stands for magnetic resonance imaging

mucus
Thick, slimy fluid. It is produced in the mouth, throat, intestines, and nose

nerves
Bundle of fibres that carry electrical signals around the body

neuron
Another word for a nerve cell. Neurons produce and pass electrical signals to other neurons and body parts

nucleus
Central part of a cell that contains the chromosomes

nutrients
Basic chemicals that make up food. Used to help the body grow, move, and repair itself

organ
Group of tissues that form a body part, such as your lungs

organelle
Small, floating, living machines that have different roles in each cell. For example, mitochondria release energy to power the cell

organism
Living thing. Types of organism include animals, bacteria, and plants

ossicles
Three tiny bones in your middle ear. They are called the malleus, incus, and stapes

oxygen
One of the gases in the air. Humans need to breathe in oxygen to live

particles
Very tiny building blocks that make up all things

protein
Particular type of complex organic building block made from amino acids

reflex
Automatic body movement, such as blinking

regulate
Control a process. For example, hormones help you to regulate many things, such as your growth

respiration
Process by which a living thing makes energy

sensor
Type of cell that helps you feel things that relate to your senses, such as taste and touch

sphincter
Ring of muscle that closes or opens to control the passage of material through it. For example, the sphincters in your bladder control the passage of your pee

spinal cord
Large bundle of nerves in your spine that connect the brain to nerve cells in your body

stem cells
Cells that can become other types of cell

tissue
Group of cells that do the same job, such as muscle tissue

transplant
Organ from one body used to replace an affected organ in another body

vertebrae
Bones that link together to form your spine

Index

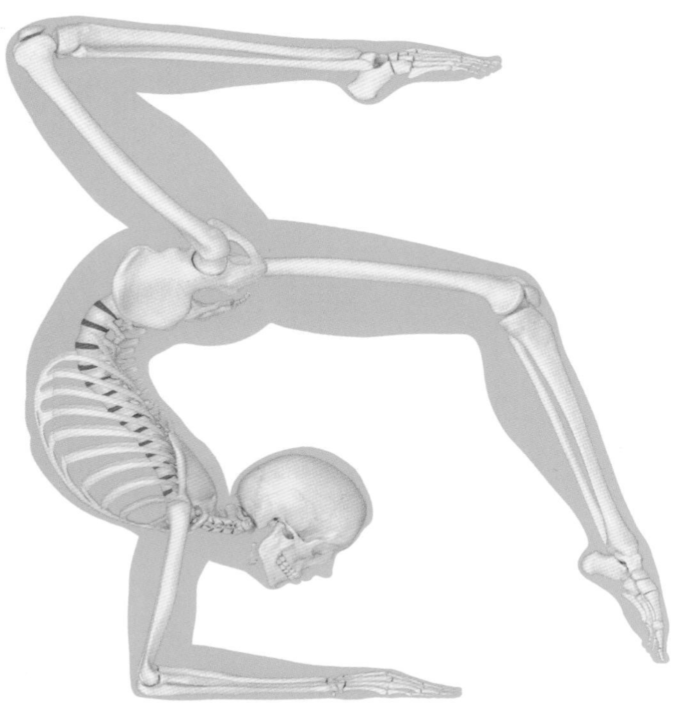

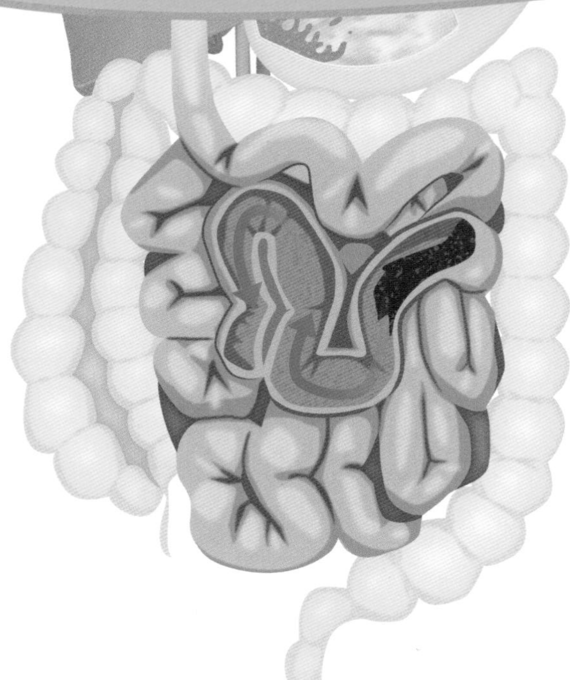

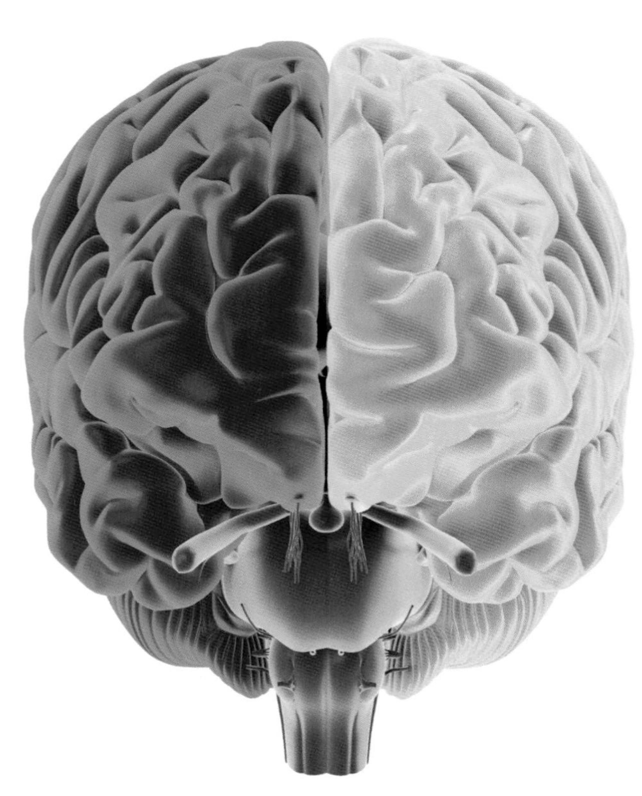

Acknowledgements

DORLING KINDERSLEY would like to thank: Polly Goodman for proofreading; Helen Peters for the index; Sally Beets, Jolyon Goddard, Marie Greenwood, and Dawn Sirett for editorial assistance; and Niharika Prabhakar and Roohi Sehgal for editorial support.

Consultant Darrin Lunde, National Museum of Natural History, Smithsonian Institution

Smithsonian Enterprises
Kealy Gordon Product Development Manager
Janet Archer DMM Ecom and D-to-C
Jill Corcoran Director, Licensed Publishing
Carol LeBlanc President

The publisher would like to thank the following for their kind permission to reproduce their photographs:

(Key: a-above; b-below/bottom; c-centre; f-far; l-left; r-right; t-top)

2 Getty Images / iStock: akesak (br). **4 Alamy Stock Photo:** Alexandr Mitiuc (cr). **Dreamstime.com:** Igor Zakharevich (tr). **5 Dreamstime.com:** Okea (cb). **Robert Steiner MRI Unit, Imperial College London:** (tr). **6 Science Photo Library:** Dr Torsten Wittmann. **6–7 Getty Images / iStock:** kali9 (tc). **8 Science Photo Library:** Dr Torsten Wittmann (b). **9 Dreamstime.com:** Sebastian Kaulitzki (clb); Mopic (cb). **10 Dreamstime.com:** Srckomkrit (clb). **11 Dreamstime.com:** Rajcreationzs (cb); Skypixel (crb). **14–15 Dreamstime.com:** Igor Zakharevich. **14 Dreamstime.com:** Florin Seitan (cra). **15 Alamy Stock Photo:** Science Photo Library (tl). **16 Dreamstime.com:** Fancytapis (ca); Sebastian Kaulitzki (tl); Skypixel (cr). **17 Dreamstime.com:** Sergey Novikov (bl). **18 Getty Images / iStock:** kali9 (cla). **18–19 Dreamstime.com:** Barbara Helgason (b). **20–21 Getty Images:** Ariel Skelley. **21 Dreamstime.com:** Didesign021 (clb); Dmitrii Melnikov (cb). **22–23 Dreamstime.com:** Axel Kock. **23 Dreamstime.com:** Mala Navet (crb); Katerina Sisperova (cb). **26 Science Photo Library:** Prof. P. Motta / Dept. of Anatomy / University "La Sapienza", Rome (b). **28 Getty Images / iStock:** BettinaRitter (bc). **29 Dorling Kindersley:** Natural History Museum, London (ca). **Getty Images:** Science Photo Library - Steve Gschmeissner (bl). **31 Alamy Stock Photo:** Phanie (cl). **32 Science Photo Library:** CNRI (ca). **36 Science Photo Library:** Astrid & Hanns-Frieder Michler (ca). **36–37 Dorling Kindersley:** Zygote. **37 Dreamstime.com:** Nmsfotographix (tr). **38–39 Science Photo Library:** Sciepro (t). **38 Alamy Stock Photo:** Science Photo Library (br). **40 Fotolia:** Zee (t). **42 123RF.com:** Langstrup (clb). **43 Dreamstime.com:** Sebastian Kaulitzki (cra). **44 Getty Images / iStock:** spukkato. **45 Alamy Stock Photo:** Kostya Pazyuk (cra). **Dreamstime.com:** Marko Sumakovic (cr). **Science Photo Library:** Steve Gschmeissner (bc). **46–47 Alamy Stock Photo:** Alexandr Mitiuc (c). **47 Dorling Kindersley:** Arran Lewis (br). **48–49 Science Photo Library:** Prof. P. Motta / Dept. of Anatomy / University "La Sapienza", Rome (c). **49 Alamy Stock Photo:** Science History Images (b). **50 Dreamstime.com:** Sebastian Kaulitzki (crb). **50–51 Dreamstime.com:** Piyapong Thongcharoen. **52 Dreamstime.com:** Andrey Armyagov (b). **53 Alamy Stock Photo:** imageBROKER (t). **54–55 Alamy Stock Photo:** RubberBall. **54 Dreamstime.com:** Oleksandr Homon (br). **57 Dreamstime.com:** Yobro10 (ca). **59 Dreamstime.com:** Timofey Tyurin (t). **Getty Images / iStock:** Freder (cb). **61 Alamy Stock Photo:** MedicalRF.com (tl). **Science Photo Library:** Dr Goran Bredberg (bc). **62 Getty Images / iStock:** stock_colors (tl). **62–63 Getty Images / iStock:** ScantyNebula (tc). **63 Getty Images / iStock:** Elen11 (tr). **64–65 Dreamstime.com:** Nataliia Maksymenko. **66 Dreamstime.com:** Berlinfoto (clb); Laneigeaublanc (cb). **67 Alamy Stock Photo:** Cultura Creative (RF) (cb); Top Notch (crb). **68 Dreamstime.com:** Jacek Chabraszewski (cb). **69 Alamy Stock Photo:** Philip Berryman (bc). **70 Dreamstime.com:** Andranik Hakobyan (cl); Valeryegorov (c); Andrey Popov (cb); Ziggymars (tr). **71 Dreamstime.com:** (tc); Ziggymars (tl). **74–75 Dreamstime.com:** Andrey Armyagov. **75 123RF.com:** Marek Poplawski / mark52 (bl). **Alamy Stock Photo:** blickwinkel (bc). **Dreamstime.com:** Fifoprod (cra). **76 Shutterstock.com:** Onjira Leibe (clb). **77 123RF.com:** Jose Jonathan Heres (cr). **78 Alamy Stock Photo:** imageBROKER (tl). **Dreamstime.com:** Ammentorp (bl); Katerynakon (tr). **Science Photo Library:** Lennart Nilsson, TT (br). **79 Alamy Stock Photo:** Science Photo Library (clb). **Dreamstime.com:** Smith Assavarujikul (tr); Magicmine (crb). **80–81 Getty Images:** PhotoAlto / Odilon Dimier. **81 Science Photo Library:** Dennis Kunkel Microscopy (bl). **82 Getty Images:** Ed Reschke (clb). **83 Dreamstime.com:** Dzmitry Baranau (cla). **84–85 Alamy Stock Photo:** imageBROKER. **85 Dreamstime.com:** Mashimara (cla); Photodynamx (ca). **86–87 Science Photo Library:** Richard Wehr / Custom Medical Stock Photo (tc). **86 Dreamstime.com:** Seventyfourimages (cb); Timofey Tyurin (crb). **87 Getty Images:** Thomas Barwick. **88 123RF.com:** Vladislav Zhukov (clb). **Dreamstime.com:** Kouassi Gilbert Ambeu (bc). **Getty Images / iStock:** kool99 (bl). **89 Dreamstime.com:** Sergey Novikov. **Science Photo Library:** Bo Veisland (br). **90 Dreamstime.com:** Lunamarina (b); Okea (t). **92 Dreamstime.com:** Decade3d (cl); Tatyana Vychegzhanina (clb). **92–93 Dreamstime.com:** Okea. **93 Dreamstime.com:** Sebastian Kaulitzki (cra). **94 Dreamstime.com:** Glenda Powers. **95 Dreamstime.com:** Golfxx (cra); Ljupco (l). **96 Dreamstime.com:** Chernetskaya (tc); Lunamarina (tl); Yobro10 (tr). **97 Dreamstime.com:** Katarzyna Bialasiewicz (cb); Famveldman (tl); Nadezhda Bugaeva (tc); Jose Manuel Gelpi Diaz (tr); Dmytro Gilitukha (clb). **98–99 Dreamstime.com:** Erik Reis. **99 Dreamstime.com:** MNStudio (cla). **100 Alamy Stock Photo:** Yon Marsh (cra). **101 Dreamstime.com:** Chinnasorn Pangcharoen (cra). **102 Dreamstime.com:** Denys Kuvaiev (bl). **103 Dreamstime.com:** Jbrown777 (cr); Monkey Business Images (cra). **104 Alamy Stock Photo:** BSIP SA (cl). **Science Photo Library:** Zephyr (c). **104–105 Dreamstime.com:** Monkey Business Images. **106–107 Alamy Stock Photo:** Alfafoto. **107 Science Photo Library:** Dennis Kunkel Microscopy (br); Steve Gschmeissner (crb). **108 Dreamstime.com:** Deyangeorgiev (crb); Wave Break Media Ltd (cra). **109 Alamy Stock Photo:** RooM the Agency (cla). **Dreamstime.com:** Chih Yuan Wu (clb). **110 Dreamstime.com:** Korn Vitthayanukarun (tc). **110–111 Getty Images / iStock:** Photodisc. **111 Alamy Stock Photo:** Universal Images Group North America LLC (bc). **Dreamstime.com:** Kts (bl). **112 Getty Images / iStock:** akesak (cla). **112–113 Dreamstime.com:** Kittipong Jirasukhanont (tc). **114 Getty Images:** SSPL (br). **115 Dreamstime.com:** Saaaaa (bc). **117 Dreamstime.com:** Georgios Kollidas (tr); Sloka Poojary (cla). **118 Alamy Stock Photo:** Westend61 GmbH (bl). Robert Steiner MRI Unit, Imperial College London: (r). **119 Dreamstime.com:** Monkey Business Images (cb); Trutta (bc). **Getty Images / iStock:** akesak (tr). Robert Steiner MRI Unit, Imperial College London: (l). **120 Dreamstime.com:** Katerynakon (clb). **121 Dreamstime.com:** Irochka (cra); Maya Kruchankova (cr). **122–123 Dreamstime.com:** Tatiana592 (tc). **122 123RF.com:** anmbph (cr). **Getty Images / iStock:** Evgen_Prozhyrko (clb). **123 123RF.com:** akkamulator (cra). **Dreamstime.com:** Per Boge (cl); Paul-andré Belle-isle (clb). **124–125 Dreamstime.com:** Juan Gaertner. **124 Science Photo Library:** Steve Gschmeissner (br). **125 Dreamstime.com:** Sebastian Kaulitzki / Eraxion (bl); Ilexx (cra). Getty Images: Ed Reschke (bc). **127 Dreamstime.com:** Edgars Sermulis (cr). **128 Alamy Stock Photo:** Edward Olive (c). **Science Photo Library:** Andy Crump (bl); Patrice Latron / Look at Sciences (bc). **128–129 Dreamstime.com:** Kittipong Jirasukhanont. **130–131 Alamy Stock Photo:** Dmitri Maruta (b); PA Images (t). **131 Alamy Stock Photo:** Universal Images Group North America LLC (br). **Science Photo Library:** Burger / Phanie (tr). **134 Alamy Stock Photo:** MedicalRF.com (cr). **Dreamstime.com:** Nataliia Maksymenko (bl). **134–135 Alamy Stock Photo:** Westend61 GmbH (bc). **Dreamstime.com:** Tirachard Kumtanom. **135 123RF.com:** anmbph (c). **Alamy Stock Photo:** Science History Images (cla). **Getty Images / iStock:** spukkato (tr). **136 Dreamstime.com:** Ljupco (bl). **Science Photo Library:** Dennis Kunkel Microscopy (cr). **136–137 Dreamstime.com:** Tirachard Kumtanom. **137 Dorling Kindersley:** Arran Lewis (tr). **Dreamstime.com:** Juan Gaertner (b); Mala Navet (tl); Georgios Kollidas (c). **140 Dorling Kindersley:** Zygote (bl). **141 Dreamstime.com:** Igor Zakharevich (tl). **143 Dreamstime.com:** Sebastian Kaulitzki (br).

Endpaper images: *Front:* **Dreamstime.com:** Juan Gaertner; *Back:* **Dreamstime.com:** Juan Gaertner.

Cover images: *Front:* **Dreamstime.com:** Ruslandanylchenko95, Skypixel crb, Studio29ro c, Igor Zakharevich br; *Back:* **Dorling Kindersley:** Natural History Museum, London tc; **Dreamstime.com:** Ruslandanylchenko95; *Spine:* **Dreamstime.com:** Igor Zakharevich ca.